THE ITALIAN AMERICANS

ALSO BY MARIA LAURINO

Old World Daughter, New World Mother

Were You Always an Italian?

THE
ITALIAN
AMERICANS

A History

MARIA LAURINO

W. W. NORTON & COMPANY

New York • London

For information about permission to reproduce selections from this book,
write to Permissions, W. W. Norton & Company, Inc.,
500 Fifth Avenue, New York, NY 10110

For information about special discounts for bulk purchases, please contact
W. W. Norton Special Sales at specialsales@wwnorton.com or 800-233-4830

Manufacturing through Asia Pacific
Book design by Chris Welch
Production manager: Louise Parasmo

ISBN 978-0-393-24129-7

W. W. Norton & Company, Inc.
500 Fifth Avenue, New York, N.Y. 10110
www.wwnorton.com

W. W. Norton & Company Ltd.
Castle House, 75/76 Wells Street, London W1T 3QT

1 2 3 4 5 6 7 8 9 0

For Bob and Henry,
and for Michael, the next generation

※

In memory of Henry M. Laurino and Constance Conti Laurino

CONTENTS

THE ITALIAN AMERICANS

Introduction

Cut to scene: Don Corleone looks into the eyes of his nervous godson, who is desperate for a coveted part in a Hollywood film. Drawing him close, the Godfather assures him that the movie mogul will do the right thing, saying in the cottony mumble that Marlon Brando made famous, "I'm going to make him an offer he can't refuse."

The easy imitation of this line from *The Godfather*—one of the most popular and parodied in movie history—has become part of the American vernacular, helping to usher in decades' worth of assumptions and stereotypes about Italian Americans. (The line was probably borrowed from the French novelist Honoré de Balzac, and a variation appears in the work of Western culture's first myth-maker, Homer's *Odyssey*.) Most contemporary depictions are as crude as that of a portraitist dabbing a canvas with a housepainter's brush: men—loud, dumb, violent; women—big hair, big mouth, make-ah the macaroni.

Myths about Italian-American culture run deep into the fabric of American life, obscuring the complicated, nuanced, centuries-long story of the Italian-American experience that demands to be told. One of the goals of this book—alongside telling this history—is to tease myth from reality and uncover a more complicated story and deeper truths.

Italian foodstuffs continue to link past and present for many Italian Americans.

Understandably, hyphenated Americans tend to romanticize the immigrant journey and present these tales through a lens of heroism in the face of hardship, leading ultimately to success. We create private myths that conform to universal ones. As the American mythologist Joseph Campbell famously patterned, the structure of myth has remained the same through the millennia: a hero with limited awareness has a "call to adventure," confronts dangers and enemies along the way and, if he survives this road of trials, rededicates himself with renewed mastery and greater awareness.

In many ways this mythic journey foreshadows the story of all immigrants coming to America. We ask ourselves, How did our grandparents or great-grandparents or great-great-grandparents summon up the exceptional courage to cross the monumental ocean—that particularly American call to adventure—and settle in the New World? How did they muster the bravery to face the isolation of leaving family behind and to accept the dangers and hardships of brute labor and the insults cast by others who saw themselves as "more American"?

Heroes surely. But often a heroism born out of desperation.

The immigrants who made this journey also carried with them the scars of the past: centuries of poverty and subjugation that wreak havoc on and deeply scar the psyche. The tension, then, in trying to honestly recount and reconstruct history is to balance both concepts: the heroic journey to modernity and the damage left behind by a feudal and impoverished past.

Unlike other nineteenth-century immigrant groups, Italian Americans had several calls to adventure, crossing the perilous ocean more than once. Although they left Italy in unprecedented numbers, most had no intention of making the New World their permanent home. They saw themselves more as migrant workers than as immigrants, and they adopted a transnational life, coming to America to earn money and then returning to Italy, much as many Latinos today aspire to spend a few years in the United States in order to build the foundations for a more stable future in the country of their birth. Many Italians stayed longer than expected; some settled down forever. But over 50 percent of those who came to America went home.

The Italian Americans begins in the latter half of the nineteenth century, explaining why the immigrants left Italy and telling the stories of those who stayed in America. This book implicitly asks why so few Italian Americans know the full range of our history and responds to these potential gaps with a narrative that touches many regions of the country.

We may know about deeply rooted family bonds in the face of American individualism, about hardworking immigrants laying the foundation for a newly industrialized country, about Little Italies and tenement living, about a tenacious mayor named Fiorello La Guardia, the Hoboken crooner Frank Sinatra, the athletic grace of Joe DiMaggio, and the graceful articulations of Mario Cuomo.

But do we know about the plight of Italian Americans working on sugarcane plantations in Louisiana or those who were lynched in New Orleans? Or the story of a banker named Amadeo Giannini, who helped rebuild San Francisco after the great earthquake? Or a labor leader and poet named Arturo Giovannitti, who was arrested for trying to change terrible factory conditions in Massachusetts? Or do we know that when Joe DiMaggio was at the peak of his baseball career, the government branded his parents, hardworking citizens of San Francisco, "enemy aliens" because the United States was at war with Italy and the DiMaggios were not naturalized citizens? This designation prohibited the DiMaggios from entering Fisherman's Wharf or visiting their son's restaurant there.

Recent psychological research suggests that children who know their family history may experience a higher self-esteem and stronger sense of control because they are able to participate in a narrative larger than the individual self and nuclear family. It seems hardly a leap to imagine that adults, too, benefit from knowing their past. Family history helps fulfill an innately human desire to replace the more somber shades of the isolated self with a color-infused pattern of belonging. Perhaps readers, intrigued by the rich, multifaceted history of the ethnic group, will embark on their own particular quest of Italian and American identity and, like the hero of the journey, emerge with a fuller sense of self.

Cent' Anni!
THE ROSETO EFFECT

To better understand the ethos of Italian-American culture—its stubborn insistence on the primacy of family and bafflement of America's ready embrace of individualism—is to trace the steps of a group of southern Italian men from Roseto Valfortore to the United States, who settled in Pennsylvania and built a community in the foothills of the Poconos that would replicate the one they had left behind. Leaving Italy in 1882, the men came to America desperate to escape the poverty of their mountain village in the region of Apulia, near the Adriatic coast.

There they labored as peasant farmers, traveling by foot for up to ten miles each day to reach land owned by the gentry. Some quarried marble from a neighboring town, and those lucky enough to have inherited a craft became stone carvers. The Rosetans lived in cramped two-story homes, the kitchen and stable on the first floor and bedroom above. Like their fellow countrymen throughout southern Italy, they heard about the promise of America.

The initial group of eleven men decided to make the journey after receiving encouraging letters from a Jesuit priest named Luigi Sabetti, who had grown up in Roseto Valfortore and emigrated to Baltimore. Eventually, eight of them, after a brief stay on Mulberry Street, found work in central Pennsylvania from a New York City employment agency. They summoned more people to join them, and each year their numbers multiplied. On a hillside they found a cheap and open tract of land empty of trees, which had been stripped for lumber. In 1887 these early residents named the town New Italy, eventually changing it to Roseto in memory of their village in the foothills of the Apennines. The ethnic enclave stayed true to its roots, speaking a regional Italian dialect and re-creating life from the Old Country.

The Rosetans had reasons to stick to their own: the Welsh, English, and Germans from the neighboring towns shunned the Italians. Slate quarries were the principal local industry, and the Anglo-Saxons, many of whom had learned this trade in the British Isles, owned the quarries and kept the best jobs for themselves. They gave the worst ones to the Italians—digging holes or throwing out rubbish—and paid them the pittance of eight cents an hour for a ten-hour workday, doled out only every three months.

So, for the ensuing decades, Roseto remained only for Rosetans, creating a safe harbor from what they perceived to be hostile outside forces. They built their own small church and eventually their own school. They built blouse mills in town where the women went to work. Two cousins ran bakeries from their home basements, producing bread loaves, pizza, and pasta for the entire town. (One of the bakeries—Le Donne's—still exists today and uses the same bread oven from the 1930s.) Nearly everyone made their own wine and grew all of their own vegetables.

By the 1960s, more than seventy-five years after the arrival of its first immigrants, 95 percent of Roseto's two thousand inhabitants were descendants of Roseto Val-

Slate quarries were the principal local industry in Roseto.

The Rosetans built blouse mills in town where the women went to work.

fortore, making it one of the most homogeneous ethnic enclaves in the nation. And at the time, Roseto received international attention as the home to a medical mystery—or perhaps medical miracle—one that would illustrate the protective effects of an emotionally supportive community in preventing heart disease.

The town had caught the attention of two doctors, Stewart Wolf and John Bruhn, after a resident cardiologist mentioned to Wolf, who owned a vacation home in the Poconos, that hardly anyone under fifty-five in Roseto had died of a heart attack or had signs of heart disease. For those over sixty-five, the rate of heart disease was about half that of the neighboring English, Welsh, and German towns and half the national average.

At the time, heart disease was the number one killer of Americans, and doctors were concerned that it was affecting men at increasingly younger ages. Wolf and Bruhn decided to study the health records of Rosetans, launching a multiyear effort that began in 1961. They discovered that although the residents indulged in salamis, cheeses, sausages, and cigarettes; although they abandoned their healthy native extra-virgin olive oil for artery-clogging lard; although they transformed traditional flatbread pizza with olive oil and salt into New World versions with sausage, pepperoni, salami, ham, and egg, the Rosetans weren't dying of heart disease.

Two cousins ran bakeries from their home basements.

The curious doctors ruled out other possibilities. They didn't believe that the reason for this phenomenon was genetic; the doctors studied relatives of the Rosetans in other parts of the country and found they weren't as healthy. And it wasn't environmental; the same water supply, doctors, and hospitals served Roseto and the neighboring towns. After years of study, Wolf and Bruhn concluded that the town's communally supportive behavior—later dubbed the "Roseto Effect"—made all the difference.

Rosetans chose to live a family- and community-centered egalitarian life. Those who had prospered didn't flaunt their wealth and lent support to the less fortunate, residents almost exclusively patronized local businesses, and they predominantly intermarried.

Doctors couldn't tell wealthy from poor Rosetans because everyone dressed alike and lived in modest homes.

Southern Italian culture and peasant mysticism reinforced the Rosetans' actions and template for living. Southern Italians—from illiterate peasants to cultured Neapolitans—believed deeply that other people, especially through the power of their stare, had the ability to bring grave harm to them and their families through what they called *malocchio*, the "evil eye." The homogeneity and isolation of the community kept practices like warding off the evil eye common ones, passed through the generations. Rosetans conjured up potions with water, olive oil, and iron tools or wore amulets (a horn around one's neck was typically considered the best protection), and they would never flaunt wealth—God forbid!—lest pride invite *malocchio* upon them. As one Rosetan told Carla Bianco, an Italian anthropologist studying the town during the same period as the two doctors, "The people think you're rich and they envy you. So you catch the evil eye. Envy is powerful. We say, 'If envy were fever, the whole world would be in bed.'"

In 1963, two years after the initial study, Wolf and Bruhn predicted that if this Old World culture began to crumble—as the times and the steady infiltration of American values suggested it would—so, too, would the protective benefits against heart disease. Their hunch was correct: younger Rosetans of that era, the first generation to become college educated, believed the town lacked opportunity, and many didn't return after graduation. Gradually, *malocchio* began to lose its powerful grip on the psyche, and with this demise, in crept envy: people wanted bigger homes and fancy Cadillacs. Twenty years later, when the same doctors conducted a follow-up study in 1985, they noted that competition outpaced cooperation, and the mortality of the Rosetans was the same as that of everyone else.

The story of Roseto challenges some ingrained notions about the primacy of individualism and offers a cautionary tale about the stress-related perils of materialism. The doctors were ahead of their time observing in the 1960s that communities matter—that

Southern Italian men typically wore the gold horn (cornetto) on a neck chain to protect against the evil eye.

socially supportive environments can protect against heart disease, while isolation and loneliness are risk factors for it. The idea of a mind-body connection in understanding and treating illness wouldn't gain traction for another few decades. Today, health researchers have returned to Roseto to analyze the merits of investigating disease by observing community behavior.

Similarly, more and more contemporary Americans, feeling alienated from a sterile, fast-paced, and flavorless twenty-first-century life, are also practicing some aspects of Old World ways: cultivating gardens, buying local, and even making their own wine. The Rosetans, the doctors reported, grew their own lettuce, green peppers, onions, peas, beans, endive, eggplant, tomatoes, corn, beets, cucumbers, figs, peaches, peas, apples, pumpkins, cherries, plums, parsley, oregano, basil, mallow, and other herbs—a cornucopia mirrored today at the varied stalls of local farmers markets.

The tradition continues today.

Every July, Rosetans would crown a young woman at the Celebration of Our Lady of Mount Carmel.

Italians toast one another with the words *Cent' anni!*—"May you live one hundred years!" Life in Roseto once seemed to offer the potential for that promise. A one-hundred-year look at Roseto, Pennsylvania—from the time the immigrants first arrived in 1882 until the 1985 follow-up study by Wolf and Bruhn—poses some important questions about the way we live today.

Could Old World communities like Roseto offer a countercheck to an increasingly alienated society? What's lost and what's gained, who benefits and who is harmed, by leaving the Old World clan for New World independence? If the ideology of contemporary American life is one of individualism, competitiveness, and materialism—and we know that these traits invite bad health and unhappiness—can we find the means within ourselves to change course, to choose a path of cooperation and egalitarianism over competition and inequality?

Well into the new millennium, Americans have an uneasy sense that not all of modernity is healthy or pleasing to the senses, while also knowing they would not replicate a life forged in part by Old World superstitions or one that shuns geographic mobility. One inclination would be to meld elements of the Old World with the New, but to accomplish this delicate feat without being trapped by the distorting effects of nostalgia, Italian Americans—and all other Americans—might want to explore this rich and varied past.

Un' altra cent' anni! To another one hundred years!

Adriana Trigiani

Adriana Trigiani is the New York Times *best-selling author of fifteen books that have been translated into over thirty-five languages. Her experiences growing up in Roseto, Pennsylvania, influenced her novel* The Queen of the Big Time, *based on the town's annual celebration of its patron saint, Our Lady of Mount Carmel—or "the Big Time," as the occasion is called by the young women who compete to be the pageant's queen. Trigiani's family moved from Roseto to Big Stone Gap, Virginia, the setting and title of her debut novel, which was followed by three sequels.*

Q: What was life in Roseto like when you were growing up?

Trigiani: Some of my most incredible childhood memories are from Roseto, Pennsylvania. Everything centered around the church, the Mass, the pageantry of the Mass, which I always found incredibly profound. If you go into Our Lady of Mount Carmel Church, there's a golden light in there, and I'd imagine that was what heaven would be like. Then you'd walk down the street, and you'd go to Cousin Ralph's, and they'd have cocktails after Mass or a drink. Then there would be dinner, and we'd go down to my Great-Aunt Mary's. It was fantastic because the pasta was homemade and the sauce was homemade. We'd spend hours in the basement rolling pasta.

Q: How was Roseto, Pennsylvania, similar to Roseto Valfortore in Italy?

Trigiani: It's crazy; when you go to Roseto Valfortore and then you come to Roseto, Pennsylvania, they're mirror images of each other. The double porches were part of two-family homes. They had those porches in Italy, so they built them in Roseto. The first group that came here went to work in the slate quarries. Basically, the folks hiring the Italians ghettoized them and gave them this hill. When

you go up that hill, you think you're going to see an ocean on the other side. You're in Pennsylvania. There's no ocean, but when you go up that hill, it feels like it does when you're in Italy and see the ocean. They may have tried to give us the worst piece of land, but it ended up being just as beautiful as in Italy.

Q: Doctors have been studying Roseto for decades because of its once low rate of heart disease. Do you think there are lessons to be learned from Roseto?

Trigiani: It's very interesting to me, living in our times, when we're struggling with how to take care of people. The best thing we can do for one another is provide work. In Roseto, they came up with an incredible idea, which was to put the women to work during the school hours of the day. You walked your kid to school, then you went to the factory, and you worked until three o'clock, when you would pick up your child and go home. You had every generation of the family living in the home, so you never had a babysitter. If you study Roseto, you see that the factories are right next door to the houses. There wasn't a commute. You didn't need a second car.

The men went off to work in the slate quarries, or they were farmers, or they had factory jobs themselves. We so often hear that women's working or being ambitious imperils home life, but it just wasn't true. Roseto is the perfect model to show you that there is a better way to live, where everybody benefits when everybody works.

Q: How do you think the cultural values of Roseto helped protect people from stress?

Trigiani: The Italian way of life offsets stress because in Italy, and you can still see this today, it's very intergenerational, interdependent. People didn't just move away. They stayed pretty much within a town. You, hopefully, fell in love with somebody local, and you built a family, and then your parents babysat, and they were there. The Italian way of life is so simple. It's take care of your own, keep your nose clean, enjoy the table, enjoy the gathering of your family. Make it as beautiful as you can with what you have. Invite the neighbor in. Keep your heart at ease. And work, work, work.

Q: Can you describe how the women in your family shopped and cooked?

Trigiani: You shopped local. It was grown local, but here's the thing that always got me about Roseto—there was never a want. If somebody canned peppers, they brought you a couple quarts. Also, nothing was ever wasted. Everything in the hands of these women became a delicacy. When we would come in from mowing the lawn or doing some chores for my grandmother, she would take dandelion greens that she had picked, toss them in olive oil, then poach eggs in her gravy, in the red sauce, and ladle those eggs, fresh eggs, over the greens, and serve it with bread. You will never eat anything more delicious. Think about that meal. Does that meal even cost fifteen cents? You've got the dandelions in your yard. You've got the eggs and the gravy, and everybody ate well. They took nothing and made something out of it. That's very, very Italian to me.

We so often hear that women's working or being ambitious imperils home life, but it just wasn't true. Roseto is the perfect model to show you that there is a better way to live, where everybody benefits when everybody works.

Q: Why did your family move from Roseto?

Trigiani: My dad was working for his parents at their mill in the mid-1960s. Garment manufacturing was a big business in the North, profitable and community based. My dad used to say that anyone could throw up ten sewing machines back then and make a living. Around 1966, the federal Small Business Administration did a big push to find young entrepreneurs in the North to go south to open garment factories. This was a key element of the War on Poverty programs; the idea was to bring industry to the South, using the successful model from communities like Roseto and other places in the North to provide jobs for the people who needed them most. The government wanted to model the success of these factories in a poverty-stricken place called Appalachia (which was defined as a landmass that stretched from southwestern Virginia all the way down to Georgia). The government representatives told my dad he could put up a factory anywhere he chose in the Appalachian region. Dad said the rate was so low, it was irresistible. He was thirty-three years old and ready to be his own boss.

Q: How did your grandmother take the move?

Trigiani: My grandmother Viola—my father's mother—visited us in Big Stone Gap soon after we moved down south. I asked her if she liked it, and she said, "I could never live in a place where they don't make cheese."

PART ONE

1860–1910

CHAPTER ONE

La Famiglia

For Italians during the first great wave of immigration to America, family would be their source of strength and survival, but the values that sustained them in places like Roseto, Pennsylvania, would also put them at odds with the rest of the country. Roseto's residents—like Italian Americans elsewhere—tended to wall themselves off, mistrusting outsiders and outside institutions. That self-imposed isolation made it harder for them to assimilate into mainstream American life.

The instinct to trust only the family—to believe, as parents routinely told their children, that "blood is thicker than water"—is deeply rooted in the complex history of Italy, a land invaded and conquered for thousands of years and occupied by foreign countries well into the nineteenth century. This fractured history distinguishes and separates the Italian experience from all the rest of southern Europe.

The nearly century-long project to unite Italy began after the Napoleonic Wars in 1815 and was completed with the annexation of Rome from the Papal States in 1870. But even after unification, the land and people of the north and the south couldn't have been more divided, geographically and culturally. The north offered a landscape of undulating copper hills, suitable as background to the images of fine-boned ladies in Renaissance portraits, and boasted unparalleled achievements in art, architecture, and literature.

By contrast, Italy south of Rome, known as the Mezzogiorno (literally, "midday"), was a dusty, arid land where illiterate peasants slavishly toiled for aristocratic landowners. About 85 percent of the Italians who came to the United States were from southern Italy. The bleakness of the region was immortalized in the Italian writer Carlo Levi's book *Christ Stopped at Eboli*, whose title comes from a

Unlike the lush northern terrain, the south of Italy was an arid land where peasants slavishly toiled.

A twentieth-century Italian parliamentary investigation revealed that the wages of peasants had remained the same since 1780.

peasant saying that Christ could not have traveled any farther than the fertile land of Eboli, which lies south of Naples in the region of Campania.

"We're not Christians," the peasants told Levi. They meant that they were not "human beings"; they were too far below the status of the blessed. Levi was banished in 1935 to a small town in Basilicata, then known as Lucania, because of his opposition to Fascism. The government's decision to exile its opponents to the south is a stark reminder for Italian Americans that the bleak, impoverished life of their ancestors was barely a step above imprisonment in the minds of northern Italians.

"No one has come to this land," wrote Levi, "except as an enemy, a conqueror, or a visitor devoid of understanding. The seasons pass today over the toil of the peasants just as they did three thousand years before Christ; no message, human or divine, has reached this stubborn poverty." Indeed, an Italian parliamentary investigation in the early twentieth century revealed an extraordinary fact: the wages of peasants had remained the same since 1780.

But in the mid-nineteenth century, southern Italian peasants—especially those from Sicily, considered the most revolutionary area of the country because of its extensive poverty—were holding out some hope for change. They placed their faith in a leading figure of Italian unification, the indefatigable soldier Giuseppe Garibaldi, to restore justice to their land.

The unification of Italy was Garibaldi's lifelong passion. As a young man, Garibaldi was largely influenced by the writings of the Italian radical thinker Giuseppe Mazzini, and he joined Mazzini's secret revolutionary group, Young Italy, which sought to liberate citizens from rule by kings. After being condemned to death in absentia for taking part in a Mazzini-inspired revolution in Genoa, at twenty-eight Garibaldi sailed to South America. He remained there for over a decade, leading the Italian Legion fighters during Uruguay's war with Argentina, and receiving military training that would be essential to his guerilla battle for Italian unification. Although he was exiled from Italy several times, Garibaldi always managed to find a way back, and most of his life consisted of a series of seemingly hopeless battles with an ill-supplied, ragtag army of Italian volunteers dressed in red shirts, throwing bayonets in the face of enemy bullets, or carrying rifles that, more often than not, refused to fire.

Garibaldi was one of four main players of Italian unification in the mid-nineteenth century, charting a course by rallying his vagabond army and trying to work with men who mostly detested each other—the revolutionary thinker Mazzini, the unpredictable monarch Victor Emmanuel II, and the scheming prime minister Camillo di Cavour. To add to the complexity of the quest for national unity, both Victor Emmanuel and Cavour, products of Austrian and French culture in the north, struggled throughout their lives to speak the Italian language.

In 1860, Garibaldi decided to lead his army, known as the Red Shirts or the "Thousand" (technically there were 1,089 volunteers), to Sicily to defeat the Bourbons, a dynasty that had originated in France and now ruled Italy's southern provinces. It was a bold move that may have been based on faulty information about a peasant insurrection in the provinces, which in reality had been suppressed. But a combination of Garibaldi's shrewd military skill and some extraordinary good luck created a scenario that ultimately led to the capture of Sicily and the defeat of twenty-five thousand Neapolitan troops under Bourbon rule.

After the Thousand won an astounding victory in the town of Calatafimi in Sicily, Garibaldi advanced his troops to Palermo. He thought that his only means of defeating the huge Bourbon army depended on getting his men into Palermo undetected and inciting the peasant population to revolt. It was a gamble based on the fact that not a single member of the peasantry in the north or the south had ever joined his nationalist cause. "I wish from my heart," wrote Garibaldi about the Thousand in his memoirs, "that I could have added 'and of the peasant'" to the list of the bricklayers, carpenters, cobblers, engineers, lawyers, and students who joined his army. "But I will not distort the truth. That sturdy and hard-working class belongs to the priests, who keep them in ignorance. There was not one case of them joining the volunteers."

But in Palermo, a different picture emerged. After his victory in Calatafimi, thirty miles away, the people of Palermo rose up in revolt. The peasants emerged from the streets and piazzas bearing knives and daggers. The women—"awe-inspiring," in Garibaldi's words—hurled mattresses, chairs, and furniture from their windows to form barricades against the Neapolitan troops trying to enter the city, and some even poured pots of boiling water on the soldiers who had found their way in.

Garibaldi's ultimate victory meant that the old Kingdom of Sardinia would become the new Kingdom of Italy, with Victor Emmanuel made its ruler in 1861. The final pieces of this unification, called the *Risorgimento*, would still take another ten years to put

The peasants were unwilling to join Garibaldi's nationalist cause until he reached Sicily.

into place. The populist Garibaldi had promised to carry out land reform immediately, but the new monarch preferred to keep the power in the hands of property owners. Conditions deteriorated even further after Garibaldi, who served as the temporary "dictator" of Sicily, introduced two highly unpopular measures: new taxes and a military conscription. Now the peasants, with barely enough food to live on, had to dig deeper into worn pockets to pay taxes that would rise by more than 50 percent. They also had to watch their boys leave home to join a military and defend a country that seemed as foreign to them as the divided land from before.

The Austrian Prince Klemens von Metternich's famous line that Italy was "only a geographical expression" certainly was borne out in the life of the peasants who spoke a regional dialect, knew little beyond village life, and never thought of them-

Italian peasant girl, 1861.

selves as "Italian" or had the time to daydream about any nationalist cause. They didn't even know the word *Italia*, with many believing that *"La Talia"* was Victor Emmanuel's wife. And how could the peasants wave a flag for patriotism without political say? Only about 5 percent of the male population was allowed to vote. To add to the unfairness, the south paid more in taxes, as a percentage of its wealth and economic output, than the north but received less in government aid and services. The belittlement of southerners by northerners—still acutely felt in parts of Italy today—first blossomed after unification, when the north had to pay more attention to its new brethren. "What barbarism!" declared Italian statesman Luigi Carlo Farini after visiting the south. "This is not Italy! This is Africa."

By 1880, a decade after a fully unified Italy, southern Italian peasants could barely survive. In cities and countryside, unemployment, crime, disease, and squalor had become unbearable; the lack of food and money even left some women scraping plaster off their walls to mix into dough in order to stretch the bread supply. These brutal conditions meant that the peasants became even more distrustful of outside authority. The state was seen only as the entity that robbed you of the meager amount you tried to save. "What could they possibly put a new tax on?" wrote Ignazio Silone about peasant life. "Maybe a tax on moonlight?"

Daily life also became much more dangerous: as tax revolts spread throughout the south, local brigands took advantage of the turmoil, wreaking havoc on the land by attacking farms and killing livestock. The government responded by imposing a military law that led to arbitrary arrests and executions. Garibaldi, long dispensed from his duties and discarded by those in power "like an orange peel," described his disillusionment: "The outrages suffered by the people of Southern Italy cannot be quantified. I am convinced that I did nothing wrong, but despite that today I would not take the same route in Southern Italy as I would fear that I would be attacked by stones, because the result was only squalor and hatred."

Under the miserable
conditions they had to
endure, southern Italians
began to hear and to heed
the call to America.

Under these untenable conditions, southern Italians began to hear and to heed the call to America—one that would bring five million people in the course of a century. Word spread throughout isolated villages about those brave enough to leave. American companies put up posters in villages promising pots of gold, state governments recruiting workers sent out leaflets announcing work opportunities, and letters from the earliest migrants beckoned those left behind to cross the ocean. The Italian government tried to discourage emigration, because large landowners needed the peasantry to work the land.

At the end of the nineteenth century it became clear that Garibaldi's dream of a united country had helped to spur its greatest exodus, with the population heading to other countries around the world. By 1905, over seven million people had applied to migrate; it is estimated that the country lost more than sixteen million people between the 1870s and the early 1920s. Trust no one outside the family, and concomitantly, invest all your precious resources in the family, became the credo that southern Italian peasants would bring to America and choose to live by.

Giuseppe Garibaldi

I n a tiny cottage in Staten Island, New York, home of the Garibaldi-Meucci Museum, the cherished symbol of Italian unification— the red shirt—hangs behind glass. The curious choice for a uniform— the bright color announced itself to the enemy like a modern-day traffic light—can be traced to Garibaldi's days in Uruguay, when he led the Italian Legion in 1843. The government, wanting to skimp on the costs of uniforms, found boxes of red overalls intended for Argentine cattle-slaughtering houses, the color blending with the gory work. Garibaldi liked wearing the loose-fitting tunic and decided to make it the uniform of his volunteer Italian army, earning them the moniker "Red Shirts." In the nineteenth century, fashion-crazed aristocratic British women infatuated with the iconoclastic Italian began wearing the shirt, a version of which hangs in Staten Island and marks Garibaldi's time living in exile there—one of the stranger interludes in his storied career.

After Garibaldi failed to take back Rome from papal domination in 1849, he fled north, pursued by the French, who had helped to protect the pope, and then by the Austrians. With hostile forces surrounding him, Garibaldi had to escape Italy, but his pregnant wife, Anita, who had left their other children with relatives so that she could fight with Garibaldi, became mortally ill as they marched through Tuscany and over the Apennines. Garibaldi's eventual exile to America—where friends had urged him to go—followed a huge military defeat, a perilous lengthy escape, and the sudden death of his wife.

Garibaldi's friend Antonio Meucci gave him lodging in his Staten Island cottage, but the great military hero of Italian unification could not stand to be idle or a freeloader. Instead, he persuaded Meucci to open a sausage factory that could employ him and other poor Italian refugees. (Imagine an unemployed General Ulysses Grant flipping hamburgers.) The enterprise was a financial failure, however. Meucci, a better businessman than Garibaldi, soon closed the sausage factory, starting instead a candle factory on his property. Garibaldi was also quite useless at the task of making candles, which required a particular agility in dipping the wick into the tallow. And Meucci, appalled that the famous freedom fighter was performing menial labor along with the impoverished refugees, tried to stop him from working—a move that drove Garibaldi deeper into despair.

Garibaldi found some satisfaction in helping poor refugees, and one day an Italian man came by and asked Garibaldi for a shirt, explaining that he was penniless. Garibaldi told the man that he had only two shirts: the one he was wearing and another in the laundry. Then he remembered that his trunk held the red shirt he had worn in the battle for Rome. At this point Meucci protested, saying that Garibaldi should not give away such a valuable item. Meucci gave the man one of his shirts instead and preserved Garibaldi's, which, according to local lore, is the shirt that hangs in the museum today.

After his astounding victory in Sicily, Garibaldi wore the red shirt for the rest of his life, cementing it as a lasting symbol of a unified Italy. In 1881, eleven months before his death, Garibaldi amended his will to request that he be cremated in a red shirt.

The great military hero of Italian unification could not stand to be idle or a freeloader. Instead, he persuaded Meucci to open a sausage factory.

DOCUMENTI

□

FROM CARLO LEVI'S
CHRIST STOPPED AT EBOLI

Carlo Levi was an Italian Jewish writer, doctor, and painter. Levi's book Cristo si è fermato a Eboli *(Christ Stopped at Eboli) described the time he spent in exile for his anti-Fascist beliefs. The Italian government sent Levi to the town of Aliano, called Gagliano in the book, in the province of Lucania (now known as Basilicata), once the poorest region in Italy. The book was a wake-up call to northerners about the centuries-long plight of southern Italian peasants. The town of Matera—described in the following excerpt by Levi's sister, a physician who came from Turin to visit him—was so poor that many of its residents lived in caves carved into the mountains. Today the area has been declared a World Heritage Site, and some of the grotto homes have been converted into luxury hotels. About twenty-five miles south of Matera, in the town of Bernaldo, the Italian-American filmmaker Francis Ford Coppola opened a luxury hotel in 2011 in honor of his paternal grandfather's birthplace.*

The houses were open on account of the heat, and as I went by I could see into the caves, whose only light came in through the front doors. Some of them had no entrance but a trapdoor and ladder. In these dark holes with walls cut out of the earth I saw a few pieces of miserable furniture, beds, and some ragged clothes hanging up to dry. On the floor lay dogs, sheep, goats, and pigs. Most families have just one cave to live in and there they sleep all together; men, women, children, and animals. This is how twenty thousand people live.

Of children I saw an infinite number. They appeared from everywhere, in the dust and heat, amid the flies, stark naked or clothed in rags; I have never in all my life seen such a picture of poverty. My profession has brought me in daily contact with dozens of poor, sick, ill-kempt children, but I never even dreamed of seeing a sight like this. I saw children sitting on the doorsteps, in the dirt, while the sun beat down on them, with their eyes half-closed and their eyelids red and swollen; flies crawled across the lids, but the children stayed quite still, without raising a hand to brush them away. Yes, flies crawled across their eyelids, and they seemed not even to feel them. They had trachoma. I knew that it existed in the South, but to see it against this background of poverty and dirt was something else again. I saw other children with the wizened faces of old men, their bodies reduced by starvation almost to skeletons, their heads crawling with lice and covered with scabs. Most of them had enormous, dilated stomachs and faces yellow and worn with malaria.

The peasants described the south of Italy to Carlo Levi as the place where Christ forgot to stop.

CHAPTER TWO

Who Killa da Chief?

After Garibaldi's astonishing military success in Sicily, word of his skills traveled across the Atlantic, and President Lincoln tried to recruit the Italian general for a major post in the Union army. The State Department sent an envoy to Garibaldi's home on the island of Caprera, but the encounter proved fruitless when Garibaldi insisted that he be appointed commander in chief with the power to immediately abolish slavery. Never mind that the president of the United States was commander in chief of the army. As Garibaldi knew, Lincoln was a moderate who didn't initially advocate the full abolition of slavery, but only opposed the extension of slavery into new territory. Lincoln needed the continued support of several southern states, and he had been arguing that the war was about preserving the union, not abolishing slavery. The envoy spent the night on Caprera and tried again the next morning to convince Garibaldi to fight for the North's commitment to democracy and constitutional government, but Garibaldi remained absolute in his position and the offer was rescinded.

After the Civil War ended in 1865 and Lincoln's Emancipation Proclamation could be fully implemented, the people replacing the freed African-American slaves who had toiled on sugar and cotton plantations were—ironically, given Garibaldi's lecture in Caprera—southern Italian immigrants, mostly Sicilians. They began arriving in the port city of New Orleans looking, in their words, for *pane e lavoro*, "bread and work."

There were two entry points for European immigrants coming

A mob lynching of Italians in Tampa, Florida.

to America—New York and New Orleans—and the state of Louisiana worked hard to recruit Sicilians to its port, then the second largest in the nation. The plantation owners were desperate to replace the slaves and unhappy with the demands of some African Americans who stayed on as tenant farmers. At first they tried, but failed, to attract white American farmers, as well as Chinese immigrants, who were more interested in working in the fishing industry. In 1866, the state of Louisiana formed a Bureau of Immigration and sent propaganda-filled pamphlets to Europe about opportunities on plantations. They already had some experience working with Sicilians because New Orleans imported citrus from Palermo, and Sicilians were also the only group that responded en masse to their efforts.

By successfully recruiting Sicilians, the state and plantation owners found the right match: southern Italians were used to the cyclical nature of planting, tilling, and reaping under a burning sun and willing to work around the clock. The immigrants were desperate to earn enough money to send home or, in their biggest dreams, to own a small piece of land. Here they would find better conditions than in Italy, despite the brutal nature of the work.

Even the leading advocate for disenfranchised former slaves, Booker T. Washington, noted that conditions for the southern Italian peasant were worse than for the African-American tenant farmer. After visiting southern Italy, he wrote, "I have described at some length the condition of the farm labourers in Italy because it seems to me that it is important that those who are inclined to be discouraged about the Negro in the South should know that his case is by no means as hopeless as that of some others. The Negro is not the man farthest down. The condition of the coloured farmer in the most backward parts of Southern States in America, even where he has the least education and the least encouragement, is incomparably better than the condition and opportunity of the agricultural population in Sicily."

From planting, to harvesting, to cutting and then grinding the cane, the work in Louisiana was backbreaking, but the Italians were up to the task. Growing the cane was a laborious process because the fields needed continuous irrigation and drainage to ensure that the roots wouldn't get too wet and rot. Cutting the cane later in the season meant working sixteen to eighteen hours a day, seven days a week. The Italians often labored side by side with black tenant farmers—and to the surprise and anger of southern whites—also socialized with them. They received the same wages as blacks: seventy-five cents to a dollar a day. Because the peasants had always managed to miraculously grow crops on arid land, the plantation owners were both astonished and delighted by their tireless labor and productivity working on more fertile soil.

Thousands of Sicilians began to head to Louisiana, and from the late 1800s to 1924, over a hundred thousand Italians arrived in the Port of New Orleans. Many worked seasonally and headed north for the rest of the year, but an estimated thirty thousand made New Orleans or the Louisiana parishes their home.

Plantation owners hoped that this cheap labor supply would last forever, but Italians, believing in the promise of America to improve their lot, resented working so hard for so little. They discovered that New Orleans and the Louisiana delta offered more opportunity, and they found jobs there peddling fruits and vegetables, handling cargo on the docks, and working in the fishing industry.

The Italians who settled in Louisiana found opportunities in New Orleans peddling fruits and vegetables.

Many settled in the historic market section of New Orleans. The French Quarter began to be called *Piccolo Palermo*. While Sicilians represented a quarter of all Italians who came to United States, in Louisiana they made up approximately 90 percent of the Italian population. The immigrants lived in appallingly crowded conditions and tended to stick together, displaying in the New World their historic distrust of outsiders. Meanwhile, the southern establishment was both disturbed by the onslaught of poor, olive-skinned Sicilians and resentful of the success of a few. Southerners in positions of power were also concerned about the newcomers' growing influence in local politics.

In this climate of suspicion, a crime took place that would alter and damage the community's relationship with Italians well into the middle of the twentieth century.

On the night of October 15, 1890, the popular police chief of New Orleans, thirty-two-year-old David Hennessy, was returning home late at night with a former colleague. They stopped at a saloon for a snack of oysters, and the two parted ways as Hennessy headed to the home that he shared with his mother. A few minutes later a group of men opened fire on the police chief. Hennessy pulled out his gun and fired back, but his efforts were in vain. His friend, hearing the barrage of gunfire, ran back to the dying Hennessy, who allegedly told him, "The dagos shot me."

The next day, the mayor of the town, Joseph A. Shakespeare, issued this order to his police department: "Scour the whole neighborhood. Arrest every Italian you come across if necessary, and scour it again tomorrow morning as soon as there is daylight enough. Get all the men you need."

The crime story would never be solved. Its interpretation over the years depended on who told the tale. The court documents have been lost, so the only records are the media reports that reflect the bias of the time. To the white establishment, the crime was about the growing influence of the Sicilians and a shadowy organization

New Orleans's popular police chief, David Hennessy.

called "the Mafia" that they were establishing in New Orleans. Most media outlets mimicked this thinking, and it wasn't until many decades later that criminal justice experts and journalists revisited the material and put forth other theories.

A persistent American myth, with roots in this New Orleans crime, is that the Mafia is an ancient Italian organization, highly unified and dating back to as early as the twelfth century. Scholars who have studied the Mafia explain that the word *mafia*, in existence probably as far back as the seventeenth century, originally connoted a form of criminal behavior, not an organized group. In the anarchy after unification, a mafioso was considered an *uomo di rispetto* ("man of respect") who, in the absence of law and order, upheld honor, tradition, and peasant interests and resorted to violence in order to do so. Eventually, one man would achieve dominance in a village and then form associations with family and friends, who composed a *cosche* (literally, "the leaves of an artichoke") for their territory. In this agricultural society, *latifundia* were the large estates throughout Sicily owned primarily by absentee landlords and run by *gabellotti*, estate managers exploiting the peasants who toiled the land. The *gabellotti* hired members of a mafia (or sometimes themselves were mafiosi) for a twofold purpose: to keep the peasants in line, and to acquire more lenient terms from the absentee landlord to rent the properties.

The local Mafia was involved in a range of both legal and illegal activity, and it wielded power by making clear that brutal violence would be used to achieve its ends. The Mafia's presence created a kind of alternative society, parallel to the feeble government; and eventually, the Mafia controlled elections, installing its own people and determining affairs—or at least calling for favors—not only in Sicily but also in Rome. The Mafia also managed the roads and water—charging taxes on these essential aspects of life—and took over the town's commerce, dominating fruit and vegetable markets. While flourishing in lawless Palermo and western Sicily, the Mafia was virtually absent from eastern cities such as Messina and Catania, where industry provided better opportunities and land-

ASSASSINATED

Superintendent of Police David C. Hennessy Victim of the Vendetta.

Ambuscaded at His Doorstep and Six Bullets Shot Into His Body, One of Which is Pronounced Fatal.

The Murderers Declared to be Italians of the Criminal Class.

The word *mafia* was added to the American lexicon after the New Orleans murder of David Hennessy.

lords tended to live on their estates rather than renting to unscrupulous *gabellotti*.

Since Italian immigrants first came in great numbers to the United States, Americans have imagined that what in Italy was a loose-knit organization, composed of about a dozen members in each town, was transformed here into a highly unified criminal society. This bias immediately became clear after the shooting of David Hennessy. Town people linked the murder to his involvement in a fight between Italian stevedores, two rivals named Provenzano and Matranga, who handled fruit cargo. Each wanted control of the lucrative docks, but while the stevedores were certainly thuggish characters, it's unclear whether they had any ties to Mafia criminals in Sicily. The bitter rivalry led to a shootout in which Matranga was wounded, and members of the Italian business community immediately went to the police both to press charges and to testify in court (a response typically considered "American," not the actions of Mafia men bound by a code of honor and distrusting the government). During that trial, people accused the police and Hennessy of protecting the Provenzano clan, and because of his involvement, some claimed later that Hennessy had been shot in revenge.

The rosy portrait of Hennessy after his death was that of a man of uncompromising ethics and civic virtue, but this, too, seems to be a myth in a sordid New Orleans tale. The city was a cesspool of vice and corruption, and even David Hennessy had landed in jail before becoming police chief. He and his cousin Mike had had an ongoing feud with a rival officer competing for promotions and, after being arrested for shooting and murdering the officer, they served prison time until a jury decided that they had acted in self-defense. It was also unclear why, if the white establishment considered both the Provenzanos and the Matrangas "mafiosi," David Hennessy had testified on behalf of the Provenzanos in court.

After Mayor Shakespeare's call to "arrest every Italian," 120 were rounded up—cobblers, fruit sellers, laborers, night watchmen, even a twelve-year-old student—and some were badly beaten. Ultimately, nineteen men, mostly associates of the Matrangas, were arrested, and nine were brought to trial. During the hysteria of the next four months, the press routinely publicized the prosecution theory that these men were part of a secret Italian society known as the Mafia. New Orleans's *Daily Picayune* reported that the trial was a "war between American law and order and Italian assassination." The case received national attention, and as far away as Chicago, Italian Americans contributed to a defense fund.

Finally, following much conflicting evidence and testimony, the jury cast a verdict of "not guilty" for six of the men and failed to reach one for the other three. The shocked judge refused to let the men go free and ordered them to return to the parish prison that night. Outraged community leaders didn't believe the jury's explanation of reasonable doubt about a crime committed in the dark without eyewitnesses and alleged that the jury had been paid off. They quickly organized a mass meeting calling all citizens "to take steps to remedy the failure of justice in the Hennessy case. Come prepared for action."

The next morning, thousands of people headed to the square, and a lawyer and rally leader named William S. Parkerson exhorted, "When the courts fail, the people must act! What protection, or assurance of protection, is there left us, when the very head of our police department, our chief of police, is assassinated in our very midst by the Mafia Society, and his assassins are again turned loose on the community."

The masses were furious and whipped into action. When another meeting leader, John Wickliffe, asked whether the crowds would follow him to the jail to vindicate this crime, they shouted back, "Yes! Hang the dago murderers!" The crowd asked if they should get their guns, and Parkerson told them to do so immediately.

Parkerson and Wickliffe considered themselves reformers trying to fix a corrupt system—and indeed the New Orleans political system was deeply corrupt. But at the time, the "reform" movement also consisted of white separatists, like both of them, work-

With calls to "hang the dago murderers," the masses assembled outside the parish prison.

ing to take away the vote from blacks. These men feared that the underclass would take control, and they were concerned about the Sicilians' gaining positions in local politics, believing that the Italians would poison the American political system with their nefarious Mafia organization.

That Saturday morning they rallied a crowd of over eight thousand people, many of them now armed. The mob marched to the jail, quickly overtook the prison wardens, and stormed the gates. The acquitted Italians tried to hide, crouching under benches and behind posts, but the mob riddled them with bullets while shouting, "Death to the dagos!"

The crowd waiting outside the prison wanted a piece of the action too, so Parkerson delivered two men to them. Both had been wounded and could now be lynched by the mob. They were hung from a lamppost and tree, their dying bodies dragged, kicked, and beaten with sticks and canes. Men carrying rifles and shotguns continued to pump them full of bullets; some even used their bodies for target practice. At the end of that bloody day, eleven Italians had been murdered and lynched, and the organizers told the cheering crowd that it had done its civic duty by ridding New Orleans of thugs and murderers.

The next day the *New York Times* headline announced "Chief Hennessy Avenged." The paper's editorial read, "These sneaking and cowardly Sicilians, the descendants of bandits and assassins, who have transported to this country the lawless passions, the cut throat practices and the oathbound societies, are to us as a pest without mitigation." While it continued that "orderly and lawabiding persons will not pretend that the butchery of the Italians was either 'justifiable or proper,'" the editorial concluded, "it would be difficult to find any one individual who would confess that privately he deplores it very much."

The effect of the lynching on the Italian-American community in New Orleans was profound. Many had been bullied since the start of the trial, leading them to quit their jobs in New Orleans or head back to Italy. When ships from Italy arrived packed with thousands of immigrants, they were taunted and jeered. The Italian government was furious over the treatment of men who had been acquitted by a jury, and diplomatic relations were strained for over a year. The wound festered after a grand-jury report exonerated the actions of the mob, describing its members as "several thousand of the first, best and even the most law-abiding" citizens. The press continued to sensationalize the story and frighten Americans, writing that the United States was on the verge of a naval war with Italy. Diplomatic relations were restored only after the US government agreed to pay a small reparation to some of the families of the murdered men—an action denounced by Congress.

The trial over the murder of David Hennessy and the New Orleans lynching painted a portrait of Italian-American immigrants not only as poor and downtrodden, but as the dark-skinned "other"—born criminals, violent and primitive in nature. After the New Orleans lynching, the press began to routinely describe any crime committed by Italians as Mafia activity. The Italians of New Orleans, once eager to come to this land to escape the unending cycle of poverty and desperation, were cast together under a net of criminality. They were among the first victims of a troubling and persistent American tendency to target entire immigrant communities for the crimes of the few.

The community never failed to remind Italian Americans of their presumed guilt over the murder of the city's police chief. One taunt, mimicking the Italians' broken English, began at the time of the trial and persisted for decades. Whether posed to a schoolchild desperate to assimilate into the mainstream or to a shopkeeper trying to earn a living, the question, designed to keep the ethnic group in its place, was always the same: "Who killa da chief?"

The parish prison after the lynchings.

CHAPTER THREE

Birds of Passage

n America, Italians rapidly encountered extraordinary difficulties, confined to backbreaking labor, cramped into squalid living, and maligned by accusations of an innate criminality. Yet still, with hope attached to hardship and the steady ache of desperation, they came, the majority leaving Italy from the port of Naples to arrive in New York Harbor. If their village lacked a railroad, the peasants would walk vast distances, with men, by some accounts, packing their belongings into saddlebags tossed atop tiny donkeys to travel over two hundred miles from the hills of Basilicata, then known as Lucania, to Naples. Nearly two million southern Italians came to the United States between 1898 and 1909.

While the economy in America's South languished at the end of the nineteenth century, in the Northeast workers were badly needed to fuel what some historians have called the second industrial revolution, the surge of development powered by electricity and fortified by steel. Italians came prepared to serve as the human capital in the undertaking of this immense production. Unlike immigrant groups who fled their countries because of political and religious persecution along with economic hardship, and knew they would never return home, most Italians came purely for economic reasons and hoped to return as soon as possible.

The men usually arrived first, and wives, children, and other family members would be summoned if the husbands found steady work. Poor and desperate, these men took any jobs available and put themselves in extraordinarily dangerous situations digging the tunnels and erecting the pillars of the subway and rail lines, water systems, sewers, dams, and aqueducts in the Northeast.

Mulberry Street, circa 1900.

For most immigrants, the arrival at Ellis Island followed a treacherous journey traveling in the ship's steerage.

To be successful was to send money home—dollars that could mean the difference between life and death in parts of southern Italy. As one Calabrian peasant remarked, "Without America to send us money, we would now be eating one another." In America, an Italian laborer could make $1.25 for ten hours of backbreaking work—the equivalent of a little over six lire. In Italy, a standard wage for twelve hours of work was one lira. Despite such deprivation, Italians wanted to return to Italy, convinced they could save enough money to live better there. No other immigrant group repatriated in numbers as high as the Italians; an estimated 50 percent went back permanently.

Leaving the homeland was a trauma for every family member, and the effects of the departure would shape lives for generations to come. Mothers hung on to trains pulling out from the stations bound for port cities—a futile grasp in the knowledge that they might never see their sons again. Once arriving at the port, the emigrants had to contend with a variety of hucksters offering goods. Men sold rope—an essential item—because few could afford suitcases and most had packed makeshift bags constructed of wooden frames covered in paper and cloth. Along with their belongings, the emigrants would carry favorite foods like chunks of pecorino and sacks of chickpeas that could last the long sea voyage.

Couples brought colorful balls of yarn, or thread from a favorite garment, to enact a farewell ritual. Once on board, the husband grabbed an end and tossed the yarn to his wife standing onshore. Each clung tightly as the ship slowly pulled out of the harbor and the ball unwound. The string bound the couple until they could hold on no longer; once it snapped from their grip, they watched it sway in the wind and gently descend into the vast sea.

Sadness, fear, seasickness, scant food, and the smell of vomit defined each journey, along with the pungent disinfectant phenic acid. The peasants often brought their own bowls, attached to their necks by string, because the ones used on board carried thick layers of grime. The voyage itself could take from eleven days to four weeks over rough waters. Everyone packed in steerage, located near the rudder below the ship's waterline, had the benefit of only a glimmer of light from a porthole. If someone perished during the journey, the body would be tossed into the ocean.

Italian mothers expressed their grief and skepticism in popular lullabies. A child asks for a hundred lire to go to America but the mother answers "no, no, no." Another explains, "Your mother's house is warm, is safe, is gold / Outside is dark, is black, the wolf is there."

At Ellis Island, examiners would inspect each prospective immigrant for any "defects" or health problems that would require them to mark an "X" on the person's arm. Common illnesses of southern Italy, such as the eye disease trachoma, which was caused by drinking nonpotable water, would lead to deportation. When families began to arrive together in later years, an "X" from the medical exam could mean permanent separation.

The questions asked by immigration officers posed more obstacles: Did you pay for your passage, and is a job waiting for you? A "yes" to the first question and a "no" to the second were the only

At Ellis Island, examiners would inspect immigrants for any "defects" or health problems.

At the bottom of the labor pool, Italians took whatever job was available.

This derogatory sheet music made fun of the Italian peasants' vowel-laden speech.

acceptable answers. The American government was trying to put an end to the *padrone* system, which thrived among the first wave of immigrants. The *padrone* was the labor recruiter, the "patron" or boss, who persuaded the peasant farmer to come to America, lending him money for the voyage at a high interest rate—sometimes 100 percent—and expecting a piece of his wages once employed in the New World.

Observers compared the system to slave labor, but the worker, while badly treated, was also accustomed to the client-patron relationship of southern Italy and accepted his lot. The *padrone* did not hold these men as his personal property, and the laborer was dependent on but not completely subservient to his boss. Sometimes a *padrone* would be a man from the same village in Italy who had gone to America earlier and had the knowledge and contacts to pave the way for the next group of men. Despite the Americans' interest in stopping the system, it eventually ended not from their efforts, but because enough Italians had arrived in the New World that family and friends could help bring over those who had remained.

The early immigrants' back-and-forth pattern of migration gave them the name "birds of passage." Sometimes they stayed no longer than six months and returned to Italy numerous times. The wives who remained behind, called "white widows," wore all white to signal their precarious position instead of the traditional black mourning garb. Their social status in the village was a little above that of the wives whose husbands didn't have the courage to leave. But there was also much gossip about these young women without husbands, and often families insisted that the woman live with the husband's brother or parents in order to keep a close eye on her behavior.

Although wages in the New World were extremely low, the few dollars sent back to Italy went a lot further than they did in America. This extra cash enabled mothers to feed their children and

Workers laying out the warp for weaving cloth at a Pennsylvania silk mill.

sometimes permitted them to buy meat or fish, a luxurious feast compared to a typical meal for impoverished peasants, which might consist solely of *acqua sale*, stale bread soaked in boiling water with a little salt and trickle of olive oil for some flavor.

Immigrants who came into New York Harbor and decided to remain in the city would most likely live in Lower Manhattan or East Harlem, areas that housed the majority of Italians. Each block tended to attract specific regions from Italy. For example, Sicilians lived mostly on Elizabeth Street, while Mulberry Street tended to be Neapolitan. These immigrants each spoke the dialect of their region and often had a difficult time understanding the other dialects. Their living pattern continued a way of life known as *campanilismo* (from the word *campanile*, meaning "bell tower")—the notion that a village was defined by being within hearing distance of the bell tower's chime. Its meaning was also metaphoric: *campanilismo* suggested a parochialism that trailed the southern Italian and found a place among the newly defined boundaries of Manhattan's narrow streets.

The Italians may have stayed "with their own," but they also needed the company of each other to mitigate the utter bleakness and squalor of the boardinghouses and tenements in which they lived. The tenements of New York City were shoddily built and prone to collapse, with sloping floors, improper ventilation, and almost no plumbing or heat (one tap for a floor was common, and toilets would be outside or in the cellar). These dark, narrow, vermin-ridden, severely overcrowded spaces were breeding grounds for diseases like smallpox, tuberculosis, and typhoid. Their horrendous conditions first came to light after the photojournalist Jacob Riis published *How the Other Half Lives* in 1890. "If we could see the air breathed by these poor creatures in their tenements," a prominent doctor told Riis, "it would show the air to be fouler than the mud of the gutters." Riis's work helped galvanize attention to the horrendous living conditions, but a deep prejudice toward Italians, Jews, Chinese, and African Americans oozed from the journalist's pen: "As the Chinaman hides his knife in his sleeve and the Italian hides his stiletto in the bosom, so the negro goes to the ball with a razor in his boot-leg."

Conditions in other Italian colonies, such as Boston's North End and Chicago's Near West End were similarly bleak: filth, vermin, and overcrowding created dehumanizing environments. As the Italian playwright Giuseppe Giacosa observed, "The only concern of Americans toward Italian immigrants is that of a sordid, degrading and insensible disinterest. The clothes, food and living quarters of the common Italian in New York and Chicago present a spectacle of such supine resignation to poverty."

Men assigned by their *padrone* to work gangs, such as those who built railroad tracks or labored in large factories, experienced some of the worst conditions. These men slept not in tenement slums, but in boxcars with "beds" constructed of boards placed over boxes and bags of straw serving as mattresses. The tiny, confined spaces would often be infested with roaches and bedbugs. Some men wrote of their discouragement—yes, they had come from abject poverty, but at least in southern Italy they had light and air and space, as well as a family to turn to in times of illness or trouble.

If the southern Italian peasant once had imagined that America's streets were paved with gold, soon he learned, as the old story goes, that one, they weren't even paved, and two, he was expected to pave them. Arriving in the Northeast as a giant infrastructure was being put into place, the Italians, at the bottom of the labor pool, known as greenhorns, wops, dagos, and macaroni, took whatever job was available. Even for people accustomed to backbreaking work in the fields, the labor in the New World was exponentially more difficult—and dangerous. Failure on a construction job often led to fatalities, and the unluckiest of these workers suffered horrific deaths—impaled by steel, suffocated by concrete, drowned and trapped by exploding water mains.

"Work! Sure!" a beleaguered laborer sarcasticially remarked in Pietro Di Donato's *Christ in Concrete*, a novel based on the fate of the author's father, who had been killed on a construction site. "For America beautiful will eat you and spit your bones into the earth's hole."

Digging ditches, collecting garbage, paving roads, picking rags, washing dishes, peddling fruit, chiseling bricks, laying track, excavating tunnels and mines—these men, like each generation of immigrants who have come to America, had chosen to remove themselves from the familiar patterns of the life they had known for difficult and dispiriting work. The journey crushed some, others returned, and the rest built a new life in America, forever changing the course of their family story.

Workers at a macaroni factory. Those who labored in large factories often experienced some of the worst conditions, sleeping in boxcars on beds made of loose boards and bags of straw.

DOCUMENTI

□

THE ART OF B. AMORE

So who tells the story now? . . . The people are gone but their "things" are still here. Looking at, touching, holding them, the people become present. Perhaps that is the attachment to existing objects. I am reminded of them and they are present in some way. The past and the present are intertwined. They exist simultaneously . . . The work is not about memory even though memory is a part of it. It's much more about the questions that are raised—looking into the past for clues to the present. Who were these characters who had so much influence? What in their lives caused them to take the roles they did? Why were they the ways they were which affected me so deeply?

—B. Amore, *Journal*

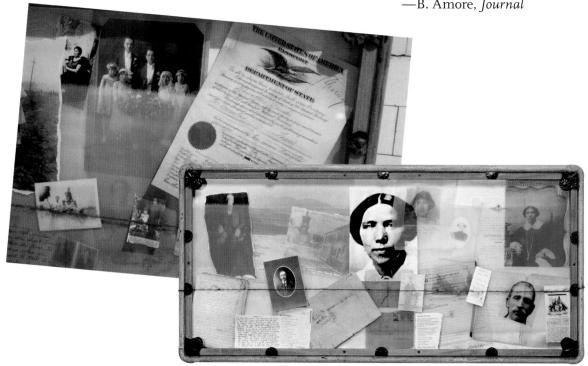

Following the thread: B. Amore connects the panels documenting the lives of her great-grandparents with a red thread, symbolizing the farewell ritual of bringing a piece of yarn aboard the ship to America and letting it go as the vessel left the Italian port city. Her family's nineteenth-century artifacts (on table) include a dowry knife, two reliquaries, a *Libro di Memorie*, passport, wedding cup, weights and measures, handmade tin-and-copper small pan, and handmade brass ravioli cutter.

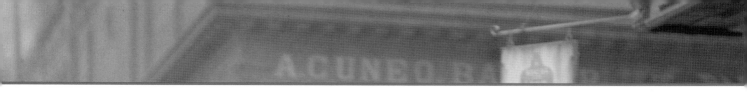

CHAPTER FOUR

A Secret History

By the first decade of the twentieth century, wives and children were joining their husbands and families and beginning to establish roots in America. Italian enclaves known as Little Italies appeared in cities across the country: Philadelphia, Boston, Providence, Baltimore, Chicago, St. Louis, Cleveland, and San Francisco. The largest by far was in New York City, and the area around Mulberry Street beat with the clamor and steady stream of urban life. Each decade, the number of Italians in New York City rose exponentially: while there were well under 100,000 Italians in 1890, by 1900 there were about 220,000, and by 1910 the already overcrowded housing swelled with more than half a million people.

The immigrants, determined to lessen the abysmal poverty of tenement life, began to re-create elements of the old *paese*. Already they were settling on streets with Italians who spoke the same dialect and worshipped the same patron saint. Soon they would try to replicate what may have been, next to their families, the ingredient missing most in their lives: the food of their regions. The Italians believed that American salt wasn't as flavorful as its Mediterranean counterpart, its tomatoes not as sweet, and its bread not as crusty, and they wanted food from the Old World in the New World.

Selling food, especially to one's own people, has traditionally been an inroad for new immigrants trying to find work, and soon pushcarts with products like bread, vegetables, and wild greens crammed the dusty, unpaved streets. As Italians saved money and could begin to afford commercial space, they elevated pushcart

A clam vendor sells to customers on Mulberry Street.

businesses into fruit and vegetable stores. Eventually they opened bakeries, live poultry markets, cheese shops, and pasta stores.

The appeal of the immigrants' first food shops in New York City has endured for over a century: The cheese shop that Basilicata native Savino Di Palo opened in Little Italy in 1910 still produces fresh mozzarella daily. In Greenwich Village, Veniero's Pastry Shop has been baking confections since 1894, Faicco's Pork Store selling meats and specialties since 1900, and Raffetto's pasta shop making ravioli since 1906—the aromatic scents of each shop preserving the flavors of the culture.

Yet pushcart vendors and store owners were prime targets of an extortion racket led by thugs calling themselves the Black Hand, successors to the violent Irish gangs, with names like the Forty Thieves, the Plug Uglies, and the Roach Guards, that once had controlled a squalid area of the Lower East Side known as Five Points. The organization sent its victims extortion letters signed *La Mano Nera* ("the Black Hand")—a name first used by nineteenth-century anarchists in Spain who terrorized the wealthy, claiming to work on behalf of the have-nots.

Bread sellers on Mulberry Street. Selling food, especially to one's own people, has traditionally been an inroad for immigrants.

The immigrants, isolated and unable to speak English, were mostly powerless against the blackmail, forced to either pay up or suffer. The threatening letters targeted wealthy Italians as well; even if the mark agreed to a negotiated amount, the Black Hand often continued its demands until the victim was drained. Gang members even tried to blackmail tenor Enrico Caruso when he came to New York to perform (Caruso went to the police, who caught all the perpetrators).

As the Black Hand became more embedded in urban life, different theories emerged as to whether these men developed ties to Mafia criminals in southern Italy. While some notorious New York gang leaders most likely did, such as Ignazio Lupo (the redundant "Lupo the Wolf"), others worked alone or in small groups. Merely using the words "Black Hand" was enough to terrorize the population, and it was easy for a few gang members to form their own extortion group and put a letter in the mail.

While the majority of Black Hand crime took place in New York because of its huge immigrant population, extortionists preyed on every city with an Italian colony. Financial envy could spur a Black Hand letter, as experienced by a fruit stand owner in Baltimore who had purchased his own home and whose son was said to have flaunted the family wealth. After the gang burned down his fruit stand, the man never purchased another piece of property, solely keeping his money in the bank. A letter to a Pittsburgh man instructed him to hand over $2,000 in gold or die by the blade of a steel knife. Dynamite destroyed produce stores and butcher shops in Chicago, where the *Daily Tribune* reported that one-third of the Italian population paid tribute money to the Black Hand. Hundreds lived in fear of receiving these creepy death threat letters with crude drawings of bones, knives, and nooses.

The Black Hand employed tactics that terrorists use today: bombing stores and public spaces, killing men, women, and children to make their statement. Random terror reigned in New York's Little Italy as Black Hand members bombed pushcarts and more than thirty stores in the course of a few years. The thugs det-

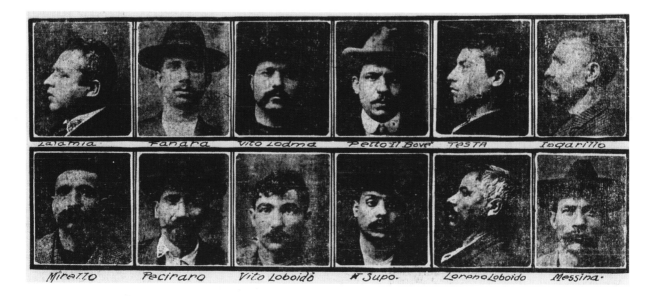

Lalamia · | Fanara | Vito Lodma | Petto il Bove | Testa | Lagarillo

Miretto | Peciraro | Vito Loboido | N Jupo. | Lorenzo Loboido | Messina ·

Thugs calling themselves the Black Hand preyed on immigrants, demanding that they pay up or their stores would be bombed. Police believed the Black Hand members pictured above were tied to a counterfeiting ring.

onated dynamite crudely, sometimes intending to target one store but bombing half a block by mistake.

They acted with impunity because the immigrants would rarely go to the police. The Italians' inherent distrust of outsiders affected the decision to remain silent, but they also acted pragmatically, seeing that those who did talk usually suffered a worse fate. A saying among Sicilians summed up their fear and unwillingness to trust anyone outside of the family: "You have eyes you no see; you have nose you no smell; you have tongue you no speak; you have hands you no touch."

Giovanna Pontillo, an immigrant from the fishing village of Scilla in Calabria, the famous town of Greek mythology where the sea monster Scylla terrorized sailors, was one of the many unlucky immigrants extorted by the Black Hand. After her husband was killed on a construction site in Brooklyn, she remarried, to a widower named Rocco Siena, a pushcart vendor. When the couple had saved enough money to open a fruit and vegetable store, the Black Hand paid a call asking for a weekly kickback. Siena refused to give up the small amount of profit he was earning and said no. After several warnings to pay up, the gang bombed his store, and Siena was lucky to survive the carnage from the destruction.

But Giovanna took a rare step. Believing that she didn't have much else to lose once their store had been destroyed, she went to a police officer named Giuseppe Petrosino, an Italian American trying to rid the neighborhood of this canker. Petrosino headed what was then known as the Italian Squad, a team of five Italian-American police officers who spoke numerous dialects, wore disguises, and tried to gather intelligence about the Black Hand. The department asked Petrosino to go to Sicily to gather information on criminals after an immigration law passed that refused entry to all those who were wanted for or convicted of a crime in their country of origin. Petrosino was hoping to use this intelligence to deport Black Hand members. But the rising star of the police department had become a well-known figure in New York and Italy; he was spotted in Sicily and murdered.

BOMB SHAKES UP BINGHAM'S OFFICE

Black Hand Explosion Wrecks Store and Tenements in Elizabeth Street.

FOUR ITALIANS ARRESTED

Men, Women, and Children Tumble Into the Street as Windows Crash About Them.

Four Italians are under arrest on suspicion that they know something about the explosion. One of the prisoners is Benedito Benigno of 196 Stone Avenue, Brooklyn. The others were arrested at the same address. Two of them are brothers of Benigno. The other gave his name as Ludovico Binconte.

A Black Hand bomb, exploded at 244 Elizabeth Street early yesterday morning, shook Police Headquarters itself, near by.

Many Italian stores have been blown up in the district around Headquarters, but yesterday morning's explosion was of such violence that the official roof tree of Commissioner Bingham came near being wrenched out of place.

The bomb was evidently not of dynamite, for that explosive drives downward, and the store of Senna & Co., at 244 Elizabeth Street, had its entire front ripped out, while across the street the tall tenements at 243, 245, 247, 249, and 251 had their many windows smashed.

Coming as it did in the quiet of a Sunday morning the reverberation, the crash of falling timbers, and the tinkling of falling panes of glass down the iron fire escapes of the tenements, set the colony of Italians in a state of panic. Out they poured from the tenements, struggling hundreds of half-clad men, women, and children, and cries for the police sounded shrilly on the air.

Lt. Joseph Petrosino (left) headed the "Italian Squad" to root out Black Hand members, pictured here escorting gang member Tomasso Petto ("Petto the Ox"), second from left.

For Giovanna, the news could not have been bleaker. With dangers surrounding her and nowhere to turn, she found herself in the predicament that defined her Calabrian village: caught between Scylla and Charybdis. Shortly after Petrosino's death, Giovanna's daughter Angelina celebrated her fourth birthday. A neighbor told Giovanna that she would take the little girl for a birthday treat—a banana, her favorite fruit. What Giovanna never could have imagined was that her neighbor was a sister of a Black Hand member. Having surmised that Giovanna had gone to the police, the Black Hand kidnapped Angelina, taking her to an isolated area of Brooklyn, where she lived in a lice-infested room, left to sleep on a pile of hay.

Kidnappings, along with bombings, were a common Black Hand

Angelina Siena on her fourth birthday. The next day, the Black Hand kidnapped her.

practice. They sent ransom notes smeared with blood; they put pieces of Angelina's hair in the envelope warning, "If you don't send the money, this is the last thing you'll ever see of her." Most kidnapped children were murdered even if ransom had been paid, but Angelina was one of the lucky ones. Four months later, after the family had been drained of its money, Angelina was returned. No longer able to bear these streets filled with vice and vermin, Rocco and Giovanna moved their family across the river to New Jersey as soon as they could afford to, eventually opening an ice cream store there. Leaving large Italian colonies was a smart choice for Black Hand victims because entering more assimilated communities where immigrants were adopting American customs and trusting the police gave them much greater protection.

When Angelina was in her eighties, her granddaughter, Laurie Fabiano, author of the historical novel *Elizabeth Street*, interviewed her about the kidnapping that had haunted the rest of her life. "She remembered every detail," says Fabiano. "She remembered the color of the blinds in the room where they had her. It was just so amazing to see how a crime could etch itself upon a person like that, and also realize how this crime had impacted my mother and her siblings and had impacted our family as well." For Fabiano, even bringing friends over to the house when she was young became a traumatic and mortifying occasion. Her fearful grandmother would tell her, "Get them out of the house. They're not blood. They're not family."

When her grandmother began to describe the kidnapping, she asked Fabiano to turn off the tape recorder because she still believed that there are some things in life you don't tell—that families are kept safe through silence. "I still feel terrible about lying to my grandmother that day when I kept the tape running," Fabiano said, "but I felt it was more important to have this story as an historical record. There's much Italian-American history that has been lost because families have refused to speak. And it wasn't even dramatic things like what happened to my family, but so many families have just lost so much of their history in the not telling."

The silence and secrets would have lasting repercussions in the nation's Little Italies. First-generation Italian Americans remained separate and isolated and had more difficulty assimilating than did other immigrant groups, such as the English-speaking Irish and the Germans, who were more comfortable with the language's Anglo-Saxon roots. The media also treated Italian crime differently from the murder and mayhem committed by Irish gangs or Russian, Jewish, and Polish criminals, who also blackmailed under the moniker of the Black Hand. Since the late 1800s, Italians in America had been branded by stereotyping with newspapers reporting that where Sicilians gathered, so did the Mafia.

The victimizing of the vulnerable Italian immigrant population by the Black Hand did not begin to diminish until around 1915. The federal government enforced laws prohibiting the use of mail as a means to defraud, and Black Hand members had to deliver notes personally, making their endeavors trickier to carry out (although professional gangs were skilled in having others—such as, in Angelina's case, the iceman—leave notes). The number of immigrants also began to drop, decreasing the pool of potential victims. By the 1920s the Black Hand had essentially disappeared, but left in its wake was a terrorized population of urban immigrants, who held serious doubts as to whether leaving southern Italy meant escaping its hopelessness and despair.

Our Ancestors

Giuseppe Petrosino

After Giuseppe Petrosino was murdered in Sicily on what was supposed to be a secret fact-finding mission, he received a tribute in America that gave him the distinction of being perhaps the most celebrated officer in the history of the New York City Police Department. Over two hundred thousand people lined the streets and crowded on balconies to witness the procession from Little Italy to the cemetery in Queens where he was buried.

"If Petrosino had died a President or an Emperor," the *New York Times* reported, "no deeper or truer show of feeling could have been manifested." The crowds were so great that from Fourteenth to Forty-Second Streets police officers were delayed repeatedly as they attempted to clear the roads.

Known as Joseph, Giuseppe Petrosino was a diminutive man of five feet three inches, with a square face marked by smallpox scars. In 1873, when he was thirteen, his family emigrated from the town of Padua in the province of Salerno to New York. Petrosino worked a series of odd jobs until he was hired by the sanitation department as a street sweeper. In the late nineteenth century, the police department ran the sanitation department, enabling Petrosino to work his way up and eventually to be hired onto the force—an unusual accomplishment for an Italian American at the time.

From his early days in the police department, Petrosino was determined to fight the Black Hand, deeply disturbed that a group of thuggish Italians was preying on its own people and preventing the immigrants from lifting themselves out of poverty. His ability to master many dialects and his penchant for wearing disguises

Once Black Hand members discovered that they were being duped by a police officer, they tried to signal to others when Petrosino was present. In several southern Italian dialects the word *petrosino* means "parsley," which prompted the peddlers helping Black Hand members to yell messages such as, "Parsley on sale today."

enabled him to infiltrate the group. Once Black Hand members discovered that they were being duped by a police officer, they tried to signal to others when Petrosino was present. In several southern Italian dialects the word *petrosino* means "parsley," which prompted the peddlers helping Black Hand members to yell messages such as, "Parsley on sale today."

The highest echelons of the department noticed Petrosino's intelligence work on both the Black Hand and anarchist groups, and Police Commissioner Theodore Roosevelt appointed Petrosino sergeant of detectives, the first Italian American to reach such a high rank. Eight years later, in 1903, the department tapped Petrosino to lead the newly created Italian Squad, later renamed the Bomb Squad. When the department told Petrosino, by then a lieutenant, about a fact-finding mission to Italy in 1909, he was nearly fifty years old and recently married, with a baby girl named Adelina. His new domestic happiness made him deeply reluctant to go, and even his parish priest begged him to stay, fearing he would be killed. The mission was supposed to be top secret, but in a colossal misjudgment, the police commissioner leaked the story to the press, perhaps to score points for an upcoming election by portraying the department's determination to eradicate violent gangs. Every major newspaper printed the story, which soon spread to Europe.

Once in Italy, Petrosino still believed that his identity had been kept secret until he arrived in his home village and his brother showed him the local paper with an article describing his trip to gather intelligence on criminal activity. Still, he didn't turn back, continuing to Sicily. Lured by the promise of an informant, Petrosino went to the Piazza Marina in Palermo and was circling an enclosed, tree-lined park called the Garibaldi Garden when he was murdered.

His standing as one of New York City's most important and renowned crime fighters has mostly been lost in the pages of history, but the 1960 movie *Pay or Die* made the savvy lieutenant its protagonist, portrayed by Ernest Borgnine, and in 2009 the Lt. Joseph Petrosino Park in New York's Little Italy was dedicated to him.

DOCUMENTI

□

BLACK HAND EXTORTION

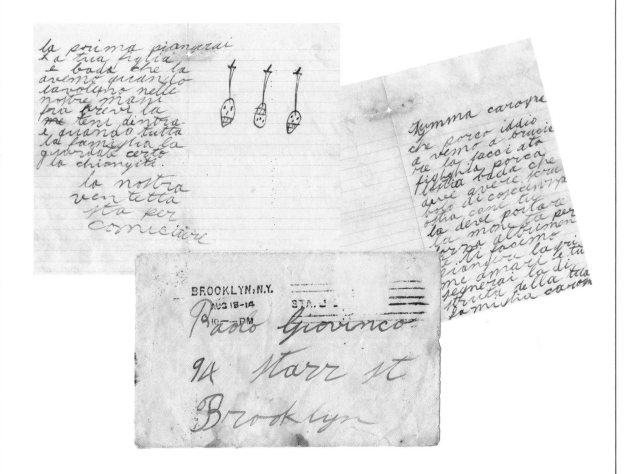

Translation of extortion letter (from the Italian American Museum): "Dirty bastard. Goddamn pig. We will burn the face of your daughter. Goddamn pig. You will find yourself with a guilty conscience you dog. You must bring the money otherwise we will make you weep bitter tears and you will be responsible for the destruction of your family. Bastard. First you will cry for your daughter and look that we can have her in our hands whenever we want. Before long, we will have her hostage and when your family will see her certainly you will mourn for her. Our vendetta is about to begin."

CHAPTER FIVE

Up from the Ashes

The Italians in San Francisco shared the plight of all poor immigrants arriving in America: they lived in shoddily built and crowded housing that exposed them to communicable diseases, they faced exploitation as unskilled and semiskilled laborers, and they suffered discrimination because they didn't speak English. Yet the western experience offered promise and possibilities that seemed merely dreams back east. By the early 1900s, Italians were shaping the economic development of California in agriculture and fishing, as well as in real estate and banking.

Was it the possibility of the West—the psychological freedom drawing so many to its vast uncharted land—that laid the path for this success? Was it the lack of interest in a class status that preoccupied eastern society? The Italians who first arrived in California had one clear advantage: they were a northern Italian population of peasants, living in an area that in the 1850s had established some of the first passenger ship service from Italy to San Francisco. They were poor certainly, but not as desperately poor as those from southern Italy.

The northerners also had fewer obstacles to overcome once they reached the New World. Prejudice existed, of course, but it was tempered by the American imagination of northern Italy as the land of Michelangelo and Leonardo da Vinci, and a promising composer named Giuseppe Verdi—far different from the image promulgated in the South and on the East Coast of a "Sicilian Mafia"

Main Street in San Francisco's North Beach, where many early Italians settled.

infiltrating American life. And it didn't hurt that the northern Italians were taller than their southern counterparts and had lighter skin and hair color—traits that matched more closely America's dominant groups.

Italians from Genoa, Tuscany (mainly from the province of Lucca), Piedmont, and the Veneto came to Sacramento, San Francisco, and the Sierra Nevada foothills as early as 1850, enticed by the great gold rush. Even when the promise of gold had vanished, its legacy of energy, possibility, and optimism remained. Northern California's verdant hills, sloping valleys, clear waters, and cinnamon and terra-cotta colors remarkably matched the home these immigrants had left behind, and they welcomed the beauty of the land, although, like most Italians entering America, they imagined it as only a temporary layover before returning home.

When southern Italians, lured by railroad agents who came to their villages with oversized promises of jobs and land, began to arrive in San Francisco in the late nineteenth century, the United States was in an economic downturn. Many fewer jobs were available, and the immigrants packed into an already crowded housing stock. For years, tensions existed between the two Italian communities, and for a while it seemed as if the beloved "Italian Colony" the northerners had created would be dismantled by the forces of poverty and illiteracy. But the northern Italians, in a mix of pragmatism and humanism, followed, for the most part, their better angels and lent a helping hand to their less fortunate brethren.

Far from the New York City nightmare of the Black Hand bombing a store owner who had just discovered the meaning of profit, the established residents helped build a community that provided opportunity, assistance, and education. The story of the Italians in California provides another template for America's immigration history, one suggesting that an ethnic group can thrive if prejudice doesn't overwhelm reason and an effective network of government, business, and community encourages immigrants to participate in civic life.

———

Once the initial wave of northern Italians had discovered the harsh realities of the search for gold, they left the mining camps in the 1850s and headed to San Francisco to work in agriculture and later in the fishing industry. They originally settled in the Latin Quarter and then moved to Telegraph Hill, whose steep terrain reminded them of home, and soon North Beach and Fisherman's Wharf filled with Italians. Those who chose to plant large farms settled in the more open space of the Mission District.

The immigrants pushed food carts and opened grocery stores, stringing salamis and hanging dried pasta by the yard. They became truck farmers, growing artichokes, lettuces, and cabbage. Some left farming to establish themselves in the fruit commission business, acting as go-betweens for the farmers and store and restaurant owners. The most successful of this group of agricultural workers established national canneries for fruits and vegetables.

An agricultural depression in Italy in the 1880s and '90s brought more Italians from Genoa to America's West. Some tried their hand at fishing, adopting methods from Italy for the California waters. They used a traditional small boat called the *felucca* that could navigate the wind and rough waters and an imported trawling net, a *paranzella*. Sicilian fishermen arrived later, and their presence created some of the worst tensions and violent conflicts between the northern and southern communities.

The Sicilians made clear that they wanted to be independent operators instead of working for the northern Italians, and in this battle for dominance, boats were sunk and nets cut. Eventually an agreement, or at least acknowledgment that the Sicilians weren't leaving, was reached and the spoils divided: the Genovese ran the deepwater and tuna fishing, while the Sicilians were left with the less lucrative inshore fishing. By the beginning of the twentieth century, many of the Genovese had turned to other industries, leaving the Sicilians in charge. In the heart of Little Italy at Fisherman's Wharf, the Sicilians brought in a wide assortment of daily catch: crab, salmon, sardines, striped bass, lobster, clams, oysters, rock cod, and herring, and they even introduced a new fish to the American palate—calamari, or squid. The Italians provided 90 percent of the fish consumed in San Francisco, and statewide they controlled 80 percent of the fishing industry.

It is difficult to piece together the early history of Italian Americans in San Francisco because many records were destroyed after the 1906 earthquake. There were roughly eight thousand Italians in the city by 1900, with twenty thousand more arriving over the next two decades. The community was tiny next to its eastern counterpart—by 1910, over a half million Italians lived in New York City—which probably helped its success. The total number of Italians in San Francisco never reached more than sixty thousand, and northerners always composed the majority of

Crab was among the wide variety of daily catch that Italian fishermen sold on Fisherman's Wharf.

Italian immigrants used boats and trawling nets from Italy. Their skill on the waters enabled them to control 80 percent of California's fishing industry.

the population, with a mix of roughly 70 to 30 percent. Most of the southern Italians lived in North Beach because the poorly built housing there was cheapest. The temperate weather and nearby Washington Square Park—*il giardino* as they called it—allowed the immigrants to hold picnics and meet others, reducing the stress of isolation and breaking the pattern of socializing with only other people from one's own region.

The southerners who were not part of the fishing industry searched for any work they could find, and established Italians eventually hired many of them. The northern Italians saw the dangers of an American prejudice that began to spread as the population grew bigger and poorer, and they decided to employ the southerners. Genovese chocolate maker Domenico Ghirardelli hired workers for his store in North Beach. Andrea Sbarboro, another leader in the community, interviewed immigrants to grow vineyard grapes for an agricultural association that he had created. Workers were to be paid thirty to forty dollars a month and given a place to sleep, as well as food and wine. Sbarboro had formed the Italian Swiss Agricultural Association in order to give workers a share in the vineyard, but to his astonishment, they balked at the collective arrangement, wishing only for a daily wage. He dropped his cooperative plan and made the vineyards into commercial enterprises.

For some Italian employers, the availability of cheap labor motivated their hiring decisions from the start. M. J. Fontana, also from the region of Genoa, discovered that spoiled fruits could be processed for canning but struggled for years to operate his plant successfully. He finally teamed up with Americans already working in the industry, and eventually he helped create the California Fruit Canners Association to produce canned fruits and vegetables

Immigrants opened grocery shops to sell the tastes of Italy that they wished to preserve in America.

under the brand name Del Monte. For his plant in North Beach, Fontana found it convenient to hire dirt-cheap Italian immigrants, paying them between sixty and seventy cents for a thirteen-hour day, instead of employing unionized American workers.

But perhaps the most famous figure in San Francisco, and the most important to the lives of the immigrants, was the banker Amadeo Peter Giannini. He not only believed in the potential success of the immigrant population, but also helped to rebuild the city when disaster struck in 1906 and one-third of San Francisco was destroyed in the fires of the Great Earthquake.

Like so many Italians in California, A. P. Giannini's parents were from the region of Genoa. His father, Luigi, was a peasant farmer who had left his tiny mountain village of Chavari, about forty miles from Genoa, in 1864 to chase dreams of gold. Luigi, too, was fast disillusioned and turned to other work. Wanting to establish a new life, he courted by mail a woman named Virginia from his hometown and went to Italy wearing a money belt with gold pieces tucked inside (to influence the parents) to ask for her hand in marriage. The newlyweds returned to northern California by taking a sailing ship to New York and then the new transcontinental railroad to San Jose.

One-third of San Francisco was destroyed in the fires of the Great Earthquake.

Eventually, Luigi saved up enough money to fulfill a peasant farmer's dream: he purchased a large fruit orchard that grew strawberries, cherries, and apricots. But when Amadeo was six, his peaceful childhood turned upside down with one unimaginable act. He watched a disgruntled worker shoot his father in front of their home over a wage dispute of a couple dollars. Amadeo's mother, only twenty-two with three young boys, found the inner resources to take over the farm and raise her children. While tending to the business of the farm, she met a produce hauler named Lorenzo Scatena, who befriended and later married her.

Lorenzo disliked farming and found work instead as a middleman in the fruit commission business. And it was here, watching his stepfather "Pop Scatena," that the young Amadeo Giannini found his first passion. He loved the 1:00 a.m. negotiations with fruit and vegetable growers, when Lorenzo would choose the best produce to sell on the docks later that day. To the horror of his mother, who wanted her son to go to high school, possibly even college, Amadeo decided that his stepfather's business best suited his interests and dropped out of school one month before graduating from the eighth grade.

By the age of fifteen, Amadeo Giannini was more than six feet tall and towered over almost everyone in the community. He thrived in his new work, negotiating consignment contracts with

farmers, assessing their motivations and needs, and persuading them to work for Scatena over others in the commission business. He was fiercely competitive, single-minded, and extraordinarily successful, building up Scatena's business, and by the time Giannini was twenty-one, his stepfather had given him a half partnership in the company. Working relentlessly for years and accomplishing the goals he set for himself, by the age of thirty-one Giannini had saved $300,000 and asked his stepfather to buy him out of the business for $100,000 (keeping an equivalent of about $10 million today).

Giannini then dabbled in politics, with a pragmatic understanding of the importance of political connections to further his business interests. He backed a reform candidate for mayor over the choice of the corrupt political boss "Blind Chris Buckley," whose cronies took bribes and routinely shook down store owners for money. Giannini also invested in real estate, but his life ambitions changed when his father-in-law died and Giannini became executor of the estate. His father-in-law had been on the board of directors of the Columbus Savings and Loan Association Society. Giannini took his seat and began observing how the banking system operated, not particularly liking what he saw.

At the time, giants like J. P. Morgan served only a tiny and select population of wealthy Americans. But Giannini had other ideas. He perceived, years before established bankers did, the potential of a huge customer base from the immigrant population. It was the "little fellow," in Giannini's words, who could transform the future of banking.

The capitalist Giannini understood the commercial potential of enrolling thousands of immigrants. He also wanted to help the population, believing that every Italian had the ability to escape poverty and achieve success, as his own family had managed to do in a couple of decades. Immigrants were stuffing their money in mattresses, and he wanted to teach them instead about earning interest in banks. Giannini also wanted to offer loans—what today would be called microcredit. Most immigrants couldn't afford to

A. P. Giannini believed in banking for the "little fellow."

seek a loan larger than five hundred dollars, and no bank in town would deal in such low amounts, forcing people to turn to loan sharks. Giannini understood that by reaching out to those who were otherwise ignored, he was not only creating a business opportunity but also earning loyalty for years, perhaps even generations.

Most of Giannini's ideas appalled the other bankers, and after a few run-ins he left the board of directors and created his own Banco d'Italia ("Bank of Italy"). The bank was having early success attracting customers when life irrevocably changed for all of San Francisco on April 18, 1906. The night before, many Italians had come to hear their beloved tenor Enrico Caruso sing at the Grand Opera House. Around five o'clock the next morning the first tremors shook. The great earthquake lasted only twenty-eight seconds, but in the next few hours exploding gas and water lines set the city ablaze. Hysterical residents ran screaming through the streets, while others simply watched in horror as the raging inferno ravaged the community that many had just begun to call home. The fires destroyed one-third of San Francisco, and in North Beach and on Telegraph Hill, the Italian communities were devastated, with over twenty thousand residents losing their homes.

Having moved his family from North Beach to the suburb of San Mateo some years before, Giannini felt the earthquake's tremors even nineteen miles away. He had to get to San Francisco to see what was happening to the beloved town of his youth and, more practically, to his bank. With chaos spreading, his train crawled into the city, taking five hours to make what was usually a thirty-minute trip. When Giannini finally reached his offices, assessing the damage as he walked, he estimated that within a few hours the Bank of Italy would be engulfed in flames. He also saw that looters were making their way through the city. Desperate to move the bank's money out undetected, he called his stepfather, still in the fruit commission business, asking for two horses and wagons and some crates of fruits and vegetables.

Waiting for night's cover, Giannini took the bank's records, cash, and about $80,000 in gold and hid them in the bottom of the wagons, piling the crates of fruits and vegetables on top. With another employee he steered the horses and wagons through the clogged streets of San Francisco, hoping to dodge the looters. It was a very long night, the journey beginning around 8:00 p.m. and ending early the next morning, when they finally reached Giannini's home. Still fearful of looters, he hid the money in his fireplace and slept in front of it for days.

The plan worked. Other than the money's smelling like orange juice, as Giannini recalled, he had saved the cash reserves of the Bank of Italy, which burned down as he had predicted.

In the next few days, the bankers of San Francisco met and collectively concurred that they couldn't reopen until at least November. They also declared a moratorium on loans. All except Giannini. Understanding the importance of providing psychological assurance to his customers, he was astounded by his peers' thinking and explained that if they waited over six months to reopen, there would be "no city or people left to serve." He also

With the city in ruins, Giannini understood the importance of providing loans for rebuilding.

knew the ways of Italians—and that their proclivity to stuff meager savings into mattresses and other hiding places in their homes meant they had just lost every penny.

With a showmanship that he perfected over the years, the next day Giannini headed to Fisherman's Wharf with two barrels, a plank, $10,000 in cash, and a sack of gold. Placing the plank on the barrels and a cardboard sign atop his makeshift desk, Giannini sat beside his institution's assets, now stuffed in a sack, and announced that the Bank of Italy was open again for business. He coaxed the lines of people to borrow smaller amounts of money than they requested, and each day he made spot judgments about who should receive loans. Giannini would shake a worker's hand, feel the calluses on his palm, and determine from the roughness of the skin that he was hardworking and creditworthy.

Giannini's decision to reopen the bank just days after the earthquake and to lend money for reconstruction transformed him in the eyes of the Italian people and created significant attention for the bank that had become his abiding and lifelong passion. He worked quickly to relocate into a new space. His fast and decisive action also helped rebuild the North Beach community faster than anyone had imagined possible.

His fame and notoriety brought envy and prejudice as well; one slur was that Giannini ran the "pope's bank." But his innovations won the lasting affection of the immigrants. He brought people who couldn't speak or write English to his banks and taught them how to save money. He served plumbers, bakers, fishmongers, grocers, and farmers. He set up a room for consultations with women, encouraging them to become involved in the family's finances. While other bank leaders insisted that money be kept in one place, Giannini initiated branch banking. Situated where the "little fellow" lived, these branches offered evening and Sunday banking hours, the only times workers had off.

Giannini also brought the Bank of Italy to schools, collecting the nickels and dimes of forty thousand schoolchildren. He made no money on the idea—the administrative costs overran any potential profit—but his instinct was to teach children to save money for their future education. Wanting to leave a lasting piece of great architecture and engineering in San Francisco, Giannini bought all the bonds (no one else was interested) for a construction project that became the Golden Gate Bridge.

Similarly, when no one invested in Hollywood, Giannini did, creating a motion picture loan division, which may be why he earned the admiration of the movie director and Sicilian immigrant Frank Capra. Two Capra films are said to have Giannini-inspired characters—the most famous, *It's a Wonderful Life*. Jimmy Stewart's character, George Bailey—modeled on Giannini, accord-

In 1930, Giannini renamed the Bank of Italy, the Bank of America.

ing to the filmmaker's son, Frank Capra Jr.—argues with a monopolist banker named Potter who detests the flexible loan policies of Bailey's father, Peter. Is it too much, George Bailey asks Potter to have the little fellow "work and pay and live and die in a couple of decent rooms and a bath? Anyway, my father didn't think so. People were human beings to him, but to you, a warped, frustrated old man, they're cattle."

Frank Capra famously erased ethnicity from his films to create a purely assimilated American landscape. And appropriately in this emerging Americana, and growing sophistication of second-generation Italians, Giannini merged his bank with the Los Angeles–based Bank of America in 1928. Two years later he renamed the Bank of Italy the Bank of America.

It seems a lost opportunity that Capra didn't give George Bailey, or the Giannini-inspired idealistic bank president in his film *American Madness*, an Italian surname. The next time a great Italian-American filmmaker, one who established his career in San Francisco, would portray a member of the community, the character would be the fictional antihero Vito Corleone, whose name would penetrate the nation's collective memory far deeper than that of A. P. Giannini. Francis Ford Coppola taught America that Italian gangsters "leave the gun and take the cannoli." But what about the Italian banker who inspired Frank Capra, one who had expanded the industry from the privileged to the masses—or in Hollywood parlance, taught them to "leave the mattress (and take the interest)"?

Giannini embodied some of the most admirable qualities of the immigrant spirit—the desire to imagine big and with unparalleled enthusiasm, using the blank canvas of California to realize his dreams. Yet many of his democratic instincts were achieved by autocratic ways; he also possessed the darker traits of cold-blooded ambition and an unbounded ego. No doubt Giannini's passion to fight anyone who, in his words, played "the big man's game" and forgot about "the small man" came from his humble past. At the time of Giannini's death in 1945, the Bank of America was the largest bank in the world, and it would be naïve to think that the institution created from his imagination could have achieved such dominance without Giannini also acting ruthlessly toward rivals.

Still, like the Frank Capra characters based on the San Francisco banker, he never forgot the little fellow. In the latter part of his life, Giannini gave away the bulk of his fortune, believing that people could become too rich. At his death, only $1 million remained in his estate, and he instructed that half of the sum be donated to a scholarship fund. A. P. Giannini, seeking to remain faithful to the values on which he was raised, was one of the most successful Italian immigrants who came to America in the nineteenth century. In the early decades of the twentieth century, the social experiment continued with an unprecedented number of new arrivals from Italy.

PART TWO

1910–1930

CHAPTER SIX

Becoming American

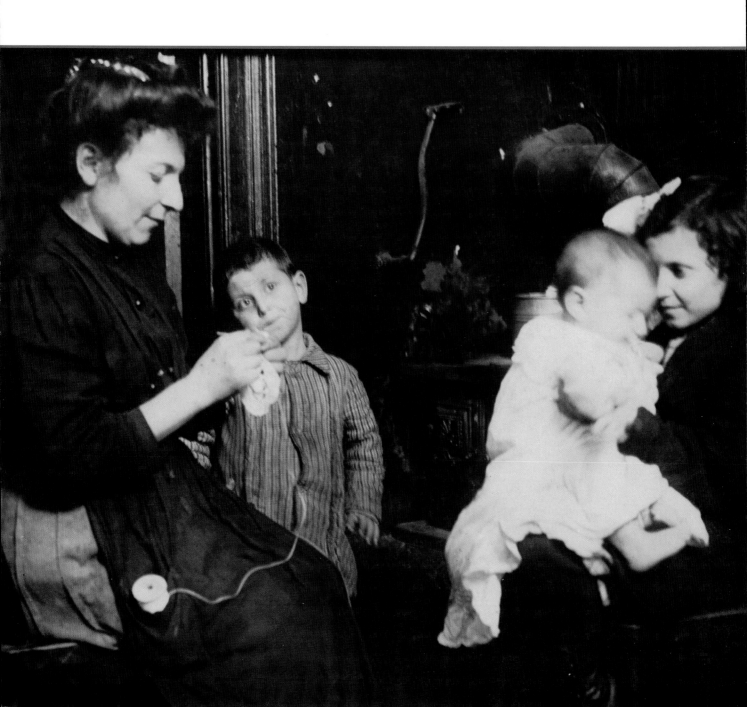

A nine-year-old boy named Leonardo Coviello felt the weight of responsibility during an interminable train ride to Naples with his mother and younger brothers, the first step of their arduous passage to America. His mother tried to remain strong when fierce waves threatened to submerge their ship, but upon reaching Ellis Island she could no longer contain her fear. Guards led the boys to another area for a physical examination, and their mother panicked. On the boys' return, her obsessive clutch and empty gaze revealed the terror of a woman who had believed the separation permanent, and signaled to Leonardo the toll this journey had already taken on her. After spending two days in Ellis Island before their discharge, mother and boys sleeping on hard benches, they finally reunited with Leonardo's father, who had been working and waiting for them in New York.

The mountain air and piercing sun of their village of Avigliano in Basilicata soon vanished to memory, replaced by the duller light of the urban skyline and the odoriferous, garbage-filled East River. They joined other tenement dwellers in East Harlem, packed together in their shabby building with one shared toilet for the entire floor. His mother, whose sorrow of leaving Italy would never dissipate, enjoyed one luxury—water from the tap, which she always treated as a wonder. Leonardo's little bit of wonder was a chocolate cream that sweetly coated his tongue—the first candy he had ever tasted after his homeland's *confetti*, sugarcoated almonds.

A laceworker and her family in East Harlem. By 1910, over a half million Italians lived in New York City, and East Harlem became their largest enclave.

The Coviellos, like so many others from southern Italy, took part in a mass exodus to pursue the dream of America. In the first decades of the twentieth century, one-third of all southern Italians left the "land that time forgot," and by 1919 over three million people had arrived here. In New York City the number of Italian immigrants rose from 545,000 in 1910 to 807,000 by 1920. The city was now home to one-quarter of all foreign-born Italians in the nation, and East Harlem became the largest Italian-American enclave in New York City.

Leonardo's father labored as a handyman when he could find jobs, his wages amounting to about seven or eight dollars a week. Everyone they knew struggled to survive; much of the available work was sporadic or seasonal, and fatalism draped households like the dark peasant shawls covering and separating the women from more modern Americans. *La volontà di Dio!*—it's God's will whether one can find work and put food on the table. Many first-generation immigrants soon abandoned the dream of transcending the life of poverty to which they had been born; the hope for a future without sweat and tears became the domain of their children.

In the Coviello family, the wager worked out. The young boy would eventually graduate Phi Beta Kappa from Columbia University, earn a PhD from New York University, teach students like future congressman Vito Marcantonio, and lead a public high school that met the needs of immigrant children better than most schools in the city. But along the way, he learned the bitter tug-of-war of loyalty between his family and his new country.

The lesson began soon after Leonardo started public school. He came home one afternoon with a bag of oatmeal given to him by his teacher, who had told Leonardo to prepare the mixture for breakfast to better meet the mental demands of the school day. Observing that Italians were shorter and skinnier than Anglo-Saxon stock, progressive teachers and social workers offered nutritional suggestions to correct what they considered the result of poor nutrition.

But to an Italian family, hardly a greater insult existed than being told how to eat. Leonardo's father, examining the oatmeal and testing it with his fingers, decided that the bran resembled nothing more than pig food. "What kind of school is this?" his father shouted. "They give us the food of animals to eat and send it home to us with our children! What are we coming to next?"

Well-intentioned gifts of "pig food" sent home were not the only way the Italians felt put upon and insulted. Protestant social workers arrived at the peasants' homes to offer instructions on the intimate matters of keeping house and raising children. They talked about the need for fresh air, opening wide the windows, to the torment of the Italian mother who feared nothing more than a draft sickening her baby. They countermanded generations, perhaps millennia, of cultural practice by telling mothers not to swaddle their infants because it was best to let the limbs move freely.

If the immigrants recoiled in anger, the children shrank in embarrassment over their parents' dress and speech. The message to the second generation became clear: the American system is far superior to your strange and mystical Old World families and their hard-to-pronounce vowel-ridden names.

The young Leonardo again experienced the dual pain of betrayal and shame when he took his report card home and asked his father to sign it. "What is this?" the father asked. "Leonard Covello! What happened to the 'i' in Coviello? . . . From Leonardo to Leonard I can follow . . . But you don't change a family name. A name is a name. What happened to the 'i'?" Leonardo responded matter-of-factly that his teacher, the eponymous Mrs. Cutter, couldn't pronounce Coviello so she snipped off the "i." His father replied, "And what has this Mrs. Cutter got to do with my name?"

Rolling pin and ravioli cutter. For people accustomed to making fresh pasta, no greater insult could be offered than instructing them in what to eat.

Protestant social workers offered instruction on the intimate matters of keeping house and raising children.

The boy, secretly grateful that the teacher had made his name sound less foreign, couldn't understand his father's ire. His father, shrugging in resignation, finally signed the report card, but the matter hissed like a steaming pot of espresso as his mother joined in. "A person's life and his honor is in his name. He never changes it. A name is not a shirt or a piece of underwear. You must explain this to your teacher. It was a mistake. She will know."

"It was no mistake," he replied. "On purpose. The 'i' is out and Mrs. Cutter made it Covello. You just don't understand!"

"I don't understand. I don't understand. What is there to understand? Now that you have become Americanized you understand everything and I understand nothing." But his mother's pleas were fruitless; from that point forward Leonardo Coviello would be known as Leonard Covello.

The personal pressure Leonard experienced in elementary school to become American accompanied a growing political concern: lawmakers fretted about the kind of stock entering the country. After 1900 the US government required that every individual who came through Ellis Island be categorized by race. For Italians, this meant that the immigration official marked down whether they were from the north or south, Alpine or Mediterranean, stamping their arrival with the distinction of superiority or inferiority—"high" Italian, from the cradle of civilization, or "low" Italian, from the cauldron of criminality. But the official demarcation of the Po River, instead of Rome, as the dividing line between north and south was an odd one, making even a person from Florence a "southerner."

Some Americans began to refer to all southern Italians as "Sicilians," and Sicilians, who represented one-quarter of the Italian immigrants who came to this country, carried much of the burden of the American prejudice. Their skin color tending a shade more olive, their hair a little kinkier than other southerners', they began to represent the new dark "other" affiliated with the Mafia, the Black Hand, and *la vendetta*.

Back in Italy, a country still grappling with the ramifications of

An Italian family in Rhode Island. Some Americans began to refer to all southern Italians as "Sicilians."

the *Risorgimento*, a nativist urge to label the southerner as inferior was also taking place. Before unification, northerners had practically no contact with the south, but now they were witnessing the chaos, banditry, and disarray of a supposedly unified country. An Italian sociologist named Alfredo Niceforo published a study in 1900 on what was being called the *Questione Meridionale* ("southern question"), and his ideas added to the growing assumption of racial inferiority. Niceforo wrote, "One of the two Italies, the Northern one, shows a civilization greatly diffused, more fresh, and more modern. The Italy of the South shows a moral and social structure reminiscent of primitive and even quasibarbarian times, a civilization quite inferior."

The educator Leonard Covello pointed out the prejudice of American academics toward southern Italians.

One of these two Italies widely embraced Niceforo's study as a "scientific" anthropological work, while the other half fumed, rejecting the notion of an innate inferiority. Niceforo's work would reverberate in America too, echoed and endorsed by sociologists and early-twentieth-century eugenicists. As an educator, Leonard Covello pointed out how Niceforo influenced academics looking for "proof" of their own prejudice. A case in point was Edward Alsworth Ross, an American sociologist and professor at Stanford and Cornell, and department chair at the University of Wisconsin. Ross, a prominent advocate of eugenics, explained in his book *The Old World in the New* that "in race advancement the North Italians differ from the rest of their fellow-countrymen." As he put it, "in the veins" of those from "Piedmont, Lombardy, and Venetia runs much Northern blood—Celtic, Gothic, Lombard, and German," while southerners possess "Greek, Saracen, and African blood."

"Rarely is there so wide an ethnic gulf between the geographical extremes of a nation as there is between Milan and Palermo," Niceforo continued. "The astonishing dearth of literacy and artistic production in the South ought to confound those optimists who, identifying 'Italian' with 'Venetian' and 'Tuscan,' anticipate that the Italian infusion will one day make the American stock bloom with poets and painters. The figures of Niceforo show that the provinces that contribute most to our immigration *have been utterly sterile as creators of beauty* [original italics] . . . I have yet to meet an observer who does not rate the North Italian among us as more intelligent, reliable, and progressive than the South Italian. We know from statistics that he is less turbulent, less criminal, less transient."

The sociologist's racial and genetic assumptions came into fuller view under a section titled "Lack of Mental Ability." Ross wrote that "steerage passengers from a Naples boat show a distressing frequency of low foreheads, open mouths, weak chins, poor features, skew faces, small or knobby crania, and backless heads. Such people lack the power to take rational care of themselves." His jaw-dropping description, drawing on the concept of phrenology popular at the time, leaves the modern reader to wonder both what is a "backless head" and what was the shape of the heads choosing university faculty in the early 1900s.

Americans were also growing angry at the Italians' high rate of repatriation, a response not unlike the reaction to Latinos today who send "good" American dollars back to their homelands. A cultural tension arose between wanting the immigrants out—a group of Harvard sociologists tried to pass an illiteracy act closing the doors to any immigrant who couldn't read or write—and wanting them to become American as quickly as possible by adopting the "better" values of Anglo-Saxon culture.

One factor that Americans failed to fully consider, amid their prejudices and eating tips, was how ill prepared the southern Italian arrived for life in the United States. Southern Italians came from an agrarian economy not as traditional farmers but as *contadini*, landless peasants, who used primitive tools working arid land. They had not the slightest idea of how to farm according to American standards. They also settled mainly in urban areas,

Passport that enabled the immigration of a *casalinga* ("housewife") with two of her children in 1920.

taking on brute industrial work for which they had no previous skills, and separating them from a rural way of life that had shaped their attitudes and ideas.

They came from a land that needed every family member, including children, to help with work, which meant their rates of illiteracy were astonishingly high, indeed higher than elsewhere in Europe. In 1901, the rate among Italian men (women were almost always illiterate) in Campania was 70 percent, in Apulia 69.5 percent, in Basilicata 75.4 percent, in Calabria 78.7 percent, and in Sicily 70.9 percent. Covello speculated that the rates were actually much higher than these numbers suggest because Italian census takers rarely ventured to the inaccessible mountain towns where most of the *contadini* lived. (Even in the mid-twentieth century, one-quarter of the southern population remained illiterate.)

Many second-generation children felt the tug-of-war between American civic values and the duty of family loyalty.

After coming to America, the immigrants were equally mistrustful of schools. Compulsory education had been introduced in southern Italy as part of the *Risorgimento* reforms, and these laws had somewhat bolstered the level of literacy early in the new century (in the late nineteenth century, the illiteracy rate hovered between 88 and 98 percent in the southern regions). Many peasants, however, deprived of the opportunities linked to education, resisted the reforms and refused to send their children to school, believing it not only useless but a disruption to the patterns of family.

Families who emigrated in part to escape such meddling by outsiders received another bitter pill when they discovered the compulsory education laws in America. For the immigrants who arrived at the end of the nineteenth century, children could receive their working papers by age twelve. But by 1903, the law had extended compulsory

Italian immigrants often believed girls were better off at home helping their mothers than in school.

This delicate embroidery reflects the skills of Italian-American women, many of whom did piecework for garment manufacturers at home.

education from the age of twelve to first fourteen and then sixteen—decisions that, in the words of one immigrant, "ruined all our hopes of a decent living, kept us poor, and destroyed the sanctity of the home."

American schools, in the eyes of the Old World peasants, didn't provide a "moral" education. The schools might teach patriotism, citizenship, and civic values, but that didn't constitute the immigrants' definition of morality, which was to respect your parents, help support them, and take care of them when they were old.

Now the "American ideas" were "going to their heads," forever corrupting the young. It was bad enough that the boys had to go to school until sixteen, but the girls! What was the purpose of sending a girl to school, to mingle with strangers of both sexes, when she was supposed to help her mother at home? The Old World structure began to dissolve further, stirring increased resentment between parents and children, because women now had to leave home for work—an anathema in southern Italian culture—in order to support the family. The immigrants were perplexed as to why parents had to do backbreaking work while the children were being "idle" in school. They had been raised with maxims like this one from Basilicata: *Fesso chi fa i figli meglio di lui* ("Stupid and contemptible is he who makes his children better than himself").

To the parents, school was *la scuola*, merely a noun, not a place in which to be actively engaged. It was uncommon for parents to know the names of the teachers—to them, faceless beings indoctrinating their children with ideas alien to their culture. Many parents simply ignored the compulsory education law, lying to truant officers by hiding their children or sending them to relatives. Working mothers would sometimes insist that their daughters had to miss at least one school day a week to keep up with the many household chores. Neighbors were also complicit in keeping children out of school, pretending not to know the names of anyone in the building if a truant officer knocked on their door.

The mistrust and anger toward the school system produced some of the lowest high school graduation rates in New York City. In 1931 a study found that only 11 percent of Italian-American students graduated high school (compared to an "American" graduate rate of 42 percent). These early attitudes would haunt Italian Americans for decades, retarding the assimilation process and creating a lasting stereotype of the ethnic group as one that didn't value education. Teachers often pegged Italian Americans, especially boys, as troublemakers or students whose only academic worth was to pursue vocational careers.

Becoming American was a difficult feat for the second generation straddling two worlds. "We soon got the idea that 'Italian' meant something inferior, and a barrier was erected between children of Italian origin and their parents. This was the accepted process of Americanization," Covello reflected in his memoir *The Heart Is the Teacher*. "We were becoming Americans by learning how to be ashamed of our parents." While the first generation could choose to retreat into their isolated Little Italies, living among *paesani* and never learning English, their offspring confronted daily the challenges of mastering a new language and weighing the values inculcated in the classroom against those taught at home.

Becoming American meant rejecting one of the two worlds. It

Italian schoolchildren ate crusty bread, like the loaves sold at this Mulberry Street bakery, distinguishing their lunches from their classmates' "American" food.

meant trying to hide the grease stains saturating the paper in which your school lunch of a fried potato and egg sandwich on crusty bread was wrapped, while the rest of your classmates ate ham on white bread with mayonnaise. Becoming American might mean dumping this sandwich in the garbage if you were too embarrassed to actually eat it in school—the act itself a blasphemy against the golden Italian rule of never throwing away good food. Becoming American meant speaking the dialect of your southern Italian region only at home, or listening to your parents but answering in English because that was your official language. Becoming American meant hearing slurs that now defined you and your people: dago, wop, guinea, spaghetti bender. And it also meant hearing your own parents and relatives reproachfully refer to you as the *"Americano."* At the heart of being a second-generation American meant feeling the shame of your heritage and the sting of family betrayal, creating an inner turmoil from which one never fully escaped.

Rudolph Valentino

As a child, Rodolfo Guglielmi wanted to escape the boredom of his village in the province of Apulia. With a little luck, a magnetic stare, and a great pair of dancing legs, the restless boy from the village of Castellaneta would transform himself into Rudolph Valentino, Latin lover. Throughout his short life, Valentino faced both anti-Italian sentiment and the wrath of men who couldn't believe that a swarthy southern European could steal the hearts of America's wives and mothers.

Rodolfo's family was a little better off than the rest of his village because his father, along with being a farmer, served as the local veterinarian. But a few years after his father's death, Rodolfo, like most immigrants, crossed the ocean in a ship's steerage.

After reaching New York and settling with relatives in Brooklyn, in 1913, he found a job as a landscaper on a Long Island estate. Always dreaming big, Rodolfo Guglielmi, like Jay Gatsby with rolling vowels, began to studiously imitate the mannerisms of the rich. The lessons were short-lived because he was quickly fired. He then supported himself through odd jobs like waiting tables, and he spent his free time in nightclubs, perfecting his tango and attracting the swoons of women wanting to be his partner. Beginning to make decent money dancing in cabarets and traveling for vaudeville tours, Rodolfo headed to Hollywood and changed his name to Rudolph Valentino.

His big career break came the next year when the influential screenwriter June Mathis insisted that he be cast as the lead in *The Four Horsemen of the Apocalypse* and the movie became a huge box office hit. There were few roles for Italians in Hollywood at the time other than villains and peasants, but Valentino carved a new niche as the romantic lead from faraway places. Soon he was living the life he dreamed of—with all the accoutrements of wealth, including limousines, paisley smoking jackets, and fawning beautiful women. When he was cast as an Arab prince in *The Sheik*, the frenzy—hysterical women begged for autographs and grabbed at his garments—was unlike any ever seen in America.

Valentino became a fantasy figure, who attracted millions of mature women, married with children, not the teenyboppers of later decades screaming first for crooners and then for rock stars. His presence on the big screen gave women in puritanical America permission to indulge sexual fantasies of the Mediterranean lover. His profile was even emblazoned on packages of "Sheik" condoms released in 1931.

But the backlash was almost as powerful as the craze. Valentino's second wife (people believed the marriage to his first dance partner had never been consummated) was badly managing his career, choosing roles that made him look more and more effeminate. His preference for European styles and silks only made matters worse. Men so detested Valentino and his pomaded, slicked-back hair—nicknamed the "Vaseline-o"—that the *Chicago Tribune* wrote an editorial called "Pink Powder Puff" blasting his mannerisms. "When will we be rid of all these effeminate youths," read the editorial, "pomaded, powdered, bejeweled and bedizened, in the image of Rudy—that painted pansy?" As early-twentieth-century Americans were articulating or subconsciously registering their contempt for dark southern Europeans arriving en masse, Valentino's stratospheric rise, fame, and riches made him a magnet for this vitriol.

Shortly after the *Tribune* incident, Valentino collapsed in a New York hotel room from an acute gastric ulcer. The world watched as his health deteriorated, and several days later he died from a severe infection at the age of thirty-one. Nearly seventy-five thousand people waited for hours outside the funeral home to see the star in a casket covered in gold cloth. Women swayed, screamed, and fainted. Across the country, fans waited for the arrival of the funeral train, kneeling in prayer when it passed.

Always dreaming big, Rodolfo Guglielmi, like Jay Gatsby with rolling vowels, began to studiously imitate the mannerisms of the rich.

D O C U M E N T I

◻

FROM JOHN FANTE'S
"THE ODYSSEY OF A WOP"

John Fante was born in Denver, Colorado, on April 8, 1909. He was the son of a bricklayer who had emigrated to the West from the region of Abruzzi in southern Italy. Fante created a deeply personal and confessional fiction about his first-generation parents, describing the conflict between trying to assimilate and retaining the values of their southern Italian village. In 1933, Fante's short story "The Odyssey of a Wop" was published in the American Mercury, *edited by his mentor, H. L. Mencken.*

During a ball game on the school grounds, a boy who plays on the opposing team begins to ridicule my playing. It is the ninth inning, and I ignore his taunts. We are losing the game, but if I can knock out a hit our chances of winning are pretty strong. I am determined to come through, and I face the pitcher confidently. The tormentor sees me at the plate.

"Ho! Ho!" he shouts. "Look who's up! The Wop's up. Let's get rid of the Wop!"

This is the first time anyone at school has ever flung the word at me, and I am so angry that I strike out foolishly. We fight after the game, this boy and I, and I make him take it back.

Now school days become fighting days. Nearly every after-noon at 3:15 a crowd gathers to watch me make some guy take it back. This is fun; I am getting somewhere now, so come on, you guys, I dare you to call me a Wop! When at length there are no more boys who challenge me, insults come to me by hear-say, and I seek out the culprits. I strut down the corridors . . .

I am nervous when I bring friends to my house; the place looks so Italian. Here hangs a picture of Victor Emmanuel, and over there is one of the cathedral of Milan, and next to it one of St. Peter's, and on the buffet stands a wine pitcher of medieval design; it's forever brimming, forever red and brilliant with wine. These things are heirlooms belonging to my father, and no matter who may come to our house, he likes to stand under them and brag.

So I begin to shout to him. I tell him to cut out being a Wop and be an American once in a while. Immediately he gets his razor strop and whales hell out of me, clouting me from room to room and finally out the back door. I go into the woodshed and pull down my pants and stretch my neck to examine the blue slices across my rump. A Wop, that's what my father is! Nowhere is there an American father who beats his son this way. Well, he's not going to get away with it; some day I'll get even with him.

I begin to think that my grandmother is hopelessly a Wop. She's a small, stocky peasant who walks with her wrists crisscrossed over her belly, a simple old lady fond of boys. She comes into the room and tries to talk to my friends. She speaks English with a bad accent, her vowels rolling out like hoops. When, in her simple way, she confronts a friend of mine and says, her old eyes smiling: "You lika go the Seester scola?" my heart roars. *Mannaggia!* I'm disgraced; now they all know that I'm an Italian.

A WOP

A pound of spaghett' and a red-a bandan'
A stilet' and a corduroy suit;
Add garlic wat make for him stronga da mus'
And a talent for black-a da boot!

CHAPTER SEVEN

Fruits of Thy Labor

The America of 1912, plump with excess and inequalities created by the Gilded Age, was a society in which the richest 1 percent controlled half of the nation's wealth—an even heftier proportion than today's 1 percent, who hold roughly a 35 percent share. With the wheels of industrialization spinning faster each year, and few laws to protect them, workers were expected to toil for whatever pittance a boss saw fit to offer.

Lawrence, Massachusetts, housed the nation's biggest textile mills, employing about twenty-eight thousand workers. The average wage varied slightly among the myriad ethnic groups working in Lawrence, with southern Italians earning on the lower end, about $6.50 a week. Among all of the textile mills, the American Woolen Company was the behemoth—a six-floor building comprising thirty acres that extended for a quarter of a mile along the Merrimack River.

The company's owner, William Madison Wood, bought an island for himself off of Martha's Vineyard, along with yachts, servants, and a vast collection of cars. Wood, whose changed name belies his ancestry as the son of Portuguese immigrants, seemed to believe that the luckiest few who make it need not look back. Had he just craned his neck, he would have seen that the vast majority of workers lived in housing so cramped, dilapidated, and disease ridden that the term "huddle fever" coined to describe the anxiety these conditions produced was quite apt.

Italian workers led the Lawrence millworkers' strike after their wages were cut by thirty-two cents a week, the cost of four loaves of bread.

The Italians who settled in Lawrence felt fooled, betrayed, and for a usually cynical people, hopelessly naïve. How could they have believed the posters the American Woolen Company had put up throughout villages and towns in southern Italy about this New England town? One poster declared, "No one goes hungry in Lawrence. Here all can work, all can eat"; it pictured a ten-member family marching into a mill, the father hugging a bag of gold. Once in Lawrence, they could barely afford to feed their families, many surviving on bread and molasses. Before they decided to take action, conditions were so bad that a typical millworker could expect to live only to the age of thirty-nine.

The spark that would lead to the conflagration—and to one of the most significant strikes in American labor history—was caused, ironically, by a progressive action. The Massachusetts legislature, recognizing the workers' untenable conditions, passed a law that reduced the workweek from fifty-six to fifty-four hours. They had passed similar legislation a few years earlier, and the mill owners had accepted its consequences; but this time, in January 1912, when the new law was to take effect, the owners refused to lose any more money and responded in marketplace fashion, cutting the workers' pay by two hours, or thirty-two cents, a week.

For the workers, any cut in pay would be catastrophic. Although they crowded into some of the most dilapidated housing stock in the nation, developers scooped up the land and rented it for high prices, charging around three dollars a week for a cold-water flat. With these meager wages it was nearly impossible to save any money and feed and clothe their families. The cut would cost them four loaves of bread. Rumors swirled for months, but once the actual deduction appeared in their checks, a group of workers entered the mills shouting, "Short pay! All out!" This call began a walkout that would last over two months and fundamentally change the way many first-generation Italians in Lawrence saw their place in American society.

In earlier strikes, Italians, the lowest on the rung and in desperate need of work, had crossed picket lines as scabs. But this time

Italians led the strike, acting from a nascent understanding that they were fighting for economic and social justice. One mill worker, a twenty-eight-year-old Italian immigrant named Angelo Rocco who had come to America in 1902, recognized that twenty-eight thousand strikers, who collectively spoke over forty-five languages, needed a strong union to keep them united after their first spontaneous walkout.

Rocco sent a telegram to the offices of the Industrial Workers of the World, the union that was nicknamed the "Wobblies" and was known for its radicalism. The IWW had formed in response to the American Federation of Labor, which at the time represented only skilled workers, not immigrant laborers. An IWW organizer and second-generation Italian American named Joseph Ettor saw Rocco's entreaty and, after discussing the situation with his colleagues, boarded a train to Lawrence. He would also recruit a fellow *paesano* to Lawrence, his friend Arturo Giovannitti, a poet and editor of a Socialist weekly newspaper called *Il Proletario*.

In the following days, the mood of the strike reflected the river's ebb and flow: the heightened joy of morning solidarity often was depleted by the terror of chance events later in the afternoon. The mayor organized a state militia (which included student volunteers from Harvard, who were given credit on their midterm exams if they helped), armed with guns and bayonets to block access to the mills and canals. The strikers responded to the blockade by marching in a moving picket line, gathering by the thousands in the town's center and singing and chanting in English, as well as their native languages of Italian, French, Polish, Russian, Portuguese, Greek, and German. The Italians waved the flags of the United States and Italy, declaring their heritage while acknowledging they were now American and would fight for the rights promised in this new land.

But as the weeks drew on, the workers' jubilant voices thinned as violent clashes between the strikers and militia intensified. Having no clear sight of an endgame, the strikers were in danger of losing their stamina and resolve. Angelo Rocco's hunch had been right:

Unified, the striking millworkers sang and chanted in their many native languages.

the organizers of the IWW provided the glue holding together this motley coalition of millworkers.

Ettor, known as "Smiling Joe," was a charismatic organizer and skilled orator who beseeched the strikers not to separate by ethnicity but to work collectively, and who enforced a strict policy of no violence, telling workers to always keep "their hands in their pockets" to escape any accusations. Ettor was fluent in several languages, which helped his ability to communicate with the workers, but it was his friend Arturo Giovannitti who proved the greatest inspiration to the crowd.

Arturo Giovannitti had come to the New World not to escape poverty, but to find a more just society than the monarchy he had left behind in Italy. He was the son of a pharmacist from the town of Ripabottoni in Molise and had received a classical high school education there. Both of his parents were inspired by the Republican values of Mazzini and encouraged their son to board a ship to Canada to study theology at McGill University. After graduating,

Giovannitti had come to the United States, first working as an assistant pastor in a mining village in Pennsylvania.

Giovannitti's theological training, which later evolved into an agnostic socialism, served him well in Lawrence. Just a few days after his arrival, he mesmerized a large crowd gathered at the Lawrence Commons with his "Sermon on the Commons," a peroration that echoed the language of the Gospel's Sermon on the Mount and applied its principles of social justice to the millworkers' struggle.

"Blessed are the strong in freedom's spirit," Giovannitti exhorted, "for theirs is the kingdom of the earth. Blessed are the rebels: for they shall reconquer the earth. Blessed are they which do hunger and thirst after equality: for they shall eat the fruit of their labor. Blessed are the strong: for they shall not taste the bitterness of pity. Blessed are the sincere in heart: for they shall see the truth. And blessed are they that do battle against wrong: for they shall be called the children of Liberty."

Giovannitti's words captivated the workers, crystallizing their inchoate feelings into a rallying cry for justice and a belief that victory was in reach. Yet the exuberance of that day would be short lived. On January 29, 1912, seventeen days after the strike began and several days after the Sermon on the Commons, someone fired a shot during a mass demonstration. Police blamed the strikers; the strikers blamed the police. Whoever fired, the untraceable bullet struck and killed a thirty-three-year-old millworker named Anna LoPizzo.

Although the police acknowledged that Ettor and Giovannitti were miles from the demonstration, they nevertheless arrested them, along with a millworker and strike leader named Joseph Caruso, and charged all three with murder by "inciting and provoking the violence," which would lead to the death penalty if they were convicted. (The prior year, a fire at the Triangle Shirtwaist Factory in New York City had killed 146 workers. The management's standard practice of locking the factory doors to stop workers from taking breaks proved catastrophic. Yet the owners were

The police arrested union organizers Arturo Giovannitti and Joseph Ettor for a murder committed at a demonstration miles from where they were that day.

In A Prison Cell Because
They Are Loyal To Their Class

TWO NOBLE FIGHTERS IN THE STRUGGLE OF TWENTY FIVE
THOUSAND STRIKING TEXTILE WORKERS WHOSE WAGES
AVERAGED LESS THAN SIX DOLLARS PER WEEK.

Our Fellow Workers
Arturo Giovannitti & Joseph J. Ettor

INTERNATIONAL ⬤ PRINTING CO.

charged merely with manslaughter, of which they were acquitted; they had only to pay a fine.)

By putting the men in jail without bail, the mayor and prosecutors conveniently removed Ettor and Giovannitti from the streets and organizing halls. The IWW filled this void by sending their noted leader "Big" Bill Haywood to Lawrence. His commanding presence, and the attention created from the leaders' arrests, brought national reporters to the scene. Haywood proved to be equally skilled, but he also had trepidation about the uphill battle the union faced with its resolute position that only a 15 percent wage increase would settle the strike. With no clear end in sight, they needed, in today's parlance, a game changer, and a few Italian labor activists whom Haywood encountered in New York City's Union Square gave him one.

The activists told Haywood that in some Italian towns, strikers employed a strategy of sending their children to families in other cities to keep them out of danger and to free up workers to meet the rigorous demands of conducting a strike. Haywood liked the idea and the attention it would receive, but he recognized the tremendous potential for something to go wrong if children were involved.

Still, he decided the risk was worth taking, and the IWW carefully mapped out a strategy to initially send over one hundred children from Lawrence to New York City. They placed ads in Socialist newspapers to help find and screen potential host families and recruited activists like the nurse and later founder of Planned Parenthood Margaret Sanger to help with the first children's "exodus." The children, registered by name, address, age, and nationality on a paper pinned to them and a duplicate kept by a secretary, were to be sent on a train to Grand Central Station. Chaperones would keep an eye on the children during the train ride and make sure that they met their host families at the station.

As anyone who has been raised by a traditional Italian mother knows, in normal circumstances she would more easily lie down on a train track than give her child to a complete stranger, even temporarily—but these were far from normal times. The strikers also feared keeping their children in Lawrence. Shortly after a bul-

The striking workers employed a tactic used in towns in Italy: they sent their children to families in other cities.

let struck Anna LoPizzo, an eighteen-year-old Syrian boy died; he had taunted soldiers by throwing ice at them, and they responded by throwing bayonets at him. Sending children to New York City to stay with screened families seemed the lesser of two evils.

And the children, donning white ribbons to stand out, were thrilled. They sang "The International" in Italian and French at the train station in Lawrence. Cheering families met them at Grand Central and placed their own coats on the children wearing threadbare garments. (Wealthy suffragettes who took up the Lawrence cause gained national attention by pointing out that the workers who made clothes for the world couldn't afford to clothe their own children.) The evening of their arrival, the children were treated to a huge dinner prepared by the Hotel and Restaurant Workers union, topped off with ice cream, cake, and fruit. The children remained well fed for the duration of their stay, for many the first time in their lives, and the host families enrolled them in local schools.

The reaction in Lawrence, led by the mayor, was one of outrage. Lawrence could take care of its own children, he insisted, and many residents fumed that the strikers had unfairly slandered the town's reputation. When the strikers attempted two weeks later to send another group of children to Philadelphia, Lawrence police tried to block them, dragging and clubbing some of the mothers. The melee, reported in national newspapers, caught the attention of President Taft, who ordered his attorney general to investigate.

Haywood's instinct had been right; sending the children away changed the course of, and public sentiment toward, the strike. Congress decided to hold hearings, and the testimony they heard awoke a nation to the horrors taking place in the mills. Children described how they had to quit school at fourteen and work frenetically all day to keep pace with the machines, their labors earning them five dollars a week. They were asked if they had ever been injured on the job—a frequent occurrence—but one girl's story captivated the hearing room. Camella Teoli was only thirteen, pulled out of school by a man who came to her parents' house to

The strikers' children marched in New York City, infuriating Lawrence officials.

recruit her. For the sum of four dollars, her father had given the man permission to forge her papers to say she was fourteen, the legal work age. Two weeks after she started, she had made the grave mistake of letting her pinned hair down, and the mill machines had scooped up the strands and torn off her scalp.

Congress asked more questions: Why was a boy throwing ice attacked with bayonets? Why could families afford only bread and molasses? Why had the looms been accelerated? The congressional hearings were a public relations fiasco for the mill owners, and they knew it. They responded by offering the wage increase the union was demanding—amounting to roughly 15 percent, with a sliding scale that gave lower-paid workers the most—and ending the strike. Not only did the Lawrence strike increase these workers' wages, but mill owners in neighboring New England towns, fearful that they would be targeted next, offered the same deal for an

When the children testified in Washington about conditions in the mills, the owners knew sympathy had shifted to the strikers.

additional 250,000 workers. It was an extraordinary victory; the people of Lawrence rejoiced and the 240 children who had been sent away came home.

But although the strike ended in March, the summer arrived with Ettor and Giovannitti still in jail awaiting trial. By fall, they were brought into the courtroom, placed in a cage for all to peer into throughout the two-month trial. The prosecutors acknowledged that the men had been nowhere near the shooting, but they hoped to win the case by using the legal precedent set in the Haymarket Square trial. The accused in that case had been put to death not for planting bombs that killed six policemen in Chicago's Haymarket Square in 1886, but for writing in anarchist journals.

The fate of the men in Lawrence would depend in part on how the jurors viewed the aims and actions of the strikers and the response of the militia. Who were the instigators of violence, and who were its victims? The trial was receiving worldwide attention, with support pouring in from trade unionists for the three men. After the defense and prosecution rested, Ettor and Giovannitti took the unusual step of asking to address the jury. Giovannitti had spent his time in jail reading the Romantic poets, Shakespeare, and Kant, and writing poetry. The courtroom was unprepared for this pale, fragile Italian who spellbound them with his eloquence.

"I, the man from southern Italy, have not told [Americans] how they should run their business," said Giovannitti in the vertiginous position of stepping out of a cage to defend his life from the electric chair. "I am not here now to tell you what the future of this country should be. I know this, though, that I come from a land which has been under the rod of oppression for thousands of years, oppressed by the autocracy of old, oppressed during the Middle Ages by all the nations of Europe, by all the vandals that passed through it. And now Italy is oppressed, I may say, even by the present authority, as I am not a believer in kingship and monarchy . . . When I came to this country it was because I thought that really I was coming to a better and a freer land than my own."

The courtroom remained hushed. Giovannitti turned to the prosecutor to remind him of the trial's location in Salem, Massachusetts. "I ask the District Attorney, who speaks about the New England tradition, what he means by that—if he means the New England traditions of this same town where they used to burn witches at the stake, or if he means the New England traditions of those men who refused to be any longer under the iron heel of the British aristocracy and dumped tea into the Boston Harbor and fired the first musket that was announcing to the world for the first time that a new era had been established—that from then on no more kingcraft, no more monarchy, no more kingship would be allowed, but a new people, a new theory, a new principle, a new brotherhood would arise out of the ruin and the wreckage of the past."

Giovannitti implored the jury to acquit Joseph Caruso, the one who could not speak English and defend himself, saying that Ettor and he himself bore responsibility—the former as the strike's leader, and the latter as "aider and abettor." And Giovannitti coura-

The spontaneous uprising in Lawrence united strikers in the sentiment that they were not machines born to work and die.

geously announced that if acquitted, he and Ettor would continue to participate and help in any future strike to better conditions of workers' lives, "regardless of any fear and of any threat."

Even some veteran reporters shed tears as they listened; no one spoke after Giovannitti returned to his cage, and the trial concluded. By evening the jury announced that it had reached a decision, and the next morning the jurors acquitted all three men.

The Lawrence strike was a turning point for Italian Americans. For the first time they had trusted themselves to challenge authority. They had not retreated in silence and suspicion. And two formidable Italian Americans, Ettor and Giovannitti, organizer and poet, had represented them and their fellow millworkers with heroism and lyricism.

The events in Lawrence would later be known as the "Bread and Roses" strike, from the James Oppenheim poem of the same name. "Hearts starve as well as bodies," read the poem, and workers needed not only bread but roses, too. The poem was published a month before the strike but later cited to express the sentiment found among the millworkers. The spontaneous uprising in Lawrence improved workers' wages but also united them in their declaration that men and women were not machines born to work and die. They needed nourishment beyond a weekly paycheck—a feat hard to achieve if bosses pressed them so hard that only sleep could mitigate the pain. The months of singing, chanting, and believing in a cause greater than any single individual gave the workers a purpose and infused their days with dignity. For a brief moment in history they could believe, as Giovannitti exhorted in his courtroom speech, "that a new brotherhood would arise out of the ruin and the wreckage of the past."

DOCUMENTI

□

PERSONAL CORRESPONDENCE OF ARTURO GIOVANNITTI

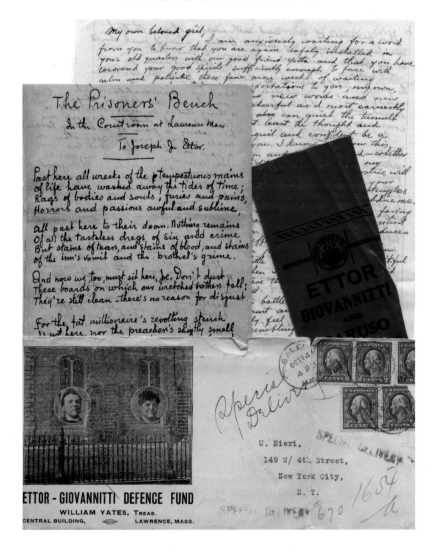

Some of the collected correspondence of Arturo Giovannitti when he was in jail awaiting trial.

CHAPTER EIGHT

Taking the Streets

f religious devotion is expressed through the prism of cultural tradition, then the more austere Irish- and German-Americans, settling in America decades before the Italians, were unprepared for, and simply mortified by, the ways in which this new ethnic group worshipped. The Italians' public displays of faith—communal, baroque, and operatic—evoked as much exoticism and strangeness as Rudolph Valentino portraying a turban-wrapped Arabian prince. Rather than Roman Catholicism providing a haven for the new immigrants and a point of commonality with others who shared the faith, their unorthodox practices made it clear that religion would become another source of conflict.

The American Catholic Church, dominated by an Irish hierarchy, held a rigid set of rules. Being Catholic meant attending sullen and subdued masses each week, officiated by a priest who was the sole intermediary between the people and the divine. The Irish Catholic Church announced its presence and its power early in America; by 1879, the huge and ornate St. Patrick's Cathedral stood in New York City as testament to the scale of the faithful's devotion.

The Italians, for the most part, did not regularly attend weekly mass in southern Italy. They held a good deal of anticlerical attitudes because village priests usually sided on behalf of the landed gentry and many were corrupt. Church attendance had been reserved mainly for baptisms, communions, weddings, and funerals, the symbolic markers of the life cycle to which the Italians paid

The Feast of San Gennaro, still celebrated in Little Italies today, began in Naples in the seventeenth century.

Receiving the sacrament of First Communion was an important ritual of Italian-American religious devotion.

due reverence. When Italians did show up in church, they were not quietly pious but boisterous, or, in the case of funerals, screamed, pounded their breasts, pulled out their hair, and even hired mourners to wail along with them.

Italians were most comfortable professing their faith in the streets. Southern Italians spent a great deal of time outdoors, and the peasants brought their faith to public spaces, routinely holding processions, or *feste* ("feasts"), to honor saints on their name days and to venerate the Madonna. Many needed to be honored—there were over one hundred patron saints, with some performing miracles and being worshipped in more than one town—and the *contadini* lovingly carried them through their villages.

When the Italians brought these rituals to the New World, the Irish Catholic Church did not know what to make of them. An earthy physicality defined the Italians' worship, literally and metaphorically, in the bend of the penitents' bodies and their depiction of saints. The hierarchy had never seen women licking the stones of a church floor in sacrifice and prostrating themselves before a statue of the Madonna. Nor did they believe that street processions in which pilgrims carried larger-than-life statues—not to mention food stands selling fried dough, nougat, and pastries, and tables hosting gambling—were acceptable ways to honor the sacred.

Madonna! Who were these people? And what was going on with their saints?

The American Catholic Church found the vivid and gory depictions of saints appalling. The patron saint of the blind, Saint Lucy, appeared in paintings holding a platter of two eyeballs, their peering dark irises served like gothic hors d'oeuvres. Arrows pierced the body of the bloodied Saint Sebastian, a favorite of soldiers. The worship of San Gennaro, Neapolitans' most important saint—whose feast day, September 19, is still widely celebrated today with street fairs in Italian-American neighborhoods—began after Vesuvius erupted in 1631. The bubbling lava killed three thousand people, and the next day, to soothe the chaos and fear, an archbishop brought out the congealed blood of San Gennaro. The blood, said to have been kept in the saint's cathedral since the fourth century, liquefied before the faithful, and the miracle is still reenacted in Naples every September.

Southern Italians sought saints for miraculous interventions, not to provide moral guidance, which frustrated the Irish Catholic hierarchy. The Church also considered saints merely representations of the divine, not lifelike statues a hairbreadth from talking back. The Italians' mystical bonds with their icons became a direct threat to the priest's role as sole intermediary with the divine.

This intimate relationship was publicly celebrated and privately bartered. Italians believed that prayers provided a direct line to heaven, and they talked to, pleaded, fought with, and even dismissed saints in anger if prayers went unanswered. A nineteenth-century Neapolitan poem 'N paraviso ("In Paradise") offers a glimpse into the Italian religious imagination. In this tale of unruly saints carping about heaven, the poet playfully suggests that even

"Our Lady of Sorrows" expresses the devotion and pain of the Italian mother.

divine icons struggle with human foibles. They gossip ("Saint Clement is jealous of Saint Pascal"), argue, and whine. While the poem might undermine the idea of a glorious heaven, it also suggests that Italians see saints as family whose billowy breath feathers the cheeks of the faithful.

Only the Madonna, the poet concludes, is just and good, affirming the traditional Latin cult of the Virgin. The Italians brought their profound reverence for the Madonna, *nostra mamma*, to America, and they celebrated her in towns throughout the United States, in some places to this day. The celebration of the Madonna through the cult of Our Lady of Mount Carmel has existed since the seventeenth century, and in Roseto, Pennsylvania, she is revered in an annual procession called the "Big Time." Every July the residents gather for this reunion and crown a local girl as queen. The largest of these early feast day celebrations took place on the streets of East Harlem, which by the 1920s attracted hundreds of thousands of Italians from along the East Coast.

The first East Harlem *festa* was held in 1882; the immigrants without their own church worshipped in a tenement courtyard ornamented only with a small painted picture of Our Lady of Mount Carmel, the patron saint of the town of Polla in the province of Salerno. Two years later, the Italians of East Harlem commissioned from Polla their own statue of the Madonna, which resembled a Mediterranean young woman and was graced with long, flowing locks of human hair. The East Harlemites adorned her gown with jewelry they donated, and she wore small pendant earrings, as might a young Italian woman. Eventually, they crowned her, the prized gold supplied from their savings.

After receiving their glorious Madonna, the Italians decided they needed a true brick-and-mortar church in which to worship her. So they built one, stone by stone, heading to a plot of land at 115th Street to throw down pickaxes after finishing a laborious day of work. Materials were carried in carts loaned by local icemen and junkmen, and by working continuously on the project—even women pitched in when a mason's union objected to so many men working for free—construction was completed in the course of one year.

Although Italian labor built the church, the hierarchy refused to fully open its doors to the immigrants. The Irish clergy, still unsure of how to treat what they called the Italian "problem," relegated parishioners to the basement to worship their Madonna from Polla. The clergy's actions were mirrored in other communities in the United States, in which Italians worshipped in the back rows behind the more established Irish parishioners. The East Harlem Italians would remain in the basement until 1919, despite their anger and conviction that the clergy's decision showed a profound disrespect to both them and the Madonna.

The Italians' most important celebration of faith and culture remained on the streets during the July 16 *festa* for Our Lady of Mount Carmel. The weeklong event meant entertaining and housing out-of-town guests, preparing large meals of Italian specialties, and getting ready for the pilgrimage. The night before, they held vigils in the church; and on the day, family, friends, and devotees of the Madonna would come from all over the East Coast. Those from other boroughs in the city often walked barefoot for miles in the sweltering heat to make the pilgrimage to the Madonna. The statue from Polla remained in the church, taken out only on rare occasions, and a large replica was in procession through the streets.

The Italians believed that the Madonna would listen to their prayers and offer her benevolent healing powers. Those who sought a healing for physical ailments had large wax replicas of body parts and limbs molded for them to carry; others lifted huge candles in her honor. The weight of the candle was meant to match the gravity of the need, and some exceeded fifty pounds. Carrying hearts, legs, and arms, these grunting and sweating supplicants made their way through the thick summer air to light the wax body parts and candles in the church. One year, a sixty-nine-year-old man who had fallen unharmed from the fifth floor of a building thanked the Madonna by carrying, with the help of others, a 185-pound candle made to match his weight. Inside the church, several people would

In America, Italians continued the practice of bringing their faith to public spaces, especially their devotion to the Madonna.

drag a woman along the church floor as she licked its stones before reaching the Madonna—a ritual that took place until it was stopped by the hierarchy in 1920.

As the years went by, the celebration grew larger, attracting five hundred thousand by the 1930s, as did the spectacle in the streets. Thousands upon thousands marched, carrying votive candles in the night. Fireworks exploded, and the smells of sautéing sausages and crispy *zeppole*, fried dough sprinkled with sugar or honey, infused the thick summer air. There were games, rides, and gambling in a Fellini-like spectacle that, as the Irish clergy saw it, mixed the sacred and profane.

But for the Italians, while the *festa* offered gaiety, it was profoundly serious, their sacrifice announced by every blistered foot and pound of wax hefted and lit at the altar. They were worshipping their most revered figure, next to Jesus: the mother who protected them and their children, and who served as a purity figure for the girls. The women were the main standard bearers of this faith during the year, although the men participated in the annual celebration. Who better than she—they said of their Madonna, witness to and carrier of the world's suffering—could understand the pain of their sacrifice and hardship in Italy and America?

She helped them as they adapted to a new land and culture, and she continued to respond to their needs as the decades marched on. During World War II, Italian mothers came to her, desperate for a sign that their sons would be safe. Those sons wore her image on scapulars as they entered battle, and the wounded would pray to her for healing. Families wrote petitions to the Madonna that were published in the parish's newsletter.

By the 1950s, the East Harlem community had begun to adopt more of the established structures of the American Catholic Church, hosting Holy Name Society and PTA meetings. They still celebrated the grand *festa*, but many social activities now took place inside the church and preoccupied them during the year. The power of the Madonna over the community began to wane by the 1960s and '70s, as Italian Americans moved out of their urban apartments to buy homes in the suburbs. Yet often they would come back for the July celebration, thousands marching, both to proclaim the form of Catholicism Italians felt most comfortable practicing and to remember the East Harlem of their parents' or grandparents' youth. The *festa* became as much about memory and nostalgia—in its most traditional meaning of a longing for one's former homeland—as a religious celebration.

Today, over 130 years later, the celebration continues, and families return to East Harlem to join a small Italian-American population. The majority of pilgrims who go to Our Lady of Mount Carmel

The devotion to Our Lady of Mount Carmel continues today.

for the annual *festa* are Haitian Americans. The Haitians share the same patron saint, adding the sounds of French Creole to the chants and susurrations. Inside the church, the Madonna from Polla presides on her altar, but the Haitians pray to another statue of the Madonna, whose skin coloring is a shade darker. Crowding their Madonna, they place petitions in her hands, along with small change, worshipping, like the Italian pilgrims before them, a spirit who listens quietly and takes heed of their suffering and sacrifices.

CHAPTER NINE

Guilt by Association

The mystical faith of Italian Americans, passionately expressed in an outreach to saints and outpouring into the streets, offered solace and guidance to millions finding their way in a newly adopted country. In the early twentieth century, however, a small group of Italian Americans practiced a secular idea with a fervor normally associated with religious devotion. This group venerated the philosophy of anarchism.

While anarchism took root in other European countries, particularly Russia, France, and Germany, in Italy the movement was abetted by a deep-seated suspicion of the government, military, and church, all of which were believed to have turned a blind eye throughout history to the desperate plight of the people. The anarchist movement was a means, its devotees believed, to restore human dignity stripped away by conquerors, monarchs, and corrupt clergy.

Anarchism established sturdier roots among Italians in America than it did in Italy, where socialist thinking was more popular. In the New World, the immigrants arrived with dreams of a just and fair American system to replace the broken one they had left behind. As those dreams turned to ash in the furnace of a newly industrialized America, the radical anarchist ideology took hold.

The anarchists held a Utopian belief that a world without rules and laws would bring out the best, not the worst, in human nature. Opposite to the Hobbesian notion that a central government was necessary to combat the "nasty, brutish, and short" life of man, the

After the anarchist bombings, the government raided the headquarters of the IWW in New York.

La Cronaca Sovversiva ("Subversive Chronicle") was the anarchist newspaper of Luigi Galleani, who wanted to abolish all civic and religious institutions. Sacco and Vanzetti developed their views about anarchism from this publication.

An anarchist movement developed in the United States in the early 1900s with the intent of improving worker conditions.

Italian anarchist leader Luigi Galleani believed that a world without government would be one of cooperation, collectivism, and liberty. By eliminating laws, private property, and the profit motive, men and women could act as creative individuals and live fulfilling and ethical lives without the constrictions of church or state.

Anarchist circles also provided a sense of community for isolated immigrants overwhelmed by the harsh demands of daily life. They gathered for picnics and weekly meetings, formed theatrical groups, and put on plays to express their ideas and imagine a life beyond the grinding workplace conditions they faced. They clung tenaciously to this "ism," the most radical challenge to capitalism, proclaiming that human beings were not machines and that the system perpetuating their mistreatment had to be abolished.

Two men, Nicola Sacco and Bartolomeo Vanzetti, would come to represent the idea of Italian anarchism in this country, and ultimately would be put to death for a crime they vehemently denied committing. Throughout the twentieth century, their dolorous faces, like a Rorschach test, would be sanctified or vilified, their piercing stares reflecting the plea of martyrs or the sneer of militants, the interpretation dependent on one's political leanings and worldview.

Ironically, these men who, in America, had abandoned religion for atheism would be remembered as Christ-like figures sacrificed on the cross of a venal and corrupt judicial system. In one of Vanzetti's prison letters, he described the seven excruciating years awaiting the promise of a new trial or the finality of death as his "ascension to the Golgotha." He wrote, "It is good for them if they succeed to loosen me . . . crushed in flesh and in spirit—a shadow of a man, a human rag—and still better to them if they will turn me out well nailed amongst six cheap planks."

Sacco and Vanzetti both emigrated to America in 1908. Sacco was from the village of Torremaggiore in southern Italy; Vanzetti, from the town of Villafalletto in the northern Piedmont region. While neither family was wealthy, both men had fared much better in Italy than the average peasant. From the beginning of their journey to America, these two men, who would be forever linked in history, possessed different dreams and dispositions. Sacco wanted to fulfill the desire of many Italian boys—to come to a new land of promise and opportunity—and after arriving in America, he soon married and had a child. Vanzetti was a loner who never married. He left Italy in deep grief over his mother, who had died in his arms from cancer. His father begged him to stay with the family and help care for his toddler siblings, but Vanzetti saw the ocean as perhaps the only vessel that could contain his vast grief.

Sacco's father owned vineyards and olive orchards, and the son would bring his inherited passion for outdoor life and gardening to the New World, even taking note in his prison cell of "the beautiful cloves and the red black beauty vivid roses" friends brought. After working in a series of construction jobs, he decided to apprentice in a shoe factory and eventually mastered the skill, becoming an edge trimmer and earning the excellent salary, for an immigrant, of roughly eighty dollars a week.

While he did not share the economic plight of his fellow Italians, Sacco deeply sympathized with them and became angered by the exploitation he saw. Living near Boston, Sacco read about the Lawrence strike and the arrests of Ettor and Giovannitti, and he committed himself to helping the strikers and their cause. He wrote to his daughter, his second child, whom he would come to know only through prison bars, that "the nightmare of the lower classes saddened very badly your father's soul."

Bartolomeo Vanzetti had a much more difficult time adjusting to life in America. Lonely, miserable, and needing work, he was horrified by the poverty and deprivation that he witnessed in New York. He found a job as a dishwasher but struggled to live on the paltry sum of six dollars a week for seventy hours of labor. The tiny steaming spaces in which he worked irritated his lungs, already damaged by pleurisy. He traveled to other states, but life remained just as bleak, digging ditches and building railroads. He returned to New York to try to find work as a pastry chef, a trade he had practiced in Italy, but employment was sporadic, and for stretches of time he ended up homeless. Eventually, Vanzetti settled in Massachusetts and seemed most content working outdoors as a fish peddler.

A pamphlet published by Luigi Galleani's radical Gruppo Autonomo urged the electorate not to vote.

Se dovessi parlare agli elettori, ecco quanto direi loro...

LO SCIOPE-RO ELETTO RALE·

VOTI

Gruppo Autonomo :: :: East Boston, Mass.

Vanzetti was raised Roman Catholic, played priest in childhood games with his sister, and staunchly defended the religion in adolescence. But his mother's illness and death began to destroy his faith, and as a teenager he abandoned it. Waiting in the New World for Vanzetti was the new belief system of anarchism, and he passionately embraced it. In his letters he described anarchism "as beauty as a woman for me, perhaps even more . . . Calm, serene, honest, natural, viril, muddy and celestial at once."

Some anarchists, like Carlo Tresca, advocated working with labor unions to effect change, but Sacco and Vanzetti followed the most radical strain of the movement put forth by Luigi Galleani, who Vanzetti referred to as "our master." Galleani, a prolific writer and mesmerizing speaker, believed that if the monarchies of Europe were inherently corrupt and capitalism devoured the possibilities of fair democracy in America, then all of these systems had to be abolished. According to intellectual historian Paul Avrich, the *Galleanisti* saw themselves as "slayers of tyrants, wreakers of vengeance, fighters for freedom."

Galleani sought "the Ideal"—a world free of government, law, and property—but this Ideal would have to be achieved by violent insurrection. He published a manual called *La salute è in voi!* ("Health is in you!"), which detailed the ingredients and recipe for bomb making. Galleani believed that bombings and assassinations were justified because the victims were capitalists and government officials. Sacco and Vanzetti were not pacifists or naïfs, as many have portrayed them. They were faithful members of Galleani's Gruppo Autonomo and planning a world that could match their anarchist dreams. The ethical ideas and whimsical musings portrayed in the hundreds of letters they wrote in prison contradict the affiliations and friendships they both kept with violent bombers, or perhaps reveal the darkest conflicts of the human soul.

As April drew to a close in 1919, thirty bombs were sent in packages labeled "Gimbel Brothers, New York" to capitalists, jurists, and political figures who had suppressed radical action and union strikes, including John D. Rockefeller, J. P. Morgan, William Madison Wood, and Oliver Wendell Holmes. Civil liberties had been severely restricted since the country's 1917 entry into World War I. Even speaking against the war could land someone in prison, and radicals under assault were determined to strike back.

Stamped on each package wrapped in brown paper were the words "novelty" and "sample," with the logo of an alpine mountain climber and the return address of the Gimbel Brothers' department store. The cardboard box contained a glass bottle filled with powerful homemade explosives. Intricately constructed and requiring significant skills to assemble, the explosives suggested that the bomb makers possessed technical acumen but lacked sophistication: they naïvely assumed that a figure like John D. Rockefeller opened his own mail.

The first person gravely injured was a black maid who lost her hands opening the deadly container. The package had been sent to an ex-senator from Georgia who had cosponsored deportation legislation. A New York City postal worker reading about the crime on his subway ride home remembered seeing packages similarly addressed. He immediately returned to the post office and discovered sixteen boxes with Gimbel Brothers labels sitting undelivered because of "insufficient postage." The anarchists' scheme and dream—to have all the bombs explode on May Day—failed because someone neglected to lick enough stamps. (This wasn't the first time the *Galleanisti* erred in attempting to carry out their revolutionary plots: In 1916, a follower tried to assassinate the new Roman Catholic cardinal of Chicago at a banquet honoring him by putting arsenic in the soup. The poisoned stock sickened the two hundred guests, but no one died. The anarchist chef, heavy-handed with the arsenic, had poured so much into the steaming pot that everyone merely vomited it up.)

By early June, the anarchists had regrouped and decided to carry out their mission personally. Across the street from where Assistant Secretary of the Navy Franklin D. Roosevelt lived in Washington, DC, in front of the home of Attorney General A. Mitchell Palmer, a handsome, nattily dressed man held a suitcase containing a powerful bomb. Echoing the macabre slapstick of "insufficient postage" and arsenic-laced soup, the assailant either tripped or improperly timed the fuse. The bomb blew him to pieces, and its powerful force shattered Palmer's windows and tossed people from

Anarchist followers of Luigi Galleani attempted to blow up the house of US Attorney General A. Mitchell Palmer.

their beds a few houses away. That same evening in other parts of the country—Cleveland, Pittsburgh, Boston, New York, and New Jersey—bombs went off, timed like tolling bells to create maximum chaos and confusion. The carefully picked destinations for the deadly devices included the rectory of a Catholic church and the homes of those who had suppressed radicals.

Flyers titled "Plain Words" that denounced capitalist abuses and declared future bloodshed and destruction blew in the wind at the scenes of the crimes. The literature eventually was traced to members of Luigi Galleani's Gruppo Autonomo in Boston. The dead man outside Palmer's house, Carlo Valdinoci, was a friend of Sacco and Vanzetti's, and his sister came to live with the Saccos after her brother's death. Another Gruppo Autonomo member and good friend of both men, Mario Buda, was tied to several of these bombings and believed responsible for the Wall Street explosions set off five days after the indictment of Sacco and Vanzetti—most likely in protest—that killed over thirty people and wounded hundreds. Buda is believed to have placed one hundred pounds of dynamite in a horse-drawn wagon along with five hundred pounds of cast-iron weights, detonating it across the street from J. P. Morgan bank and causing America's greatest terrorist disaster of the time.

Throughout its history, the US government has never taken kindly to, or sat passively before, acts of terrorism. Anarchism was outlawed in 1901, after a Polish anarchist shot President William McKinley, and Attorney General Palmer responded to the 1919 incidents with a broad sweep known as "the Palmer raids," in which he deported over four thousand people, many without due process, thought to be involved in radical activity. At the time, the country was also reeling from the Red Scare; the Bolsheviks had taken control in Russia, and people feared the revolution would spread to America.

It was under these circumstances that police arrested Sacco and Vanzetti for a robbery in South Braintree, Massachusetts, in 1920 with little credible evidence connecting the men, particularly Vanzetti, to the crime. Two men had been murdered in a payroll robbery, and a police chief decided that anarchists trying to finance their activities—not previously suspected local thugs—had committed the crime. The police chief linked a stolen car in a repair shop to the robbery and told the mechanic to inform him of anyone who came looking for it. When Sacco and Vanzetti arrived to claim the car of their friend, Mario Buda, the mechanic's wife called the police, who eventually caught up with the men after they had boarded a trolley car.

At the time of their arrest, Sacco and Vanzetti were both armed, probably because of their growing fear that the feds were closing in on Gruppo Autonomo. One recently arrested member had jumped to his death from the window of a federal office building after breaking the anarchists' code by revealing the names of coconspirators. Sacco and Vanzetti later said they had intended to gather and hide anarchist literature that evening (Upton Sinclair, who researched the case, argued that "literature" was merely a euphemism for explosives). After being arrested, and not knowing what crime they had been accused of, both men repeatedly lied when questioned about their evening activities. Their responses and evasions would be held against them during the course of the trial.

The presiding judge, Webster Thayer, declared that the conviction of both men would rest not on a positive identification—indeed there were far too many conflicting testimonies—but on a "consciousness of guilt" to the South Braintree crime, which the prosecution argued the men had displayed upon arrest. Yet Sacco and Vanzetti lied probably to avoid being linked to their anarchist circle and activities that evening, not, as the judge implied, to distance themselves from the payroll crime.

Or, as Sacco later told the journalist Mary Heaton Vorse, "If I was arrested because of 'The Idea,' I am glad to suffer. If I must I will die for it. But they have arrested me for gunman job." The evidence against both men for this "gunman job" was so weak that it exposed the prejudices and limitations of the American judicial system and created a worldwide outrage over the men's eventual executions.

Nicola Sacco (right) and Bartolomeo Vanzetti (middle) would become the face of Italian anarchism in this country.

Judge Thayer decided to try Vanzetti for another payroll robbery, a botched and unsuccessful earlier incident in Bridgewater, Massachusetts. Despite conflicting testimony—bystanders thought the assailants were either Russian or Polish—Vanzetti's dark, "foreign" countenance created enough suspicion for people to change their original identification. The attempted robbery took place on Christmas Eve, yet Vanzetti's alibi—he had been selling the traditional fish that Italians devour that night—did not convince the jury, despite the testimony of sixteen witnesses who said they had bought eels from him. The jury determined that the Italians, who could barely speak English, were merely assembling a group alibi to protect one of their own. Even the governor of Massachusetts commented that the word of Italians couldn't be believed. The Italians, on the other hand, were shocked that their words, no matter how unpolished, weren't deemed credible. Once the jury declared a guilty verdict, the wheels were set into motion: the trial for the Braintree robbery was bound to produce the same verdict, despite a substantial lack of evidence against Vanzetti and a case against Sacco that left many doubts.

Their trial, which lasted six and a half weeks, called on a dizzying 167 witnesses. Many eyewitnesses could not identify either Sacco or Vanzetti. Vanzetti was accused of driving the getaway car, but the driver had been heard to speak perfect English, unlike Vanzetti's heavily accented tongue. Witnesses supported Sacco's alibi that he was at the Italian consulate that day obtaining a passport to return to Italy. A bullet traced to Sacco's gun was said to have killed the payroll guard, but there was credible evidence that the bullet had been substituted during a test firing. While reasonable doubt existed, the jurors, charged to find a "consciousness of guilt," quickly reached a guilty verdict.

Defense lawyer Fred Moore, a flamboyant labor attorney from California who had helped secure the release of Ettor and Giovannitti and never failed to make the staid Judge Thayer wince, requested a new trial. The subsequent odyssey for both men would last seven years. During this time, a hardened criminal named Celestino Madeiros confessed to the Braintree robberies while in jail. Although Madeiros wouldn't name his gang, his description fit a group of thugs led by Joe Morelli, who were among the original suspects. Morelli's mug shot bore a striking resemblance to Sacco's profile, their Buick getaway car matched the vehicle the police sought, they possessed the type of guns used in the crime, and Madeiros had been found with nearly $3,000 in cash, while no money had ever been traced to Sacco and Vanzetti.

The Sacco and Vanzetti case received international attention as unions and activists around the country rallied to the two men's defense.

The bias of Judge Thayer was also revealed: after denying Sacco and Vanzetti another trial, he was overheard at a Dartmouth football game (the judge's alma mater) saying to a professor, "Did you see what I did with those anarchist bastards the other day? I guess that will hold them for a while! Let them go to the Supreme Court now and see what they can get out of them!"

The case's many inconsistencies and the government's determination to prosecute radicals without sufficient evidence prompted Felix Frankfurter, who would later become a Supreme Court judge, to write an article for *Atlantic Monthly* in 1926 that challenged the conduct of the trial and detailed its many weaknesses. Frankfurter later expanded his article into a book, which further enraged the clubby Boston establishment, furious that a Jewish outsider would suggest a tainted legal system in the commonwealth.

Despite the overwhelming amount of new material, the Massachusetts Supreme Court would not reverse Thayer's denial of a new trial. Pleas were then taken to the governor of Massachusetts, Alvan T. Fuller, who appointed a three-man commission headed by the president of Harvard. But the bias against the men was too strong—despite a swelling support in the United States and worldwide rallies, protests, and strikes—to make any difference. Fuller's commission ultimately upheld the conviction, and after seven excruciating years, all pleas were exhausted.

The denial of the right to a new trial sent supporters into despair because they believed that America's judicial system had been badly, if not irreparably, tarnished. As Katherine Anne Porter explained in *The Never-Ending Wrong*, a reflection written fifty years after her participation in the protests, "It was a silent assembly of citizens—of anxious people come to bear witness and to protest against the terrible wrong to be committed, not only against two men about to die, but against all of us, against our common humanity and our shared will to avert what we believed to be not merely a failure in the use of the instrument of the law, an injustice committed through mere human weakness and misunderstanding, but a blindly arrogant, self-righteous determination not to be

moved by any arguments, the obstinate assumption of the infalli-
bility of a handful of men intoxicated with the vanity of power and
gone mad with wounded self-importance." Porter was among those
who stood vigil the night of the execution, watching the light in the
prison tower flicker shortly after midnight on August 23, 1927—
the sign that powerful voltages of electricity had been charged
through the bodies of Sacco and Vanzetti.

The passion surrounding the case only grew more intense as
the men became worldwide martyrs. Cities feared reprisals, and
police were sent to guard subways, railroads, and ship terminals.
Hundreds of thousands of people poured into the streets for their
funeral. Over the years, in addition to Porter, the painter Ben
Shahn, writers John Dos Passos and Upton Sinclair, poet Edna St.
Vincent Millay, and folk singer Woody Guthrie created works about
them. A year after their execution, supporters published the *Letters
of Sacco and Vanzetti*, and both Sacco's tentative English prose,
which had grown more graceful through years in prison, and Vanzetti's often lyrical passages won more hearts. "The truth is that
not only have I not committed the two crimes for which I was
convicted, but I have not stole a cent nor spilt a drop of human's
blood—except my own blood in hard labor—in my whole existence," wrote Vanzetti.

The truth about the information Sacco and Vanzetti possessed is
shrouded in mystery. The majority of their supporters knew little
about the depth of their anarchist activity; they were protesting the
lack of evidence against the two men for the payroll robberies.
Sacco and Vanzetti became a parable of justice denied: the judicial
system will be merciless; no one will believe your innocence if you
are swarthy, speak accented English, and are accused of a crime.

The actions of the American elite, the Dartmouth judge, the
Harvard-led commission, and the prosecutors in the Commonwealth of Massachusetts reflected the warning President Woodrow
Wilson had made a decade earlier: "Hyphenated Americans," he
said, "have poured the poison of disloyalty into the very arteries of
our national life." The fanatical actions of militant anarchists, a

tiny fraction of the millions of Italian Americans then residing in America, tainted the community and helped to fuel anti-Italian prejudice.

In 1924, three years before Sacco and Vanzetti's death, Congress passed the Johnson-Reed Act that put into place large-scale immigration quotas, drastically cutting the number of people who could emigrate from southern and eastern Europe. A key expert witness to the congressional panel and the man largely responsible for getting the legislation passed was Harry Laughlin, a eugenicist and vowed proponent of eugenic sterilization, who believed that the American stock had been polluted by "alien hereditary degeneracy." Congressman Albert Johnson, who chaired the Committee on Immigration and Naturalization, was himself an honorary president of the Eugenics Research Association. The actions of Congress deepened the perception of "good" Americans and "untrustworthy," biologically inferior foreigners who were now, to the lawmakers' dismay, rapidly reproducing. President Calvin Coolidge concurred, explaining, "Biological laws tell us that certain divergent people will not mix or blend."

After the execution of Sacco and Vanzetti, the message to Italian Americans became clear: any dissent or difference will no longer be tolerated. Blending fully into American life, a difficult dance for southern European Catholics struggling to understand Anglo-Saxon culture, could be the only path ahead.

Our Ancestors

Angela Bambace

I t was the end of a long day on March 25, 1911, when a fire broke out at the Triangle Shirtwaist Factory, trapping the workers who occupied the top three floors. The fire claimed the lives of 146 garment workers, mostly Italian and Jewish immigrant women. Bystanders on Greenwich Village streets noticed smoke and saw bundles falling from the top-floor windows. To their horror, they realized these were the bodies of young women, mostly between the ages of sixteen and twenty-three, leaping to their deaths. Many had been fighting the previous year for better working conditions during a citywide garment strike, but the Triangle owners refused to let them unionize.

The horror of the Triangle Shirtwaist Factory fire became a galvanizing force for young immigrant women, whose sorrow turned to rage and then to a purposeful anger. One of those future leaders was Angela Bambace, who was thirteen at the time of the incident and by the age of eighteen had begun organizing garment workers.

Angela Bambace grew up in East Harlem, and like her mother, who trimmed hat plumes and worked in a shirtwaist factory, she became a seamstress. Both Angela and her sister Maria began to attend Italian socialist and anarchist meetings and decided to organize workers to improve factory conditions. Their mother, Giuseppina, supported her daughters but also feared for their safety, knowing that hired thugs often roughed up union advocates. Giuseppina accompanied her daughters to their union activity, always carrying a rolling pin to ensure that a protective motherly swing was in arm's reach.

In 1919, when Angela was galvanizing women garment workers to go on strike, she also agreed to her father's wish that she marry Romolo Camponeschi, a Roman-born immigrant who worked as a waiter. The mismatched pair—Romolo sought the normalcy of domestic life while Angela set out to improve the lives of the working class—grew further apart after Angela gave birth to two boys, Oscar and Philip. It was boring, she would later admit to her grandchildren, "to stay home and make gnocchi and take care of the kids."

Angela Bambace and sons Philip (left) and Oscar.

The marriage ended a few years later, followed by a bitter custody battle. Because of her organizing activities and involvement in socialist and anarchist circles, the judge ruled Angela an unfit mother and awarded custody to the father. Luckily for the distraught Angela, her mother lived near Romolo and agreed to help raise the grandchildren, allowing Angela to see them.

Through the years, the boys had to endure their mother's frequent absences and the many causes she supported. When Oscar celebrated his seventh birthday, he discovered the bad luck of being born on the date set for the midnight execution of Sacco and Vanzetti. His "party" consisted of a roomful of heartbroken adults gathered around the kitchen table, underneath which Oscar spent the evening.

After a long day's work as a factory seamstress, Bambace took on the perilous activity of union organizing. She was thrown down a flight of stairs by an enraged employer and even landed in jail. In the 1930s the International Ladies' Garment Workers' Union (ILGWU) sent her to organize small factory shops in Maryland and Virginia. Never learning to drive, she was chauffeured to these southern towns by a union worker. The two formed a motley pair: an Italian-American woman who spoke like a longshoreman and an African-American driver who had only one eye. They often had to sleep in the car because hotels refused to accommodate a black man.

Angela Bambace became the first Italian-American woman elected into the male-dominated labor hierarchy, as vice president of the ILGWU. During the half century that Angela Bambace worked for the union, she recruited and organized thousands of workers, shaping the ILGWU into a powerful force. She dedicated her life to improving conditions for garment workers and helping to ensure that tragedies like the Triangle Shirtwaist Factory fire, the worst industrial accident in New York City's history, would never take place again.

It was boring, she would later admit to her grandchildren, "to stay home and make gnocchi and take care of the kids."

CHAPTER TEN

A Shortcut

anicked by the addition of millions of immigrants, the incipient rise of organized labor to counter the brutalities of industrialization, and the emergence of radical politics, white Protestant lawmakers resorted to a more zealous moralism. Detesting what they saw as the menace of alcohol and its effects on the ethnic working class, they became determined to enact the "noble experiment" of restricting it. But the reformers could never have imagined that their impulse to control human behavior by forbidding a five-cent saloon beer at the end of a long day would lead to the creation of a sophisticated organized crime network that operated successfully for the rest of the twentieth century.

On January 16, 1920, the Volstead Act, named for Minnesota congressman Andrew J. Volstead, became law, forbidding "the manufacture, sale, or transportation of intoxicating liquors." From the start, the law was almost completely unenforceable, with roughly thirty-three hundred agents to patrol a population of nearly 106 million people. Many of these agents were political appointees, the products of patronage machines, which meant they could be easily bribed. Prohibition did stop working-class people from socializing in neighborhood saloons. But it also whet the appetite of the middle and upper classes, especially young and newly emancipated women, ready to flaunt convention and rebel against an oppressive moralism, as they stepped into unlicensed bars known as speakeasies.

Protestant lawmakers, detesting what they saw as the menace of alcohol, enacted legislation to restrict it. Any drink with a standard alcoholic content could no longer be legally sold.

Before Prohibition, a clear demarcation existed between a dangerous criminal element and the majority of the hardworking citizenry, with the two rarely, if ever interacting. Prohibition erased this line, allowing gangsters the ability to socialize with the affluent in speakeasies and nightclubs. In cities like New York, indulging in Prohibition nightlife and its aura of gentle illegality not only was titillating but defined cosmopolitanism. Keeping the social set wet by stocking speakeasies, cabarets, and nightclubs with liquor, as well as becoming the private bootlegger for parties held by the elite, helped legitimize gangsters, earned them hundreds of millions of dollars, and provided them with the accoutrements of a successful life: cars, women, and fancy homes.

Italian-American criminals in the earlier part of the century, like the Black Hand gangs, had made their money through prostitution, gambling, and extortion schemes. In states that had been dry before Prohibition, Italian Americans controlled a bootlegging business; in the formerly dry state of Colorado, for example, that

For middle-class and wealthy women, drinking at a speakeasy defined cosmopolitanism.

Members of the Italian-
American Monte Vulture
Social Club celebrate with
wine in the dry year of
1929. As an old proverb
had it: "Six months a year
Italians drink wine; the
other six months, they don't
drink any water."

business centered in Denver. But Italian Americans did not dominate the national crime scene until Prohibition, which turned previous hoodlums, muggers, and robbers into gangsters—cunning,
brutal, and enormously successful.

As soon as the law went into place, criminal activity soared,
starting with the robbing of warehouses stocked full with spirits
that could no longer be legally sold. After that supply ran dry,
some bootleggers worked with brewery owners willing to skirt
the law. Breweries continued the usual distilling process of producing spirits with a standard alcohol content of 3–4 percent, and
then "de-alcoholized" the product to 0.5 percent, the legal limit
under Prohibition. This process enabled the owners, or the gangsters who now fronted for them, to siphon off the harder stuff from
the original production.

The Genna brothers, members of a Chicago gangster family, raise a glass together.

Much of the alcohol consumed during Prohibition was smuggled from Canada and overseas via trucks, trains, boats, and airplanes. Bootleggers also used homemade stills, and criminals like former Black Hand member Frank Yale (Americanized from "Uale") paid residents of the Bay Ridge section of Brooklyn to produce spirits with one-gallon home stills—and shot those who seemed inclined to squeal about the practice. In Chicago, the Genna brothers paid neighbors fifteen dollars a day to produce moonshine in every home so that the brothers could sell the home stills' production of roughly 350 gallons of raw alcohol a week.

The original bootleggers were Irish and Jews, with Italians following behind. Italian-American criminals ran bootlegging businesses in Los Angeles, Kansas City's Little Italy, Boston's North End, Detroit, Chicago, and New York. These children of immigrants thought school a burden, not a means to success, and most dropped out when they were fourteen or even younger, finding a shortcut to the American dream of wealth and power.

Because the money to be made was enormous, so was the amount of blood shed. Former Black Hand members, now newly minted bootleggers, understood how to employ brutal and unpredictable violence to eliminate rival gangs and consolidate their power. One of the most famously violent of this new crop of gangsters was Chicago's Al Capone. He assumed control of his syndicate from a mastermind named John Torrio, who had both politicians and police on his payroll and managed competing criminal interests like a savvy CEO. Torrio advocated cooperation among gangsters instead of competition, and the arrangement lasted until a mayor was elected who wouldn't succumb to the syndicate's tactics. When Torrio was finally arrested, the tenuous gangster peace ended, eventually replaced by a bloody free-for-all.

The loud and crude Capone, who was born in Brooklyn and had dropped out of school after the sixth grade, pushed violence and mayhem to a new degree. Torrio had started by taking over the production of once-legal breweries; under his guidance, Capone helped expand their enterprise to gambling and prostitution.

Capone arranged the shocking killings known as the St. Valentine's Day Massacre.

Capone, lacking the patience and calm of Torrio, did not take lightly to violations of peace arrangements made by warring gangsters divvying up these businesses. When George ("Bugs") Moran refused to honor one such arrangement, Capone responded by sending four men (two were dressed as police officers) into a garage to murder seven members of Moran's group.

With over a thousand bullets fired, the shockingly gruesome murders, known as the St. Valentine's Day Massacre, appalled the public. This reaction eventually pushed the federal government to act, arresting Capone for tax evasion two years later, in 1931. Capone, spending most of the decade in prison and suffering from the effects of syphilis, never recovered, but the power of his organized crime syndicate carried on.

Besides Capone, no Italian-American gangster matched the power and viciousness of New York's criminals competing for the most lucrative illegal liquor market in the country. New York—"Satan's seat," in the words of a Protestant minister and temperance leader—was home to over thirty-two thousand speakeasies and nightclubs. The fight for dominance resulted in the murder of over a thousand gangsters in the 1920s. The ugliness of these murders—machine gun firing squads, burlap bags dropped into cement and sea, bodies burned in automobiles—was also unparalleled.

The most influential mobster of the 1950s, Frank Costello—who owned a lavish Central Park West apartment and appeared on the cover of *Time* and *Newsweek*—made his way up the ranks through bootlegging. Born Francesco Castiglia in Calabria, he had come to America as a young boy with his parents, who settled in East Harlem. From the age of seventeen he had been arrested several times for robberies, but the early cases against him had been dismissed. At twenty-four, he was arrested again and spent nearly a year in jail. After his release, Costello married a Jewish woman and worked easily with Irish and Jewish gangsters, enabling him to branch out from the world of solely Italian-American thugs.

By the 1920s, Costello and future mob head Charlie ("Lucky")

Luciano, the man later credited for creating the organizational structure of the modern American Mafia, were both members of a powerful bootlegging gang. Costello worked as a rumrunner, meeting boats off the coast of Long Island, transferring the liquor to his trucks, and making sure troublesome competition stepped out of the way. Both men came under the influence of Jewish gangster Arnold Rothstein (known as "The Brain"), who tutored them in how to make large sums of money in illegal alcohol and expand to other businesses.

Costello bore a tremendous grudge over the ways in which poor Italians accepted their sorry lot in America. Unlike radical leftists, such as the *Galleanisti*, who believed that American capitalists deserved letter bombs for their abuse of workers, Costello's attack on "the system" came through a criminal version of capitalist entrepreneurship. Like the twenty-first-century fictional mobster Tony Soprano, who confessed to his shrink about his demanding mother, Costello complained to his Park Avenue psychiatrist that he hated the humility and meekness of his father, who had settled for poverty and poor treatment. He also deplored his inability to be accepted as a legitimate businessman, despite investing over the decades in legal pursuits.

Along with fellow New York bootleggers Lucky Luciano and Joe Bonanno, Costello ran speakeasies and nightclubs, mingled with rich New Yorkers, and aspired to at least the appearance of legitimacy—a far cry from street thug, gang, or Black Hand members. By the time Prohibition ended in 1933, these local mob leaders had made partnerships with bootleggers across the country. Seeking new streams of revenue, the gangsters expanded into business and labor racketeering. Unions like the International Longshoremen's Association and the Teamsters were particularly vulnerable. The gangsters demanded kickbacks for finding jobs and secured payments from businesses that depended on truck deliveries. Rich and unaffected by the Depression, they also returned to their earlier sources of income—gambling, loan-sharking, prostitution, and the expanding market for narcotics.

Over the next few decades these Italian Americans, along with Jewish gangsters like Meyer Lansky and Ben ("Bugsy") Siegel, dominated the criminal landscape, leaving the ethnic ghettos they had come from to establish multimillion-dollar illegal empires. Prohibition taught them that crime did pay—if you were shrewd and ruthless enough to get out alive.

If only the sincere but inept Protestant reformers, trying to shape how immigrants became American, could have stuck to suggesting oatmeal and left their efforts at the breakfast table. By successfully stopping the legal production of alcohol for thirteen years, they spawned a savvy organized crime network that grew rapidly and exponentially in sophistication and reach.

In East Harlem in the first decades of the twentieth century, there couldn't have been a greater moral and intellectual divide between tenement coevals, the revered educator Leonard Covello and the wily mobster Frank Costello. Sadly, popular culture, with its attraction to Italian-American criminals, made Costello, not Covello, the more famous of the two. Another man, however—a short, stocky, and pugnacious politician representing East Harlem as a congressman—would also capture the country's imagination and soon come to symbolize the early extraordinary achievements of Italians in America.

PART THREE

1930–1945

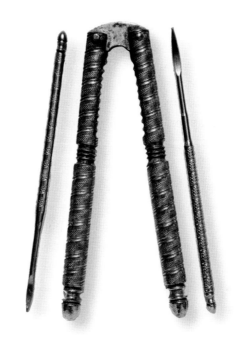

CHAPTER ELEVEN

The Little Flower

When Fiorello La Guardia was sworn into office on January 1, 1934, as mayor of New York City, it was the first wet New Year's Eve after fourteen interminably dry ones under Prohibition. The inauguration was particularly thrilling for Italian Americans, now numbering over one million in New York City and exuberant that one of their own had reached this pinnacle, ending the control of a corrupt band of Tammany Hall politicians that had drained the city's coffers. La Guardia wasn't the first Italian-American mayor of a major city—Angelo J. Rossi of San Francisco beat him by two years—but he was the first Italian American in Congress, and as mayor of New York he became the nation's best-known political figure after President Franklin Roosevelt. For an ethnic group that had been the target of an increasingly virulent nativist prejudice during the previous decade, La Guardia's election was monumental.

Fiorello La Guardia was, in many ways, the perfect representative for a beleaguered Italian people. The indefatigable politician, who reached just over five feet in height, had suffered his own share of indignities and personal tragedies. Unlike the anarchists intent on destroying a system that they believed caused only misery, La Guardia channeled his anger and grief into creating effective and lasting change through government action.

Born in a four-story building in Greenwich Village, Fiorello

Fiorello La Guardia (left) wasn't the first Italian-American mayor of a major city. Angelo J. Rossi, mayor of San Francisco (seen here with La Guardia), was. But as mayor of New York, La Guardia became the nation's best-known political figure after Franklin Roosevelt.

(which means "little flower") spent most of his childhood in Arizona. His parents, Achille La Guardia (a musician born in the town of Foggia in southern Italy) and Irene Luzzatto-Coen came to America after Achille had been offered the opportunity to play and arrange music here. Although a talented cornetist, Achille never found permanent work with an orchestra and eventually joined the army as a bandmaster—a decision that took the family west.

Fiorello's mother was a Sephardic Jew born in Trieste when the city was under Austrian rule. As part of a prominent Italian Jewish family, though, she always thought of herself as Italian. With Achille a lapsed Catholic and Irene not particularly religious, they raised their children as Episcopalians, adding to the mixed cultural and religious heritage that shaped La Guardia's outsider status.

The family moved around to follow Achille's military assignments, and while stationed in Florida during the Spanish-American War, he became ill eating rancid beef, which had been returned from England a year earlier, embalmed with preservatives, and sold to the army for its rations. Thousands of others similarly suffered food poisoning in what became known as the "embalmed" beef scandal, and Achille developed hepatitis, further complicated by malaria. The realization that disreputable contractors out to make a profit had sickened his father, along with thousands of other soldiers, made a profound and lasting impression on the adolescent Fiorello. His father retired from the army a weakened and angry man, and died several years later from a heart attack.

Before La Guardia's father died, the family returned to Trieste to live with Fiorello's maternal grandmother. Fiorello stayed for a few years to help support his mother, but eventually he became anxious to return to America, and he found employment in Ohio. The job didn't last long. Fiorello longed to live in New York, and his knowledge of several languages secured him a job at Ellis Island working for immigration services as an interpreter and caseworker. La Guardia never finished high school or attended college, but he took courses to acquire a high school diploma and enrolled in night classes at New York University Law School, where he earned a degree. At Ellis Island, La Guardia witnessed the cruel treatment of immigrants and arbitrary permanent separations that took place after family members failed the medical inspection. These incidents stoked his rage. By the time La Guardia arrived in Washington, he was ready to fight for social justice.

The political career of Fiorello La Guardia—which began with his first election to Congress in 1917—combined tenacity, improbability, and luck. He was a die-hard progressive, sympathetic to immigrants and labor, but he ran on the Republican line because the brazenly corrupt Irish political machine known as Tammany Hall dominated the Democratic ticket. The Republicans, composed mostly of New York's gentry, considered La Guardia crude and loud. But they also needed the pugnacious and overwhelmingly popular politician because there was little Republican representation in the state.

La Guardia's first bill in Congress—a surprising move for a freshman, who is supposed to be seen but not heard—sought penalties for anyone who knowingly sold inferior supplies to the army or navy: a prison term in times of peace and the death penalty during war. The bill never went any further than the Judiciary Committee, the usual fate of legislation for a junior congressman without strong party backing. But it became clear from the beginning of his career that La Guardia meant to be seen *and* heard.

La Guardia briefly left Congress to serve as a fighter pilot during World War I. Strongly patriotic at a time when his ideological colleagues remained pacifists, he enthusiastically applied to a training camp. The congressman had learned to fly several years earlier, when he served as the attorney for the airplane company of a man named Giuseppe Bellanca. La Guardia was sent to Italy as the lieutenant of a bombing squadron,

La Guardia ran as a Republican because the brazenly corrupt Irish political machine known as Tammany Hall dominated the Democratic ticket.

and returned to the States a major. While some of his supporters denounced his decision to leave the people of his district to fight in the war, he won reelection, returned to Washington, and spent the remainder of his time there putting forth a progressive agenda that prefigured major themes and ideas of the New Deal.

An attractive Italian dress designer whom La Guardia had courted before the war, Thea Almerigotti, from his mother's hometown of Trieste, finally agreed to marry him. The next year Thea gave birth to a baby girl, Fioretta. The sheer happiness of this time was extremely short-lived; both wife and daughter developed tuberculosis, a disease commonly acquired from living in tenements, as the couple did. Two years later, Fiorello's daughter died of tuberculous meningitis, and his twenty-six-year-old wife, of pulmonary tuberculosis.

When a newspaper reporter asked La Guardia shortly after his wife's death how he would spend $1 million a day—the daily sum of New York City's annual budget—La Guardia responded with the fury and passion that would define his tenure in Congress and as mayor. "First I would tear out about five square miles of filthy tenements, so that fewer would be infected with tuberculosis like that beautiful girl of mine, my wife, who died—and my baby . . . Then I would establish 'lungs' in crowded neighborhoods—a breathing park here, another there, based on the density of population . . . Milk stations next. One wherever needed, where pure, cheap milk can be bought for babies and mothers learn how to take care of them. After that the schools! I would keep every child in school, to the eighth grade at least, well-fed and in health. Then we could provide widows pensions and support enough schools for every child in New York on what we saved from reformatories and penal institutions . . . I would provide more music and beauty for the people, more parks and more light and air and all the things the framers of the Constitution meant."

A significant and popular Progressive Party existed in

Within two years after La Guardia married Thea Almerigotti, both she and their baby girl, Fioretta, would die from diseases commonly acquired from tenement living.

America in the 1920s that vigorously challenged the status quo and culminated in the effort to elect Robert La Follette as president. La Guardia was a member of this movement, which he described as "the arousing of a united protest against conditions which have become intolerable"—conditions such as the high cost of food and rent, vast economic inequality, a tax system that significantly favored the rich, and the exploitation of workers.

Although the Progressive movement made fighting for economic equality a keystone of its agenda, most of its members came from the Midwest, which meant that one of La Guardia's most salient issues—immigration—was barely on their radar screen. Having grown up in the West and watched how Italian organ-grinders were mocked (kids would cry out, "A dago with a monkey!"), and having spent his career in the East combating the stereotype of the "crude wop," La Guardia championed immigration reform. He wanted to remedy the abusive treatment of families at Ellis Island and change the restrictive quotas placed on southern and eastern Europeans. Learning that an Italian girl diagnosed with trachoma had been denied the right to a delayed deportation, which would have allowed her to return to Italy with her mother rather than alone, La Guardia sent a telegram to the secretary of labor, condemning the department's action as "cruel, inhuman, narrow-minded, prejudiced."

When, in 1924, nativists in Congress supporting the Johnson-Reed Act declared that "we have too many aliens in this country . . . we want more of the American stock," La Guardia responded, "Is not this country made up of immigrants no matter what period of history you take?" By setting quotas based on immigration rates from 1890, the legislation ensured the drastic reduction of Italians and Jews. La Guardia fought to have quotas pegged to 1920 immigration levels, but the bill overwhelmingly passed by a vote of 323 to 71.

La Guardia detested the stereotype of the Italian organ-grinder. Growing up in the West, he had heard kids cry out, "A dago with a monkey!"

Many Italian-American women were talented seamstresses, and the ethnic group dominated the garment industry in the 1920s and '30s. The black velvet dress and prom dress pictured here were designed and sewn by Nina Piscopo, a daughter of immigrants who had the good fortune of attending an art and design college in the 1930s.

Fearless of special interests, La Guardia refused to cater to them. He supported a rent control bill despite the urgings of the powerful Real Estate Board of New York to vote against this "radical" act. The undeterred congressman wrote back, "I have read the arguments contained in your memorandum and it is the same old whining, cringing pleas presented by the New York landlords who have thrived on the housing situation . . . Nothing better in support of the bill could have reached the memberships of Congress than a protest from the landlords of New York City. Please keep up your good work."

Throughout the decade, La Guardia warned of the nation's excessive inequality and sought to ameliorate rural and urban poverty. He introduced legislation to establish unemployment insurance. He advocated government ownership of power, railroads, coal, water, and oil to protect the public good over private profit. He was called a socialist and a radical, although his Old World values belied the second label. La Guardia could also be culturally conservative, especially toward the arts: he was suspicious of free-form jazz and modern art and dance, and preferred classical music and other more traditional art forms. While supportive of women's rights, he had old-fashioned expectations of women as wives and mothers.

Such traditionalism was a luxury, however, for the majority of urban Italian-American women. In the 1920s, Italian Americans represented the largest group of women working in the manufacturing sector, and this number continued to grow in the following two decades, a time in which they dominated the garment industry. Seamstresses in factories, hat plume and piece workers at home—Italian-American women took needle to thread to help their impoverished families survive. As a congressman, La Guardia backed organized labor and joined workers on the picket line during the 1926 garment strike in New York.

La Guardia masterfully detected hypocrisy and shone best decrying it. He fought against the Volstead Act and continually made fun of it by mixing two "legal" substances at a drugstore—malt extract (with an alcoholic content of 3.5 percent) and near-beer—drinking his homemade concoction, and waiting for the cops to arrest him. Such theatrics, which he mastered throughout his career, illustrated the deeply troubling aspects of a law he found ridiculous. La Guardia understood that the rich and the middle class never lost access to alcoholic drinks—that Prohibition, as was intended, punished the immigrant masses and the working class. And he saw how young immigrants found bootlegging an easy way into illicit activity—a path that would haunt Italian Americans for decades.

La Guardia made fun of Prohibition, mixing two legal substances, drinking his homemade concoction, and waiting for the cops to arrest him.

After the 1929 stock market crash and subsequent bank run, the country entered the Great Depression and the economic promise of America vanished as if a vague dream. By 1932, the majority of the nation would come to agree with La Guardia's views, favoring the kind of legislation that he supported but had been vetoed by Herbert Hoover. Ironically, with the public furious at the phlegmatic Hoover, a Democratic majority swept the country, ushering in Franklin Delano Roosevelt as president and his New Deal as policy—and voting a Republican congressman named Fiorello La Guardia out of office.

The despondent La Guardia returned to New York with his devoted secretary (now his second wife), Marie Fischer, upon the completion of the 1933 lame duck session of Congress. Within weeks he began talking about running for mayor. The first time La Guardia ran for mayor, in 1921, he was told, "The town isn't ready for an Italian mayor." Eight years later, trying again, he was called a "crazy little wop," and the dashing and refined Jimmy Walker soundly defeated him.

Walker may have been elegant, but he was also a crook. Forced to resign in 1932 on charges of graft, he fled the country with his mistress. Now it was La Guardia's turn to defeat the corrupt Democratic Tammany Hall. Once again he would have to solicit Republican backing, which meant the endorsement of a WASP gentry that had repeatedly rejected him. Or as one party leader said, "If it's La Guardia or bust, I prefer bust!"

But through a combination of skillful maneuvering and a little luck, La Guardia became their reluctant choice. His political club in East Harlem served as the base to organize Italian Americans throughout the city. Vito Marcantonio ran the club, nicknamed the *Gibboni* (it took on this name after a baseball victory—someone called the group *campioni*, "champions," and a member quipped that they looked more like *gibboni*—that is, gibbon apes).

Marcantonio, elected to the East Harlem congressional seat the same year that La Guardia became mayor, was, like his mentor, smart, progressive, and extremely hardworking. In their district office they listened to the problems of thousands of immigrants who marched each year through its doors seeking relief from their

La Guardia (left) and his smart and liberal protégé, Vito Marcantonio.

woes. Marcantonio, along with Leonard Covello and another East Harlemite, named Edward Corsi, was in charge of rallying the Italian-American base.

Not that they had to do much convincing. The jubilant Italian-American population embraced Fiorello La Guardia and his message of social justice. Who better to clean up the slums than the man who had lost his wife and child to diseases contracted from tenement living?

La Guardia campaigned to convince the rest of the citywide electorate, who had grown used to an annual free turkey from Tammany Hall, that this cheap vote-buying trick meant little to their daily life. What they needed was good government and a benevolent welfare state—a city with balanced finances, which would make it eligible for federal money and the massive jobs program that President Roosevelt was creating. With Tammany in charge, the city would forfeit these funds because the federal government knew of its deep and pervasive corruption. The people needed a city in which tenements would be cleared for decent housing and parks built to rid the streets of their relentless urban blight.

On Election Day it became clear that Tammany wouldn't give up without a violent fight. They sent out criminals and thugs wearing brass knuckles to intimidate and in some cases beat up the slum dwellers to support the Democratic candidate. Still, La Guardia won by over 250,000 votes. The overwhelming support of more than 300,000 Italian Americans enabled La Guardia to end the twenty-year reign of Tammany Hall.

La Guardia's victory was a transformational moment in the history of New York and the identity of Italian Americans who, up until this time, held the least wealth, status, and power compared to other immigrant groups of equivalent size. Now they played a significant part in the political process. Tammany leaders, using taxpayer money for their personal trough, had nearly bankrupted the city's finances. After La Guardia cleaned house and brought in top-notch commissioners, he restored the city's credit rating, clearing the way for Washington to give New York badly needed New

Deal money. The popular La Guardia became head of the United States Conference of Mayors, and his close connection to Washington brought billions of dollars to New York.

The money was desperately needed to repair a city still deep in Depression woes. Tens of thousands of people remained unemployed, and thousands more were starving and homeless. In 1935, Congress allocated $4.8 billion for President Roosevelt's massive jobs creation program, the Works Progress Administration. La Guardia immediately began drawing up plans for $300 million in new projects, and New York became the first city to be awarded two hundred thousand WPA job slots.

The WPA gave employment to thousands of Italian Americans and placed them in jobs doing what they knew best: digging tunnels, drilling concrete, and laying bricks. These jobs in construction and other artisan trades gave Italian Americans a significant lift, and the means to enter a middle-class life. Because of the WPA programs, Italian Americans continued to contribute their talents to defining, in bricks and mortar, the visual texture of the city. Italian Americans already had sculpted some of the city's most memorable landmarks, such as the stone lions guarding the New York Public Library, which La Guardia nicknamed "Patience" and "Fortitude," created by the talented Piccirilli Brothers, whose workshop was located in the Bronx.

Plasterer's union card and WPA assignment slip.

East Harlem artist Daniel Celentano, hired by the Public Works of Art Project (PWAP), the precursor to the WPA, painted *Festival* in 1934, depicting the neighborhood's annual *festa*.

With federal money pouring in through the WPA and other programs, the creation of New York as a modern, well-run cosmopolitan city began. La Guardia built the nation's first public housing, along with bridges, tunnels, and the city's first commercial airport, which would be named after him (La Guardia fondly called the project "the airport of the New World"). He established health clinics and created parks to give weary residents space to relax and breathe. He purchased privately owned subway lines to unify the city's piecemeal mass transit system. He promoted symphony music, once even conducting the New York Philharmonic as its renowned leader Arturo Toscanini stood beside him. He created the City Center, which offered opera, theater, and the symphony at prices that ranged from twenty-five cents to a dollar, enabling the working-class to patronize the arts.

The famously hands-on La Guardia ran to fires with his own fireman's helmet and read the comics over the radio to the kids during the newspaper strike. He created a legitimate police force, throwing out Tammany's gang of bribed cops and significantly reducing crime. He took on organized crime, ordering the arrest of any known gangster who appeared in public, and he made a showy display of smashing slot machines and tossing them into the ocean. La Guardia understood that these rigged machines preyed on the poor, creating false dreams and draining them of the few dollars they had. He also continued his practice of taking political action to absolve private hurt. He was merciless toward Italian-American organ-grinders, removing them from the streets to rid the city of a stinging stereotype from his childhood.

Fiorello La Guardia served for three terms and, with his exhaustive list of accomplishments, remains the most effective mayor the city has ever had. His hiring policies, based on merit not political friendship, opened the doors for Italian and Jewish Americans to enter government, and eliminated barriers for the promotion of African Americans to supervisory positions. Fundamentally changing the perception of government from an excuse for graft to a force of good, he set a model for the nation. When he died of pancreatic cancer in 1947 at the age of sixty-four, New York experienced for the first time in over thirty years the shock of his silence, unable to imagine that their beloved Little Flower would no longer voice his passion for the city and its people.

La Guardia took on organized crime and made a showy display of smashing slot machines.

DOCUMENTI

ART RENEWS A PEOPLE

Italian Americans chiseled and sculpted many of the nation's
leading landmarks (e.g. the figure of Abraham Lincoln at the Lincoln Memorial, carved
by the Piccirilli brothers). Union workers celebrated their pride in craftsmanship, an
Italian virtue they feared was threatened to become obsolete in America.

CHAPTER TWELVE

Faith in the Fatherland

Columbus Day, the fall celebration that contemporary Italian Americans either gently note or easily forget, first became a federal holiday under President Franklin Delano Roosevelt on October 12, 1934. The Italian-American bloc had become formidable—ushering in La Guardia as mayor the previous November—and Roosevelt, the consummate politician, understood the importance of recognizing the ethnic group's emerging political and civic voice. The presidential proclamation represented a moment of great pride and growing confidence, yet coinciding with this new patriotism, a troubling nationalism was brewing in the Italian-American community. For over a decade, nonstop propaganda from a Fascist Italy had been saturating Italian-American newspapers, community centers, and after-school programs.

Columbus Day became a focal point that revealed clashes within the Italian-American community. In 1925, the dictator Benito Mussolini had made Columbus Day a national holiday in Italy, using the celebration to reaffirm the special nature of its people, descendants of the great Roman Empire. In the United States, throughout the thirties, Columbus Day brought with it bloody and violent confrontations between Italian-American Fascist sympathizers and a much smaller but belligerent coalition of anti-Fascist protestors. Governor Herbert Lehman presided over a ceremony at New York's Columbus Circle in 1937, where more than five thousand people

A Fascist gathering in New Jersey. Marginalized Italians felt that Mussolini could lessen their humiliations.

had gathered. Generoso Pope, the publisher of *Il Progresso*, the largest Italian-American newspaper in the country, and a fervent supporter of Mussolini, chaired the Columbus Citizens Committee. Many who gathered shouted "Fascisti!" and when Italy's Fascist anthem, the "Giovinezza" (meaning "youth"), played, the massive crowd raised arms in the famous salute to the dictator.

Mayor Fiorello La Guardia, also on stage, gave a perfunctory and platitudinous speech praising Columbus and the contributions Italian Americans had made to the country. Later that day, La Guardia returned to the same platform to speak at a much smaller anti-Fascist event organized by his protégé, Vito Marcantonio. The second gathering, Marcantonio explained, was to support "the preservation and extension of democratic rights and civil liberties."

Fascist sympathizers, like Pope, saw Columbus Day as a way to reaffirm the message of Mussolini. Anti-Fascist leaders, such as Luigi Antonini of the International Ladies' Garment Workers' Union, saw Columbus Day as an opportunity to better recognize Italian Americans as part of mainstream American society, a group worthy of its own day. By 1938, Pope's Columbus Day events were attracting upwards of thirty-five thousand people and routinely received the imprimatur of political leaders and the media. Many Americans viewed Fascism as the antidote to Communism, and as the *New York Times* reminded its readers, anti-Fascist gatherings included "Communists."

La Guardia was caught in a political predicament: he despised the Italian dictator but didn't want to offend the Italian-American masses supporting Mussolini. By the late 1930s, President Roosevelt found himself in a similar spot, afraid of offending the powerful publisher Generoso Pope and the votes his paper could deliver, but growing increasingly concerned about the situation in Europe. This fraught relationship between Pope and Roosevelt had international repercussions, thwarting the president's initial attempts to stop the growing Fascist aggression in Europe.

———

It would be impossible to understand the adulation of the Italian-American masses for Mussolini throughout the 1930s without recognizing America's initial enthusiasm for the dictator. After the "March on Rome" in October of 1922, in which hundreds of his followers demanded a Fascist government and the weak King Victor Emmanuel III relented, America was quick to celebrate Mussolini as a winner. Politicians, journalists, and businessmen believed that Mussolini's new political program, with its brutal intolerance of strikes taking place throughout the country, would restore order and stem the tide of the growing Bolshevist threat.

Americans lapped up Mussolini's rhetoric about restoring the greatness of the Roman Empire. Even the name of his party—the *fasces*, a bundle of wheat bound to an ax—symbolized Roman authority. Finally someone would impose structure on an undisciplined nation and make the trains run on time.

The magazine of Middle America, the *Saturday Evening Post*, praised Mussolini and serialized the dictator's autobiography in 1928. The *Chicago Tribune* declared that Fascism represented "the most striking and successful attempt of the middle classes to meet the tide of revolutionary socialism." Reporters like *New York Times* correspondent Anne O'Hare McCormick worked themselves up to a high pitch of adulation: "It is easy enough for Americans to comprehend the Fascisti. Direct action is intelligible in any language. A nation that thrilled to the Vigilantes and the Rough Riders rises to Mussolini and his Black Shirt army. They have done more to make Italy understood in the United States than three million Italians coming over to dig ditches."

"A land of mothers is a land of sons, and the mothers of Italy have great power over their sons," continued McCormick. "Mussolini himself is the son of a strong peasant mother, to whose devotion and self-sacrifice he is said to owe much. Women understand the old-fashioned, masterful sort of government which he re-establishes. They rally to the old-fashioned hierarchies, of religion, authority, obedience which he restores."

The most nefarious aspects of Mussolini's regime were still a decade away, but each of these journalists in the twenties turned their backs on the loss of Italy's free press, its wrathful nationalism, the extreme violence of the Blackshirts who beat their opponents to death (or at a minimum beat and force-fed large doses of castor oil to any who showed disobedience), and the placing of faith in a man who radically and opportunistically changed his political positions.

Mussolini had been a fervent socialist and atheist journalist who denounced capitalists like John D. Rockefeller and J. P. Morgan in his articles about America. The young Mussolini wrote about the millworkers strike in Lawrence, Massachusetts, sympathizing with the workers and condemning the "crimes of capitalism." Once in power, however, he abandoned these positions, brutally suppressing strikes and embracing and winning the support of American capitalists and the Vatican. Eventually, the head of J. P. Morgan bank would become one of his most influential backers. The humorist Will Rogers, after interviewing Mussolini for the *Saturday Evening Post*, affectionately explained, "Dictator form of government is the greatest form of government; that is, if you have the right Dictator."

America's nativist prejudices played into this adoration. Elite Americans had always admired the beauty and artistic achievements of northern Italy, even if they found the people less diligent and hardworking than Anglo-Saxon stock. Now the moment emerged in which they believed Mussolini could mold an Italy that combined these achievements with their own more rigorous standards of work. It would take a dictator, so this thinking went, to accomplish such a herculean task.

Italian-American immigrants, typecast as stolid manual laborers or radicals (either "three million . . . coming over to dig ditches" or troublemakers like Sacco and Vanzetti), found solace in America's embrace of the new Italian leader. Here was a man who could lessen their humiliation, illustrate their devotion to religion and country, and restore pride and glory to the Italy of their imagination. Nothing helps the confidence of a marginalized and maligned ethnic group more than recognizing that a new American idol is one of your own.

Mussolini was greatly preoccupied with how America saw him. The American press, for the most part, accepted the fact that the Italian government controlled the news and printed its own favorable versions of Italy's progress and growth. But Mussolini found a way to spread his propaganda even more deeply through the Italian-American press.

Kansas City's *La Stampa*, Philadelphia's *L'Opinione*, Stockton, California's *Sole*, Boston's *Gazzetta del Massachusetts*, Chicago's *L'Italia*, and Detroit's *La Tribuna d'America*—all proudly served as propaganda machines, printing dispatches from the Italian news service controlled by Mussolini's government. Pro-Fascist newspapers also promoted the creation of Italian language classes, which essentially became propaganda centers instituted under Mussolini's orders to indoctrinate Italian-American youth. Parents, increasingly concerned that their children were losing ties to their homeland by not knowing Italian, enthusiastically signed up their children for these classes.

Meanwhile, the small anti-Fascist opposition, composed mostly of Italian-American labor groups, tried to get its word out under increasingly difficult circumstances. The Italian embassy alerted the US State Department about "the notorious Italian labor agitators Carlo Tresca, Arturo Giovannitti . . . and other social-communist elements in New York." After Giovannitti's imprisonment during the Lawrence strike, he continued to write political poetry and eloquently spoke out against Fascism, but his words, revered by the Italian-American left, never reached the masses.

In 1923 the Italian government tried to stop Carlo Tresca from publishing his leftist Italian-American newspaper *Il Martello* ("The Hammer"). The American government, concurring with the Italian embassy's description of Tresca as an agitator, arrested and jailed him for publishing in *Il Martello* a two-line advertisement for a book written by a physician about birth control. The literary critic H. L. Mencken was so incensed by this assault on free speech that

After Giovannitti's imprisonment during the Lawrence Strike, he continued to write political poetry.

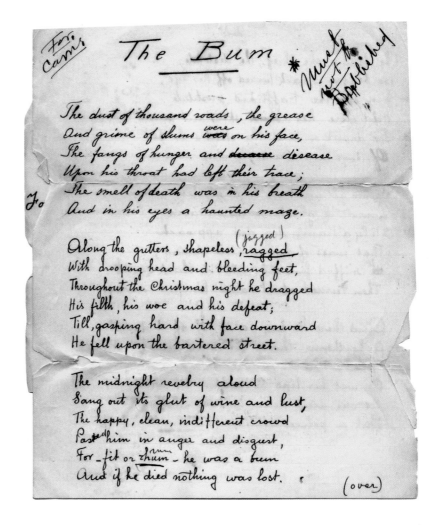

he ran the same ad in his magazine, the *American Mercury*, and, to no avail, challenged the government to arrest him. The mounting criticism of the government's actions influenced President Coolidge's decision to commute Tresca's sentence of a year's imprisonment to four months.

Of all the pro-Fascist Italian-American newspapers, the most important propaganda vehicles were San Francisco's *L'Italia*, published by Ettore Patrizi (both A. P. Giannini's Bank of America and Di Giorgio Fruit Corporation bought ad space in this publication), and New York's *Il Progresso Italo-Americano*, which had the largest national circulation.

Generoso Pope had come to America from southern Italy penniless. As a young man he had hauled water to workers in New York City building the Pennsylvania Railroad, worked his way up to foreman, and eventually made his fortune as the owner of the Colonial Sand & Stone Company, the largest supplier of sand and gravel in the country. Along the way he befriended gangsters like Frank Costello, who was godfather to one of Generoso's sons.

In 1928, Pope bought *Il Progresso* for over $2 million. Before he purchased the paper, the Italian ambassador and counsel general both became personally involved with the sale, each expressing concern that the paper needed to fall into sympathetic hands. They had nothing to worry about with Pope; he accepted its "free telegraph service," went to Italy to receive a private audience with Mussolini, and faithfully printed Fascist falsehoods until 1941.

Pope also helped organize one of Mussolini's biggest propaganda stunts in the United States: the overseas flight of the Fascist air marshal Italo Balbo. In 1933, during a time when trips across the Atlantic were still considered perilous, Balbo led a squadron of twenty-five seaplanes flying to Chicago's World's Fair. On the shores of Lake Michigan, tens of thousands of Italian Americans eagerly waited to see the fleet's pageantry as it flew in a perfect V formation. Balbo then headed to New York, where he would be welcomed by two million people with a ticker tape parade organized by Pope, followed by a lunch at the invitation of President Roosevelt. The Italian-American masses, thrilled at this American recognition of Italian strength, listened rapturously as Balbo used the opportunity to reinforce Mussolini's key propaganda message: "Be proud you are Italians," he told the cheering crowd. "Mussolini has ended the era of humiliations."

Italian Americans believed that Fascism celebrated the glory of being Italian. "You've got to admit one thing," a young anti-Fascist Italian-American woman observed at the time. "He has enabled four million Italians in America to hold up their heads, and that is something. If you had been branded as undesirable by a quota law, you would understand how much that means."

But what Italian Americans didn't know, watching Balbo's show and expressing a love for the motherland, was the increasingly militaristic and oppressive nature of the regime. Mussolini, now known as *Il Duce* ("the leader"), directed his secret police to spy on and imprison dissenters—or the next-worst fate, exile them to southern Italy. Militaristic Fascist rallies took place each Saturday for schoolchildren because Mussolini wanted to condition every child and citizen to prepare for a perpetual state of war. And still, President Roosevelt welcomed Balbo to the United States and called Mussolini "that admirable Italian gentleman." The following year, *Fortune* magazine ran a feature praising Fascism's "ancient virtues" of "discipline, duty, courage, glory, and sacrifice."

Only when Mussolini invaded Ethiopia in 1935, his first step in restoring Italy to the greatness of the Roman Empire, did Americans take a second look. When Ethiopia's leader, Haile Selassie, pleaded for the world's help, America was shocked to learn about the Italian dictator's dive-bombing raids and use of mustard gas on the Ethiopian people. Yet, conservative publications like Henry Luce's *Time* magazine still had plenty of laudatory words for the dictator. The readers of *Time* learned that "Mussolini is a spellbinder . . . [He] is more controlled, more disposed to reticence, less expansive than the average Italian . . . He gives the impression that confidence will be well placed in him, and power turned to good uses . . . It is this un-Italian steadiness which marks him off from the rest."

Italian Americans continued to buy this kind of praise. When Mussolini declared a "Day of Faith" in Italy, telling every woman to give up her gold wedding ring to raise money for the country's war efforts, rallies were held in Philadelphia, Chicago, Boston, and New York. Italian-American women handed over their precious gold wedding bands and in return received steel ones blessed by local parish priests. Generoso Pope led a huge Madison Square Garden rally in support of the war, declaring that he had sent a check of $100,000 to Mussolini's government in Rome.

Roosevelt wanted to stop the aggression and agreed with the

League of Nations' decision to impose economic sanctions on Italy, calling for a "moral embargo" on trade. Generoso Pope, most likely working with the Italian embassy, ran a campaign in *Il Progresso* urging Italian Americans to protest the embargo, including a template protest letter. The government was barraged with tens of thousands of letters, and Roosevelt backed down. While the United States didn't ship weapons, it continued to send exports to Italy.

Nonetheless, Roosevelt refused to recognize Italy's conquest of Ethiopia. Republicans tried to capitalize on his position, telling the Italian-American community not to reelect a man who refused to support Italy and instead backed the wishes of African Americans to support Selassie. These two communities, which had coexisted, if at times uneasily, now found themselves political enemies. Combined with the Depression and competition for jobs, neighborhoods like East Harlem became rife with racial taunts, street brawls, and an increased police presence in the streets.

Mussolini was stripping away civil liberties in Italy, but many Italian Americans remained blind to his actions.

Mussolini personally told his Italian-American mouthpiece, Generoso Pope, that Italy would not discriminate against Jews, and the publisher dutifully reported the dictator's words. Yet Italian Jews soon discovered the reality behind Mussolini's blatant lie as their rights were slowly eroded. By the time Mussolini's racial laws fully came into effect, Jews had been stripped of their citizenship and prohibited from public jobs, skilled professions, and schools.

Even Generoso Pope couldn't accept the 1938 racial decrees, and while he continued to support the dictator, he criticized Mussolini's regime for the first time in decades. With atrocities rapidly taking place in Europe, in the following years anti-Fascist Italian-American groups finally began gaining ground against pro-Fascist publications. In California, anti-Fascists took on San Francisco's *L'Italia*; Carlo Tresca continued to devote his energies to writing against Pope and denouncing Mussolini; and Carlo Sforza, a former count

President Franklin
Roosevelt (left) and *Il
Progresso* publisher
Generoso Pope. In 1941,
FDR finally insisted that
Pope rein in his support
for Fascism in the Italian-
American press.

and foreign minister, became a leading member of the anti-Fascist
Mazzini Society (founded in 1939 by the historian and Italian exile
Gaetano Salvemini), and had the ear of top members of Roosevelt's
administration.

Fiorello La Guardia, fed up with the Fascist propaganda in *Il
Progresso*, decided it was time to play hardball with Generoso Pope,
whom La Guardia referred to as a *cullo di cavallo* ("horse's ass"). He
asked the FBI to investigate Pope's tax returns and grill him about
his Fascist activities. The FBI balked until Roosevelt granted his
permission. In 1941, Roosevelt asked Pope to come to Washington
for a private meeting and told him that it was time to rein in his
support of Fascism. Whatever FDR said, or threatened, during the
meeting, Pope stopped praising Mussolini in his editorials and
finally, several months before Pearl Harbor, denounced Mussolini
in *Il Progresso* in both Italian and English.

Not until Mussolini attacked France in 1940 did the majority of
Italian Americans begin to understand the regime's brutality and
the true meaning of Fascism. For a year the community waited in

fear, worried about the events taking place in Italy, and wondering if America would enter the war. Four days after the Japanese attacked Pearl Harbor, on December 11, 1941, they received their answer: Mussolini, standing on the balcony of Rome's Piazza Venezia, declared war on the United States, forever ending the decade-long romance with America and Italian Americans.

Our Ancestors

Arturo Toscanini

After Mussolini's March on Rome, Arturo Toscanini—then fifty-five years old and considered one of the most illustrious conductors in the world—was not impressed. As most of Italy and America embraced the daring of the would-be dictator, Toscanini reportedly said to a friend before the march that if he were capable of killing a man, he would kill Mussolini.

Toscanini had met Mussolini in 1919, and even briefly flirted with a form of radical socialism that Mussolini first supported. Toscanini's roots were antimonarch—his father, Claudio, had been a soldier under Garibaldi and had fought among the Thousand in Sicily. Arturo, perhaps inheriting his father's political sense, feared Mussolini's ambitions earlier than others, and as an artist he inherently understood the dangers of authoritarianism to freedom of expression.

Toscanini had a famous temper to match his perfectionism, and he refused to tolerate the slightest bit of laziness or slack on the part of musicians or staff. His embrace of rigor and excellence in pursuit of artistic freedom would clash magnificently with Fascism's crudity and heavy-handedness. From the earliest days of

Mussolini's rule, Fascists began requiring that the "Giovinezza," the party anthem, be played during concerts. In one performance of *Falstaff* at La Scala, members of the audience demanded the "Giovinezza" before the third act. The conductor refused and their chants continued, leading Toscanini to smash his baton and leave the pit.

Toscanini's renown enabled him to escape the Fascist stranglehold, and he traveled often to America, serving as a conductor for the New York Philharmonic and the Metropolitan Opera. It wasn't until 1931 that Toscanini's position would have personal repercussions, after Mussolini wrote into law that the "Giovinezza" had to be played at public events. When the sixty-four-year-old conductor refused to play the anthem for a concert in Bologna, Fascist thugs surrounded and attacked him outside the theater, punching him in the face and neck. In the next years, life became intolerable for

Toscanini had a famous temper to match his perfectionism, and he refused to tolerate the slightest bit of laziness or slack.

Toscanini, whose phone was tapped and movements monitored by the secret police.

A well-timed offer provided another opportunity to live and work in America. Trying to improve its radio content, the National Broadcasting Company invited Toscanini to create and conduct an orchestra for weekend broadcasts. Beginning in 1937 on radio and lasting until 1954 on television, Toscanini was America's "maestro," conducting the NBC Symphony Orchestra. The first classical conductor to become a household name, Toscanini brought the music of Verdi, Wagner, Vivaldi, Brahms, and Beethoven into millions of homes. Combining technical perfection with bold imagination, he famously elicited brilliant performances from his musicians.

Toscanini enraptured American audiences, but his defiance of Mussolini continued to endanger him. During one of his return trips to Italy, Mussolini, furious that the conductor had traveled to Palestine in protest of the newly implemented racial laws, seized his passport. Friends feared imprisonment or death, and a Swiss journalist seeking to help posed as a Fascist informer. The journalist suggested that the American press was on the verge of learning about Mussolini's actions. *Il Duce*, still concerned about his image in America, fell for the ruse and had Toscanini's passport returned.

Returning to New York, Toscanini settled permanently in the Riverdale section of the Bronx. On July 25, 1943, an announcement interrupted one of his NBC broadcast concerts: Mussolini had been toppled. The aging conductor clasped his hands and looked to the heavens.

CHAPTER THIRTEEN

Why We Fight

n schoolyards, kids booed Italian boys, called them "Mussolini," and flung the words "dago" and "wop" as easily as brown-bag lunches. For older boys, wearing the uniform of the US military was the ultimate show of patriotism, and huge numbers of Italian Americans answered this call by enlisting. Even more responded dutifully to the draft. By 1942, US Attorney General Francis Biddle acknowledged that half a million Italian-American men were serving the country, a high percentage for an ethnic group numbering five million. The Italian-American newspaper *Il Progresso* now performed a 180-degree turn, trumpeting the call of American patriotism against Fascist Italy, and featuring page after page of Italian Americans participating in the war effort. The war had tested the meaning of the hyphen, and the answer was clear: one's heritage might be Italian, but one's allegiance was to America.

Ambivalence, however, coincided with this allegiance, causing Italian Americans much grief. As author Jerre Mangione wrote in his memoir *An Ethnic at Large*:

> Anxiety was a common trait of all my relatives, myself included, and the war worried them as nothing else in the United States ever had. Even the years of the Depression, when many of them lost their homes to the banks, were not as fraught with anxiety. It worried them that their adopted country, the birthplace of their children, was at war with their

Albert Onesti (left) had second thoughts about the enemy after visiting his family's ancestral village.

native land, dropping American bombs on their own kin. They worried that their sons might be drafted, killed, wounded, or taken prisoners, all of which was happening with increasing frequency. They were not the only ones in the nation who had such worries, of course, but their capacity to emotionalize their anxieties seemed to surpass that of any other people I knew, and I could not help wondering if this was a peculiarly Mediterranean legacy of theirs, an instinctive anticipation of tragedy germinated through the centuries by frequent traumas and tears. In any case, their worries loomed distinctively large and black compared to the general mood of the nation which was bizarrely optimistic.

But lingering doubts and dark fears had to be kept private, or among closest family, certainly not shared with the larger population. This "two-ness" dilemma, as it was labeled, affected many second-generation Italian-American enlisted men, as well as those who watched their brothers and neighbors sent to Italy. Alberto Onesti, a World War II private, articulated this predicament more than seventy years later as he recalled his basic training in South Carolina in 1943. His superiors had asked if he would have any objection to killing Italian soldiers. "Absolutely not," Onesti had replied. "He's wearing a different uniform than I am. I don't care if he's Italian, Polish, German. I'm going to kill him."

The answer satisfied the commanding officers, who sent Onesti to Italy. But upon reaching the same roads once traveled by his ancestors, Onesti's initial reaction grew more nuanced. He decided to track down his family's former village in Umbria and met a man who asked Onesti what town he was looking for. "Olveto," Onesti responded, prompting more questions from the man. "He heard my name and he went crazy. He says, 'we talk about you all the time.' The whole town came out—they gave me such a welcome. You can't ever believe it, like a hero walked in. I met my aunts, my cousins. I still was against Mussolini and Fascists. But I had a whole family out there."

As Italian-American soldiers grappled with this dilemma, at home the ethnic group worked hard to suppress anything that announced one's "Italianness." Along with the Germans and Japanese, Italians spoke the "enemy's language," and the FBI had been monitoring Italian publications because so many of them had been pro-Fascist. One result of this intense scrutiny was that the Italian language and its numerous dialects, once part of the polyglot of America, began to fade. Italian-American newspapers changed the names of their publications to English or stopped publishing altogether; store owners put up signs announcing, "No Italian spoken for the duration of the war"; and the number of high school and college Italian language classes dropped precipitously.

Italian Americans understood that to be American meant helping with the war effort, and they found many ways to contribute. At home, Italian-American women, with their dominant presence in the garment industry, worked tirelessly in large cities around the country. Many of them were employed by Italian-American dress and suit store owners who manufactured and supplied uniforms to the GIs, specializing in popular styles like the short-cut Eisenhower jacket.

Italian-American merchants showed their support for the war effort. Some even posted signs announcing that Italian couldn't be spoken for the duration of the war.

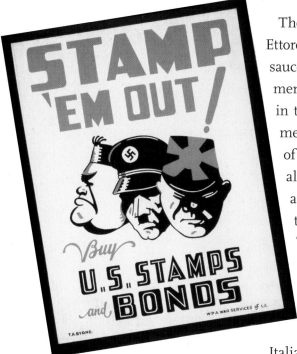

STAMP 'EM OUT!

Buy

U.S. STAMPS *and* BONDS

W P A WAR SERVICES of L.A.

T.A.BYRNE.

The US military approached the Italian immigrant chef Ettore Boiardi, who had been mass-producing his own sauces and spaghetti, to provide supplies for the servicemen. His factory employees, working seven days a week in twenty-four-hour shifts to produce enough spaghetti, meatballs, and tomato sauce, became the largest supplier of rations to US and Allied troops. Boiardi's company also made other items popular with the troops, like ham and eggs and hot dogs, and it supplied fat-laden staples to the Russians to get them through the harsh winters. The American troops liked the canned pasta and sought it out once the war was over, finding the product under its easier-to-pronounce phonetic label: Boy-Ar-Dee.

Il Progresso found its new mission in promoting Italian-American war efforts and regularly ran features of newsworthy men and women. The newspaper introduced readers to Margaret Ferrone, inventor of a machine that accelerated the production of fuses used to detonate bombs; Teresa Daniello, who wrote not only to her five sons in service but to their fellow servicemen as well, penning thirty-two hundred letters; and Carmela Zarillo, a senior citizen who repaired asbestos gloves for factory workers.

Italian Americans even gave the country a "Rosie the Riveter." As the song of the same name played on the radio and the "We Can Do It!" poster—whose iconic face later became known as Rosie the Riveter—inspired women to join the war production effort while the men fought overseas, Rosina ("Rosie") Bonavita was working at a GM plant in Tarrytown, New York. Her future husband had joined the navy, three of her brothers were in combat zones, and Rosie saw it as her duty as a riveter to assemble war equipment at record-breaking speed. Morale in the plant had been terribly low, and, according to her son, Rosie decided to "perk everyone up" with some assembly-line wizardry. She and her partner set a national record in 1943 for building the wing of a Grumman Avenger torpedo bomber. Between the hours of midnight and 6:00 a.m., Rosie and her partner Jennie Fiorito, bandannas tied around their heads like the determined woman in the famous poster, drilled over nine hundred holes and drove in 3,345 rivets to assemble the bomber's wing. Another pair of riveters eventually broke this record, but Rosie was not one to give up her title. She set a new speed standard, assembling a wing in a mere four hours and ten minutes with another partner, Susan Esposito. Bonavita, however, always disliked the iconic image of Rosie the Riveter that was depicted in the "We Can Do It!" poster, designed to inspire women to join the war production effort. She said that she never had those kinds of muscles.

A few prominent Italian Americans aided the war effort by trying to coax Italians to join the Allies. The Roman-born journalist Natalia Danesi Murray worked at NBC studios and broadcast *The Italian Hour* via shortwave radio to Italy. Murray began her broadcasts earlier in the dictator's regime to expose Mussolini's oppression and to introduce an American voice to Italy (conductor

Rosina ("Rosie") Bonavita, Italian Americans' own "Rosie the Riveter" (right), saw it as her duty to assemble war equipment at record-breaking speed.

Italian Americans showed their patriotism at World War II parades.

Arturo Toscanini was a frequent guest on her radio show). After Italy declared war on the United States, Murray reminded Italians of their close ties to America and their many relatives here, trying to win their support for the Allies. Mussolini's team branded Murray "the voice of Italo-American anti-Fascism." Her son, the writer William Murray, nicknamed his mother "Tokyo Rosa."

Similarly, New York's indefatigable mayor began a shortwave radio program, *Mayor La Guardia Calling Rome*, in which he roused Italians to free themselves from the Fascist yoke of Mussolini. Beginning and concluding each broadcast with the words "Patience and Fortitude," La Guardia spoke enthusiastically about American advances while encouraging the Resistance by telling Italians that Hitler intended for their country to fall so that he could assume control of its machinery, ships, and industry. La Guardia's exhortations were extraordinarily popular among Italians yearning for a voice from America.

The filmmaker Frank Capra joined American propaganda efforts, putting together a series of films for servicemen called *Why We Fight*. Capra's films were careful to exclude traditional stereotypes and took the point of view that Mussolini, not the Italian people, was the enemy to be stopped.

There were also many Italian-American war heroes, and the pages of *Il Progresso* well documented their deeds: the ace pilot Don Gentile from Ohio; the Minnesotan Willibald C. Bianchi, among the first servicemen to win the congressional Medal of Honor fighting in the Pacific; New Jersey war hero John Basilone, who plowed through Japanese enemy fire to rescue two other marines; and Californian Allen V. Martini, a World War II pilot who dubbed his plane the "Dry Martini" and was credited with shooting down twenty-two Nazi warplanes in only fifteen minutes.

The government, reaching out to Italian-American anti-Fascist organizations, also recruited Italian Americans for secret intelligence missions. One of the largest operations took place in Sicily, where Italian-American soldiers used their knowledge of the language, customs, and local dialect to gather information. The Sicilians, much more comfortable with the presence of Italian

The singer Tony Bennett, who served in World War II, with his mother.

Italian-American wives waited patiently while their husbands served in the US military. In this photo, an Italian-American mother celebrating the second birthday of her son placed a picture of her husband stationed in the South Pacific on the table.

Americans than that of German troops, provided the men with invaluable information as the Allies ultimately liberated Sicily.

The Battle of the Bulge and the Battle of Normandy in Europe, Guadalcanal and Iwo Jima in the Pacific—in all the major battles of World War II, Italian Americans played vital roles. When, on September 2, 1945, the Allies declared the war officially over, Italian Americans, overwhelmed with joy and finally seeing an end to years of oppressive anxiety, welcomed back their fiancés, husbands, and sons.

The war broadened the lives of servicemen in ways previously

With Italy's surrender, Italian Americans were joyful, welcoming back their fiancés, husbands, and sons.

unimagined. Sent across the world, they learned foreign customs and saw exotic lands, perhaps for the only time in their lives. Some married European and Asian women; others took advantage of securing an education or a coveted home through the GI Bill. Italian Americans would also need to put behind them the jeers they had heard and marginalization they had experienced during the lowest point in their New World history, but now their American identity felt more tangible than ever.

Our Ancestors

Hector Boiardi

Second-generation Italian-American mothers, accustomed to their mammas rolling dough for the pasta, usually harrumphed at their children's request for Chef Boy-Ar-Dee canned ravioli, America's version of Italian food. Did they realize that beneath the white toque on the label was a talented immigrant Italian chef who had begun his career making a sauce that used only imported olive oil and Parmesan cheese?

Ettore Boiardi was a fifteen-year-old orphan in 1914 when he came to America from Piacenza in Emilia-Romagna, today considered Italy's leading food region. His older brother Paul had found a job as a waiter at New York's Plaza Hotel and soon became maître d' of the hotel's stylish Persian Room restaurant. He sent for his brothers, Ettore (who would anglicize his name to Hector) and Mario, both eager for a fresh start in the New World. Paul found Ettore work in the hotel kitchen, which started him up a ladder of jobs that included sous-chef at a New York Italian restaurant called Barbetta; a stint at the Greenbrier hotel in West Virginia, where he catered the large wedding for President Woodrow Wilson's second marriage; and head chef at a hotel restaurant in Cleveland, the city he would make his permanent home.

In 1924, Hector opened his own restaurant on the side, Il Giardino d'Italia. The customers loved the fresh ingredients in his sauce, and Hector began making them take-home packages: he poured the tomato sauce into glass milk bottles, wrapped up some dried spaghetti, and threw in a container of Parmesan cheese. Soon he realized the potential market for the jarred sauce, and with his two brothers he formed the Chef Boiardi Food Company. The triple vowel combination proved too difficult for Americans, so they changed the name to its phonetic spelling, Boy-Ar-Dee (Americans emphasize the last syllable, while Italians stress the penultimate).

"Secret of magical meals...real Italian-style sauce"

In 1936 they moved the plant to Milton, Pennsylvania, the home of an abandoned silk mill. The brothers chose the predominantly German town to be near acres of farmland, space to grow enough tomatoes to process twenty thousand tons of sauce a season. At the company's height, it produced 250,000 cases a day, sold exclusively through the A&P super-market chain.

After the war, the Boiardi brothers sold the company to the American Home Foods Company. The market had already demanded that the Boairdis use less expensive ingredients than imported olive oil and cheese, but with increasing mass production, the Chef Boy-Ar-Dee brand came to mean the goopy canned goods lamented by Italian-American mothers, stunned that anyone would consider this Italian food. No wonder kids in the 1980s taunted Anna Boiardi, Hector's great niece, for her "weird" lunches when she brought mozzarella, prosciutto, and tomato sandwiches to school, made by her Italian-born mother.

Hector continued to advertise Chef Boy-Ar-Dee to millions of Americans up until the 1960s. In a 1953 commercial, he peers through an open door to announce, "Hello, may I come in?" part of the intimate approach that made the brand a household name.

The customers loved the fresh ingredients in his sauce, and Hector began making them take-home packages: he poured the tomato sauce into glass milk bottles, wrapped up some dried spaghetti, and threw in a container of Parmesan cheese.

Gay Talese

Gay Talese, who was born in 1932, is the best-selling author of eleven books. His book Unto the Sons *traces the origins of his family, who emigrated from the town of Maida in southern Italy. Talese recounts the stigma of an Italian-American childhood during World War II and the dilemma of dual loyalties that his father, who worked as a tailor in Ocean City, New Jersey, experienced during those years.*

Q: You had relatives in Italy fighting the war?

Talese: I had Italian uncles who were in Mussolini's army, and the only reason I knew that was because on my father's bureau in his bedroom, there were pictures of these two brothers. In 1942 and 1943, they were fighting the Americans who were invading at that time the southern part of Italy by way of North Africa.

Q: How did your father feel about all of this?

Talese: Well, he spoke to my mother, not to me, not to my younger sister, but to my mother. He would express a certain misgiving about what his mother and other female relatives must be under-

going, the sisters or wives of those people who were in the army. He would then reveal his affiliation and his concerns about his native country, as he would not during the daytime in the presence of anyone in the store, including the two employees they had. In the privacy of their apartment, they were more candid and more revealing of their place in society and their fears about where their ancestral traces were.

Q: He was concerned about revealing these feelings to others who weren't Italian?

Talese: He became a citizen in 1928, but he didn't feel that he was a citizen. He'd felt maybe before the war he was, but during the war, he felt he was on trial. He felt he was a marginal American citizen, a half American citizen, and he had to behave himself, and he did.

He felt he was a marginal American citizen, a half American citizen, and he had to behave himself, and he did.

CHAPTER FOURTEEN

Enemy Aliens

talian-American servicemen fought in record numbers for America abroad, but at home the US government deemed the parents of many of these soldiers "enemy aliens" and restricted their parents' civil liberties. The servicemen considered the government's decision nonsensical at best, destructive and demoralizing at worst.

More than a year before Pearl Harbor, the government, fearing war might be imminent, created the Alien Registration Division to register and fingerprint Americans who had never gone through the process of becoming citizens. Not wanting to alarm millions of aliens in the country (with Italian Americans representing the largest number of them), the government tried to soft-pedal the process, urging celebrities who were noncitizens to register and changing registration centers to post offices rather than the originally designated police stations.

The day after the attack on Pearl Harbor, Franklin Delano Roosevelt issued Proclamation 2527, which rendered the country's six hundred thousand unnaturalized Italians enemy aliens, subjecting them to restrictions, apprehension, and detention (another proclamation was similarly issued against German nationals), and requiring them to carry pink identification cards.

The War and Justice departments decided that any Italian who lived here for decades but did not seek citizenship performed an inherent act of disloyalty. Yet the majority of immigrants in that category were illiterate, and many still lived in isolated ethnic con-

Six hundred thousand Italian Americans were registered as enemy aliens, 1,500 were arrested, and over 250 were kept in internment camps like this one in Missoula, Montana, for the duration of the war.

Deemed an enemy alien because she never applied for citizenship, Celestina Stagnaro Loero was forced to move from her home for the duration of the war.

claves where they never learned English, the essential prerequisite for passing a citizenship test. Hundreds of thousands of these enemy aliens were mothers and grandmothers, women who saw the purpose of their lives as cooking, cleaning, and caring for their children to help them live the promise of this new land.

Restricted from traveling more than five miles from their homes without permission, enemy aliens had to report to the police a move in residence or change in job. They needed to surrender to the local police office shortwave radios and cameras, two items on a list of contraband. Their homes were subject to spot searches, and violation of any of these restrictions carried the risk of arrest. Nearly three thousand spot searches took place (mostly in New York, Pennsylvania, California, and Louisiana), over 1,500 Italian Americans were arrested, and more than 250 were kept in internment camps for the duration of the war.

Along the Pacific Coast, the War Department forced an estimated ten thousand Italian Americans to move from their homes near strategic waterfront areas and subjected another fifty thousand to a strict 8:00 p.m. to 6:00 a.m. curfew. The government's actions, especially the forced relocation of elderly residents, treated grandmas as if they were spies sautéing bombs for the gravy or packing pistols in Sunday purses, alongside the rosary beads. Terrified families feared what the next step might be. In the weeks preceding the relocation program, four Italian men committed suicide. Italian Americans only narrowly escaped the plight of the Japanese in internment camps—also originally planned for Italians and Germans. A 2001 report to Congress admitted that much of the information about the treatment of Italian Americans during World War II remains classified and "never acknowledged in any official capacity by the United States government."

At the time, many believed that a fifth column existed in the United States that was taking its orders from "Roberto"—that is, Rome, Berlin, and Tokyo. Since 1936, FBI director J. Edgar Hoover had been compiling a "Custodial Detention List," which categorized potential security threats. Roosevelt gave the FBI permission to arrest anyone on Hoover's list without the protection of the Bill of Rights. When the police came knocking on doors, they stated simply that it was "by order of President Roosevelt."

Teachers at schools that taught Italian (once supported by Mussolini) and World War I veterans, known as *ex combattenti*, were marked as dangerous subversives, some sent to internment camps or forced to relocate hundreds of miles from their homes. Filippo Molinari, who sold subscriptions for San Francisco's pro-Fascist newspaper *L'Italia* and was a World War I veteran, was taken from his home on the same night of the Pearl Harbor attack. Wearing only slippers and a thin garment, Molinari was put on a train to Missoula, Montana, isolated, unable to contact anyone, and freezing as the midwestern temperature dipped far below zero.

For West Coast Italian Americans, this government treatment must have come as a particular shock. California Italians had been a great immigrant success story earlier in the twentieth century; many had secured a place in the American power structure. But the man placed in charge of the War Department's Western Defense Command, Lieutenant General John DeWitt, was a militaristic bureaucrat determined to treat Italian and German Americans as badly as the Japanese. Convinced that a large number of fifth columnists existed in each community that could sabotage key military areas and bridges, he vetoed the more moderate plans of the Justice Department. DeWitt persuaded Roosevelt to relocate Italian Americans who were living in what he considered "restricted" zones of the West Coast.

The Western Defense Command announced in January 1942 that it had created eighty-six prohibited zones affecting almost the entire Pacific Coast—from the Pacific Ocean to the Sierra Nevada. The next month, Roosevelt signed Executive Order 9066, which authorized the army to exclude anyone it chose from these restricted areas. In the counties of Monterey and Santa Cruz, thousands of Italians west of Highway One had to move. In Pittsburg, Califor-

Italian-, Japanese-, and German-American internees stand with officers in Missoula, Montana. Without the protection of the Bill of Rights, police could haul enemy aliens away to internment camps following a mere knock on the door.

nia, a third of the residents, nearly three thousand people, were forced to leave their property. In San Francisco, Fisherman's Wharf and other areas near the water were off limits to aliens.

The government moved Italian-American noncitizens a few blocks from waterfronts, steel companies, and other production facilities. DeWitt's initial plan went well beyond this relocation, which took place two months before the internment of the Japanese. He intended to put the Italians and Germans in camps as soon as the Japanese had been cleared from the area.

Many ludicrous elements defined this quickly implemented policy, beginning with the premise that moving nearly ten thousand Italian Americans a few blocks from where they lived would be in the interest of national security. In addition, if one parent was a citizen and the other an enemy alien, the citizen could stay in the home but the alien had to move. In one case, a man could no longer enter his business—a pool hall and soda fountain located in a restricted area of Eureka in northern California—so he stood across the street (which wasn't restricted) and yelled instructions to his son on how to keep things running. If a doctor's office was located on the restricted side of the street, a permit from the local police office had to be obtained before an enemy alien could get medical attention.

For preternaturally anxious Italians, their worst fears vividly unfolded before them. Reading the newspaper meant learning they had to leave homes often built with their own hands. With scant information, people didn't know if they would ever return. Some families stayed with relatives, but others futilely searched for places to live because many landlords wouldn't rent to enemy aliens. Being old and poor meant moving to ramshackle houses and waiting for further news of one's fate.

Fishermen suffered terribly. Since the late 1900s, when they had begun supplying food for the California coast, these men, many illiterate, had tested their command of choppy waters, not the

Many Italian-American fishermen were unnaturalized citizens, now deemed enemy aliens. Because of this status, they could not step onto wharves, piers, or their own vessels.

English language. Having secured steady work, they never imagined learning to read and write in English to prepare for a citizenship test (in the era before Social Security and Medicare, there were few benefits to being a citizen). Enemy aliens could not step onto wharves, piers, or their beloved fishing vessels.

Giuseppe DiMaggio, the father of Joe DiMaggio, was a Sicilian immigrant who had come to America in 1898 and brought his wife Rosalie several years later. Like so many Californians of Sicilian origin, he worked as a crab fisherman while Rosalie raised their nine children. Neither could read or write. Their home on a hill above Fisherman's Wharf didn't fall in the restricted zone, but because of Giuseppe's enemy alien status, he could no longer work on the wharf or enter his son Joe's restaurant. Giuseppe's specialty, spicy crab *cioppino*—a fish stew invented in San Francisco—which he liked to prepare for Joe's friends, was now officially off the menu.

Yet just the year before these restrictions, Joe DiMaggio had given the nation its summer pastime as they watched "Joltin' Joe" pop home run after home run in a remarkable fifty-six-game hitting streak for the Yankees. While his panicky government declared his parents enemy aliens, Joe left the Yankees to fight in the war (along with three of his brothers who also played major league baseball).

No one on the West Coast escaped suspicion. The mayor of San Francisco, Angelo J. Rossi, was subpoenaed by his own chief of

Joe DiMaggio and first wife, Dorothy Arnold, with his parents, Rosalie and Giuseppe. Both of DiMaggio's parents were deemed enemy aliens during World War II.

police and questioned about his loyalty before a state senate fact-finding committee on un-American activities. Although there was no evidence that Rossi had any Fascist connections, the committee's accusations were among the factors that contributed to his defeat in 1943.

On the East Coast, where a much larger Italian-American population had achieved substantial political power, it proved harder to isolate and target individuals. Ettore Patrizi, the editor and publisher of San Francisco's *L'Italia*, had been forced to move from his home; but Generoso Pope, the publisher of New York's pro-Fascist and more widely circulated *Il Progresso*, never faced any government sanctions or restrictions, no doubt because of his political clout and personal relationship with Roosevelt.

No one on the West Coast escaped suspicion. A state senate committee questioned the mayor of San Francisco, Angelo J. Rossi (standing on the right with his siblings), about his loyalty.

Roosevelt's attorney general, Francis Biddle, favored selective rather than mass internment and disagreed with many of DeWitt's plans. But he didn't have enough clout to veto the demands of the War Department in the middle of a war. Biddle and the Justice Department knew, however, the political, social, and economic nightmare that would ensue if the East Coast Italian-American enemy aliens—over 50 percent of the Italian population in New York, New Jersey, and Connecticut—had to be relocated or interned. Such a policy would affect millions of people and disrupt the nation's economy and wartime production.

As months passed, Roosevelt recognized that the military's plans for West Coast Italians were also out of the question. He couldn't afford to further alienate a huge voting bloc of over five million people, with higher enlistments in the military than any other ethnic group, from the Democratic Party.

Having made Columbus Day a national holiday eight years earlier, the Roosevelt administration reached for its symbolism to announce the reversal of the government's policy. On October 12, 1942, Attorney General Biddle, introduced by Mayor Fiorello La Guardia in Carnegie Hall, declared that Italian Americans had proved their loyalty and would no longer be under restrictions. Their enemy alien status had been lifted.

If a pattern exists to the immigrant experience—an isolated first generation dedicates itself to finding work and raising a family; a more secure second generation, recognizing the chasm between its parents and the culture, seeks to eliminate ethnic traits; and the third and fourth generations set about reclaiming ancestral roots to better define the self—World War II added a much darker dimension to this universal passage of American selfhood.

The government's imposition of an enemy alien status went far beyond the standard humiliations of eating unrecognizable food or uttering a foreign word in place of an English one. The profound stigma of the enemy alien designation and the humiliation of

KNOCK 'EM ON THEIR AXIS!

WESTERN PRODUCTION

Western VICTORY DRIVE

With Mussolini now the enemy, being Italian-American carried a new stigma.

restrictions and relocations kept most Italian Americans silent about the experience. When drawn out in oral histories of the time, Italian Americans typically described themselves or family members as "aliens" not "enemy aliens," as if combining each loaded term was too much to bear—better an extraterrestrial association than that of the traitor.

Joe DiMaggio's astounding fifty-six-game hitting streak taught Americans not to take their eyes off the lithe batter at the plate or risk missing his athletic grace, yet the predicament of his parents taught Italian Americans to keep their heads down.

D O C U M E N T I

ENEMY ALIEN RESTRICTIONS

Alien Registration No. 1864815
Name Steve Ghio, Jr.
(First name) (Middle name) (Last name)

RIGHT
INDEX FINGERPRINT

(Signature of holder) Steve Ghio Jr.

Birth date Sept. 19 1889
(Day) (Year)
Born in or near Ge...
Citizen or subject of
Length of resid...
in United S...
Address of residence
Santa...
(City)
Height
Weight
Color of
Distincti...

Alien Registration No. 2598410
Name Grazia none Cerulli
(First name) (Middle name) (Last name)

RIGHT
INDEX FINGERPRINT

Appli...
filed

Birth date July 2 1881
(Month) (Day) (Year)
Born in or near Faeto Foggia Italy
(City) (Province) (Country)
Citizen or subject of none East of Italy
(Country)
Length of residence in United States 28 yrs., 10 mos.
Address of residence 73 Stillwater Ave
(Street address or rural route)
Stamford Fairfield Conn
(City) (County) (State)
Height 5 ft. 4 in.
Weight 202 lb.
Color of hair Black-grey
Distinctive marks none

STAMFORD, CONN. FEB 14 1942 REGISTERED

T. Roger Hart
(Signature of Identification Official)
...ation filed in Alien Registration Division. Copy
...ith Federal Bureau of Investigation office at
New Haven, Conn.
10—26150-1

Birth date Nov. 1865
(Month) (Day) (Year)
Born in or near Bexh Drieno, Genova Italy
(City) (Province) (Country)
Citizen or subject of Italy
(Country)
Length of residence in United States 41 yrs., 2 mos.
Address of residence 17 Laguna St
(Street address or rural route)
Santa Cruz-Santa Cruz Cal.
(City) (County) (State)
Height 4 ft. 10 in.
Weight 140 lb.
Color of hair Grey
Distinctive marks NONE

(STAMP)
SANTA CRUZ FEB 8 1942 REG. DIV

(Signature of Identification Official)
Application filed in Alien Registration Division
filed with Federal Bureau of Investigation offic...
SAN FRANCISCO CAL.
10—2...

UNITED STATES DEPARTMENT OF JUSTICE

★

NOTICE TO ALIENS OF ENEMY NATIONALITIES

★ The United States Government requires all aliens of German, Italian, or Japanese nationality to apply at post offices nearest to their place of residence for a Certificate of Identification. Applications must be filed between the period February 2 through February 7, 1942. Go to your postmaster today for printed directions.

EARL G. HARRISON,
Special Assistant to the Attorney General.

FRANCIS BIDDLE,
Attorney General.

Alien Registration No. 4622126
Name FRANCES MAGGIO
(First name) (Middle name) (Last name)

RIGHT
INDEX FINGERPRINT

(Signature of holder) FRANCES X MAGGIO
HER
MARK
10—26150-1

Witness: Anne F. Gibson 7416-2...

Birth date Oct. 1862
(Month) (Day) (Year)
Born in or near Palermo Italy
(City) (Province) (Country)
Citizen or subject of Italy
(Country)
Length of residence in United States 27 yrs., 10 mos.
Address of residence 1561 68 Street
(Street address or rural route)
Brooklyn, Kings, N.Y.
(City) (County) (State)
Height 5 ft., in.
Weight 145 lb.
Color of hair Grey
Distinctive marks None

BROOKLYN (STAMP) FEB 28 1942

Rose E. Wodensky
(Signature of Identification Official)
Application filed in Alien Registration Division. Copy
filed with Federal Bureau of Investigation office at
NEW YORK, N.Y.
10—26150-1

PART FOUR

1945–Present

CHAPTER FIFTEEN

American Dreams

At the end of World War II, life in America held astounding promise. As the liberator of Europe from Nazism and Fascism, the United States had won the admiration of the world; war production lifted the country from its Depression woes, boosting confidence beyond imagination. With the outlook sunny and the step light, America was eager for a new tune—sung by a slightly built, dreamy, blue-eyed singer named Frank Sinatra.

In the early 1940s, tens of thousands of teenagers ran screaming "FRANKIEE!" through Times Square when the young Sinatra played at the Paramount Theatre. Inside, they swooned with such intensity that the owner worried the building would collapse from the fervor. By mixing street swagger with stylish vocal lilts and the graceful phrasing of the bel canto tradition of Italian singing, Sinatra created an entirely new brand of urban cool.

Sinatra's astounding musical success helped pave the way for a group of Italian-American crooners who would dominate the pop charts for the next decade. Between the years of 1947 and 1954, twenty-five Italian-American singers had major hits; and between 1956 and 1959, more Italian Americans were on the Billboard charts than ever before or since, their upbeat tempo and easygoing style perfectly matching the mood of the country. Until the Beatles redefined music in the early sixties, these soothing voices filled the airwaves.

Not all of these crooners could be recognized as Italian-American,

Tens of thousands of teenage fans swooned over Frank Sinatra.

because show business called for changing one's name or tightening mellifluous vowels: Vic Damone was born Vito Farinola; Frankie Laine, Franceso Paolo LoVecchio; Perry Como, Pierino Como; Tony Bennett, Anthony Dominick Benedetto; Dean Martin, Dino Crocetti; Jerry Vale, Genaro Louis Vitaliano; and Connie Francis, Concetta Franconero. Each of these singers transcended their immigrant roots to become national stars with hits such as Martin's "Volare," Bennett's "Because of You," and Como's "Prisoner of Love."

Perry Como racked up an astounding seventy-three chart-topping songs in the 1950s. One of thirteen children born to immigrant parents in Canonsburg, Pennsylvania, near Pittsburgh, Como had a pleasant face, low-key manner, and cardigan sweater that defined laid-back style. Como was a barber who liked to sing and play guitar, and he would have contentedly stayed that way, but for a chance occurrence: a musician heard him sing when he was on vacation with a mutual friend and asked him to join his band. He almost quit his newfound career because he disliked the travel, but he decided to continue after he was offered a steady contract at the Copacabana nightclub. By the 1950s, his easy voice and style had garnered him a fifteen-minute television program, *The Perry Como Show*.

Dean Martin, born in Steubenville, Ohio, epitomized the rakish 1950s man with a cigarette in one hand and scotch on the rocks in the other. When he sang "That's Amore," America readily shared the love. Tony Bennett began his singing career as "Joe Bari," thinking the two-syllable name of an Italian region might be easier on the ear than his family name. Bob Hope disliked the choice and urged him to change Benedetto to Bennett instead of Bari. Growing up in Astoria, Queens, Bennett acquired his earliest musical memories listening with his family to the great tenor Enrico Caruso and performing in front of cousins who stopped by every Sunday. After serving in World War II, he turned to the sounds of jazz and bebop—Charlie Parker, Count Basie, and Billie Holiday. Like many of the fifties crooners, Bennett's singing

Dean Martin (Dino Crocetti) epitomized the rakish 1950s man.

Tony Bennett (Anthony Dominick Benedetto) dominated the pop charts in the 1950s.

idol was Frank Sinatra. As a young man, Bennett would stay all day at the Paramount Theatre to watch the singer known simply as "The Voice" perform each of his seven shows.

Francis Albert Sinatra was born in Hoboken, New Jersey, on December 12, 1915, in a breech delivery so difficult that he was first taken for dead. The women birthing his mother were preoccupied trying to save her life, but luckily someone had the presence of mind to grab the baby and run cold tap water on his head. His shrieks announced survival. The doctor's forceps, however, had left permanent scarring along the left side of his face, neck, and ear, prompting Sinatra to avoid being filmed from the left and to wear pancake makeup throughout his adult life to cover the disfigurement.

Sinatra spent his childhood gazing across the Hudson River and imagining himself on its glittering New York side. It wasn't until 1939 that talent, ambition, and sheer will led him to New York City's nightlife and fame. He took a job as a singing waiter in a New Jersey restaurant called the Rustic Cabin because it had a hookup with the radio station WNEW that broadcast in New York City. The wife of the famous bandleader and trumpet player Harry James heard Sinatra on the radio and told her husband to go see him in person. Sinatra wasn't supposed to sing the night James came by, but good fortune befell him in the last-minute cancellation of a peer. After Harry James had heard the singer handle the challenging note variation of Cole Porter's "Begin the Beguine," he offered Sinatra a contract on the spot. But James's next words fell flat: he told Sinatra to change his name to "Frankie Satin." Sinatra famously replied that if he wanted the singer, he had to take the name.

Decades later, Sinatra told the writer Pete Hamill that the exchange with Harry James had stirred up memories of the prejudice he had encountered as a child. "Of course, it meant something to me to be the son of immigrants. How could it not? How the hell could it not? I grew up for a few years thinking I was just another American kid. Then I discovered at—what? five? six?—I discovered that some people thought I was a dago. A wop. A guinea. You know, like I didn't have a fucking *name*." Besides, Sinatra added, a name as oily as Frankie Satin would have doomed him to playing cruise ships.

The fortuitous meeting with James changed Sinatra's life. Soon the young man was trying hard to mask his lack of education (Sinatra had dropped out of school before he reached sixteen) and his New Jersey accent. Diction lessons bolstered his confidence, and he began to create his own style. After six months with Harry James, an even bigger swing bandleader, Tommy Dorsey, offered Sinatra a contract.

In a few short years, the voice of Frank Sinatra had become a mega-phenomenon, and on October 11, 1944, the commotion around him grew so great that, as the press dubbed it, a "Columbus Day Riot" erupted. This riot, far from the earlier Columbus Day political melees when Fascists and anti-Fascists had faced off, was strictly about entertainment. Sinatra had been playing all day at the Paramount, and the overly packed theater held five thousand fans, far more than its maximum capacity of thirty-five hundred. Many of the fans wouldn't leave after the first show, intensifying the craziness. By the end of the day, thirty thousand hysterical girls waited outside—screaming, crying, pushing—and causing a commotion over a celebrity the likes of which had never before been seen in America.

Not everyone appreciated the young man who made girls swoon, particularly servicemen. Sinatra had received a 4-F classification for a perforated eardrum, excusing him from military service. Many soldiers didn't like this singer making love to their girlfriends with his microphone. They labeled him a draft dodger and threw tomatoes at him when they could. While few people questioned the

Frank Sinatra would redefine urban cool.

4-F status of famous Americans like John Wayne, many resented this son of Italian immigrants who had made it so big.

The draft-dodging charge hounded Sinatra throughout his career, and by the late 1940s a series of missteps seemed to doom the once invincible singer. Sinatra had a few too many run-ins with the press and even punched a newspaper columnist. He took a trip to Havana, Cuba, where he was photographed with the mobster Charlie ("Lucky") Luciano—a decision that would forever link him with the Mafia in the public's mind. He also began an affair with the sultry movie star Ava Gardner while he was still married to his wife, Nancy, the mother of his three children. The teenagers who once had been crazy for Sinatra had grown to be wives disgusted by infidelities that were particularly shocking for an Italian-American Catholic.

Only five foot seven and, at 130 pounds, already a slight man, Sinatra was rapidly shedding weight from the stress of the public's ire. He even lost his voice for a while: one night in 1950 simply no sounds came out. The Italian-American singers for whom Sinatra had paved the way were now entertaining the country and topping the charts, while Sinatra was without a hit in both 1952 and 1953.

Yet, as everyone who remembers Frank Sinatra from the latter part of the twentieth century knows, the "Chairman of the Board" returned to have the world on a string. If the Sinatra story has a happy Hollywood ending, it also contains a pervasive myth that remains in the public's imagination, no matter how many biographers have tried to debunk it. The myth centers on Sinatra's longing for a comeback role in the movie *From Here to Eternity* and the belief that the Mafia told the studio it had to hire Sinatra—or else.

Sinatra was desperate to play army private Angelo Maggio for the movie version of the James Jones novel because he felt he understood, and perhaps shared a few character traits with, this troubled but charismatic Italian-American man. He even sent Harry Cohn, the founder of Columbia Pictures, who had bought the rights to the film, telegrams signed "Maggio." But it was the glamorous A-list movie star Ava Gardner, by then his second wife,

Rat Pack members Sammy Davis Jr., Dean Martin, and Frank Sinatra—the ultimate bad boys having fun.

who most likely secured the role for him. She visited Harry Cohn's wife and begged her to let Sinatra have a screen test. Gardner went even further, telling Cohn that if he agreed to the screen test, she would do a picture for him for free. Cohn eventually called Sinatra, and the screen test went so well that a part of it ended up in the final cut of the film.

In his novel and later screenplay *The Godfather*, Mario Puzo decided to embellish the highly publicized story of how Sinatra got the part. One of America's most famous movie lines—"I'm going to make him an offer he can't refuse"—is from a scene in which Don Corleone reassures Johnny Fontane, the Sinatra-inspired character, that a movie role he desperately wants will be his. After the studio head, resembling Harry Cohn, insists the singer will never get the part, he wakes up to bloodied sheets and the severed head

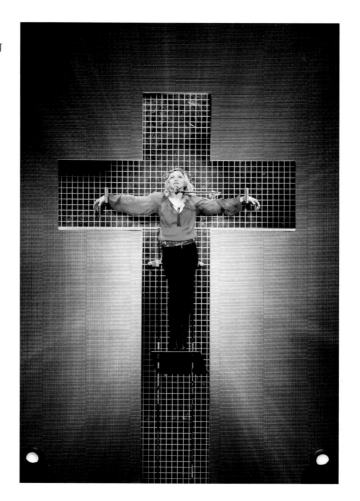

The singer Madonna performing on stage during her Confessions Tour in 2006.

of his prized racehorse. The arresting psychic power of the horse's head used as warning and revenge has been emblazoned on the American imagination, even if this narrative had no bearing on reality.

Luckily, Sinatra's instinct that Maggio was the right role for him panned out: his portrait won him an Academy Award for best supporting actor in 1953, and his comeback began. A contract with Capitol Records put his singing career back on track, and the mature voice of Frank Sinatra, combined with the lush orchestration of Nelson Riddle, created hits like "I've Got the World on a String."

Over the next twenty-five years, Sinatra would record more than three hundred songs. The middle-aged Sinatra with the tilted fedora (to hide thinning hair), slightly wrinkled white shirt, and skinny tie personified an urban style that hipsters imitate today. He became the ultimate bad boy having fun, cavorting with his Rat Pack friends: Dean Martin, Sammy Davis Jr., Peter Lawford, and Joey Bishop. The appealing and lasting cool of the Rat Pack's *Ocean's Eleven* film capers convinced Steven Soderbergh to direct a remake and two sequels in the new millennium, starring George Clooney and Brad Pitt. One hundred years after his birth, Frank Sinatra's elegant vocals continue to be admired by superstar singers: Jay-Z declares in "Empire State of Mind" that he is the new Frank Sinatra, ready to make it anywhere. Sinatra remains the first Italian-American singer to have given millions of immigrants a taste of what it meant, with its impossible highs and feverish lows, to live the American dream.

The next time Italian-American singers became pop culture icons, two women created the phenomenon. By the late twentieth century, worldly cynicism had supplanted American promise. Third- and fourth-generation rebellion had replaced immigrant determination. Enter Madonna Louise Ciccone, born to an Italian-American father and French-Canadian mother, who in 1983 released her first album and in the following decades would sell over three hundred million—more than any other female singer.

Madonna, raised in Bay City, Michigan, by her father after his wife, the mother of six children, died young of cancer, has said that Sinatra was an important influence while she was growing up. But Madonna was referring to Nancy, Frank's daughter, whose 1966 hit, "These Boots Are Made for Walkin'," made a big impression on the eight-year-old Ciccone. Walking over someone with pastel-colored go-go boots—the image stuck with the future megastar Madonna, who made female power and sexuality prominent motifs in her songs and music videos.

In the 1980s, Madonna's signature style of dressing included lacy underwear and giant crosses, turning the sacred icon of her Catholic upbringing into mass-marketed jewelry for a vast female following. The Catholic hierarchy that had once protested the

Stefani Joanne Angelina Germanotta, known to the world as Lady Gaga.

blending of the sacred and the profane during religious street processions was made apoplectic by Madonna's use of religious symbols to promote her pop music. Her videos and stage performances, beginning with the 1984 recording of "Like a Virgin," have included burning crosses, the use of stigmata, and even a crucifixion of her on stage during the Confessions Tour in 2006. Critics called her crass and attention-getting, while fans defended Madonna as brave and boundary-breaking.

A similar desire to flaunt convention and turn Christian symbolism on its head became even more shocking in the work of Stefani Joanne Angelina Germanotta, known to the world as Lady Gaga (the stage name came from the song "Radio Ga Ga" by the group Queen). Madonna and Lady Gaga are frequently compared, and both are recognized more for their dance music and outré performances than their vocal range.

Gaga, who attended the elite all-girls school Convent of the Sacred Heart in New York, determinedly broke free of her thirteen years there. Her music video "Judas" depicts the pop star riding on the back of a motorcycle driven by a man in a crown of thorns as she looks longingly at a biker wearing the name Judas on his leather jacket. In another scene, she cavorts in a tub reminiscent of a baptismal font with both men. The music video "Alejandro" includes scenes of sadomasochistic sex juxtaposed with Gaga dressed as a nun in a latex habit sucking and swallowing rosary beads.

Since her debut single "Just Dance" in 2008, Lady Gaga has become an international superstar. Her third album, *Born This Way*, sold over one million copies in a week. Presenting herself as the friend and fellow traveler of outcasts, Lady Gaga has a huge following among the lesbian, gay, bisexual, and transgender community.

Both Madonna and Lady Gaga grew up surrounded by Roman Catholic imagery, and they have made religious pageantry a central element of their performances. Both are part of a cultural inheritance that has never shied away from the baroque. As far back as the sixteenth century, Italy's popular art shocked its more subdued European neighbors: a Neapolitan painting of the Madonna depicts her with lactating breasts delivering milk to souls in purgatory. Saints like the willowy Sebastian appeared as gender ambiguous as some of Lady Gaga's fans. Both women have changed the nature of music and stagecraft by aggressively using these symbols and flaunting their own sexuality. They have made Frank Sinatra's bad-boy behavior and the Rat Pack serenading a woman to spend the night because "baby, it's cold outside" seem as tame as a glass of warm milk and cookies.

Dion DiMucci

Dion DiMucci helped introduce rock and roll in the 1950s, leading his doo-wop group Dion and the Belmonts and later singing solo. His chart-topping hits included "The Wanderer," "Teenager in Love," and "Runaround Sue." Dion grew up in the Belmont section of the Bronx (hence the group's name) and found his early inspiration not in Italian-American crooners, but in the blues guitar of Jimmy Reed and the country music of Hank Williams. Bruce Springsteen once remarked that Dion's music was the bridge between Frank Sinatra and rock and roll.

Q: What was it like growing up in the Bronx in the forties and fifties?

DiMucci: It was great. All the tenement buildings were built by my relatives, and they were carving out marble for stairs. My grandmother would come down with a pot of hot water and soap and actually clean the stoops because the kids would sit on them. Everything revolved around the church. Mount Carmel Catholic Church was the hub of Little Italy in the Bronx. As a kid growing up in the forties, on those cold winter December nights, with the snow on the ground, and it's silent and you walk into the church—there were the candles, the choir, the awe, the wonder, the majesty. It felt like you were home in the arms of God.

Q: Did your extended family live nearby?

DiMucci: I used to run out of my house to practically any apartment building and I had an aunt or an uncle who lived there with my cousins. As soon as you'd knock on the door, there'd be food on the table. I'd run over to my grandmother's house, and she'd open the door, and she'd say, "Jesus, Mary, and Joseph, thank you for this lovely boy," and she'd grab my cheeks and feed me oranges and provolone cheese. Oh, God, it was good. It was good.

Q: You were always very aware of being Italian?

DiMucci: My grandfather came to this country in 1907 when he was sixteen. He didn't have any money. He educated himself. He had eight children. My mother was the oldest. My mother always said, "I left school at fourteen to work and help my family, and I was so proud when I could help them." Today, you'd get arrested for that. My grandfather Tony would take me to a theater called Windsor in the Bronx. In the forties they had the operas there—*La Boheme, La Traviata, Pagliacci*. We would sit in the balcony. I'd say, "What does that all mean?" He'd explain to me the clown in *Pagliacci*. The clown made its way into some of my rock-and-roll songs.

Q: The Italian-American crooners of the time were on the top of the charts. But you were playing Hank Williams.

DiMucci: Yeah, I was into something totally different. I ran home from school just to catch maybe twenty minutes of the Don Larkin

I'd run over to my grand-mother's house, and she'd open the door, and she'd say, "Jesus, Mary, and Joseph, thank you for this lovely boy," and she'd grab my cheeks and feed me oranges and provolone cheese. Oh, God, it was good. It was good.

show that came out of Newark, New Jersey. He played country music. I wasn't into the Italian singer.

Q: You've said that Hank Williams brought you beyond your neighborhood. As you grew older, did the nurturing aspect of your neighborhood feel at all suffocating?

DiMucci: I think some of my friends got threatened that my world was opening up. There was maybe a fear of the outside world—just stay close—but I was breaking out of that. That's what rock and roll was all about: expressing your individuality and your freedom.

Q: Why do you think there were so many Italian-American singers in the fifties?

DiMucci: I think in the culture, there's a rhythm. It's like there's a rhythm in the way they talk and the way they express themselves. It's very demonstrative. I think there was a rhythm of the city, the rhythm of Italians, the church, the music. Music was part of the fabric of being Italian and part of growing up.

CHAPTER SIXTEEN

Cultural Outlaws

THE POCKET POETS SERIES

GASOLINE

GREGORY CORSO

INTRODUCTION BY

ALLEN GINSBERG

NUMBER EIGHT

n the late 1950s and early 1960s, a few radical voices heralded a call about the dangers of a too complacent and self-satisfied America. In the literary world, counterculture writers riffed on paper like jazz artists improvising on stage, and on university campuses dissent movements blossomed, sending students from the ivory tower to the streets. Poet Gregory Corso and student activist Mario Savio played leading roles in these movements, and their voices against conformity and injustice recalled those of early-twentieth-century radical *paesani*.

Along with his pals Allen Ginsberg, Jack Kerouac, and William S. Burroughs, Gregory Corso formed a group of hipster poets known as the Beats, who experimented with drugs, declared free love, and decried capitalism and materialism. When Corso's book of poetry titled *Gasoline* was published in 1958, Jack Kerouac described him as "a tough young kid from the Lower East Side who rose like an angel over the rooftops and sang Italian songs as sweet as Caruso and Sinatra, but in *words*." Yet this sugarcoated description seemed off-note for the in-your-face Beat, who was closer in spirit to the Italian anarchist than to the crooner.

The worldview of anarchist forebears had its corollary in the Beats' rejection of authority and search for transcendence from a tainted world. And in the lyrical symmetry of history, the son of an Italian-American anarchist made the publication of *Gasoline* possible. Peter Martin—who cofounded the City Lights Bookstore in

City Lights, cofounded by Lawrence Ferlinghetti and Peter Martin (the son of anarchist Carlo Tresca), helped establish the careers of the Beats by printing their early work.

San Francisco with another free-spirited half Italian, poet Lawrence Ferlinghetti—was Carlo Tresca's son. (Martin was the progeny of an affair between Tresca and Bina Flynn, the sister of Tresca's longtime lover, Elizabeth Gurley Flynn. Elizabeth had become Tresca's partner after the two met in Lawrence, Massachusetts, rallying striking millworkers.) City Lights helped establish the career of the Beats by printing their work under its publishing wing, City Lights Books.

Corso's poetry was rooted in the hardship and squalor of his youth, wounds carried from parental abandonment and teenage imprisonment. Born Nunzio Corso at 190 Bleecker Street in Greenwich Village on March 26, 1930, he was the son of Italian immigrants—sixteen-year-old Michelina Colonna Corso and seventeen-year-old Fortunato Samuel Corso (known as "Sam"). Michelina left Sam when Nunzio was an infant, depositing her son on the doorsteps of Catholic Charities. The boy bounced from foundling hospital to foster homes. Sam Corso eventually remarried, but Nunzio, who later went by his confirmation name Gregory, had a difficult relationship with his father and stepmother. Forced by Sam to leave school in the sixth grade, Gregory ran away at the age of twelve, and after spending time on the streets, he was placed in a boys' home.

At thirteen, Gregory was arrested for stealing a radio and spent five months in the notorious Manhattan prison known as the Tombs, the first stop on a horrid childhood odyssey. He was also sent to Bellevue Hospital's psychiatric ward for three months. At seventeen, he stole a used suit, worth less than fifty dollars, to wear on a date. The crime earned him a three-year sentence at Clinton State Prison in Dannemora, New York, near the Canadian border—the same facility that had housed mafia boss Lucky Luciano in the 1940s.

Corso dedicated *Gasoline* to "the angels of Clinton Prison who, in my seventeenth year, handed me, from all the cells surrounding me, books of illumination." Corso told the story, which might be one of the poet's elaborate yarns, of Lucky Luciano donating money for a library at Clinton State after he left the facility, which provided young Gregory with the education he'd never had. The poet also liked to talk about a high-level mob figure who helped protect him in prison. (In one of Corso's collected letters, he railed against, after seeing the movie *Goodfellas*, "wop mafia ignorant Ginszo pain hurt and hard-headedness, true to such false life," adding, "Glad when I left prison I made friends with Bohemians, not hoods. Can't bear dumb talk. Even in prison, the hoods I knew were the head guys, with the smarts.")

From this prison library, Corso read the poetry of Percy Bysshe Shelley and Arthur Rimbaud, along with Stendhal's *The Red and the Black*. He devoured the poetry and prose, as well as the contents of a 1905 dictionary, and left prison knowing that he would become a poet. Shortly thereafter, Corso met Allen Ginsberg in Greenwich Village and shared with him his writing.

Corso also became friends with a poet named Violet ("Bunny") Lang, who took him with her to Cambridge, Massachusetts. She put him up in housing for five dollars a week, but when the deal fell through, Lang approached a Harvard student named Peter Sourian and asked if he could lodge Corso in his dorm room. Sourian and his five roommates at Eliot House took Corso in, cordoning off a space in their living room with tie-dyed sheets. Corso sat in on Harvard classes, and the college boys pilfered food from the dining hall for their yearlong stowaway. Sourian, a former professor at Bard College, remembers Corso as a considerate roommate, careful not to wear out his welcome, who recited reams of Shelley's poetry with a near-photographic memory. The Harvard students admired Corso's verse and helped him publish his first collection, written between 1954 and 1955, *The Vestal Lady on Brattle*.

Corso's poetry, which combines the dark and the sublime, can matter-of-factly describe a woman who eats children or the suicide of an unnamed girl in Greenwich Village. Yet a playful humor, surprising imagery, and gratitude toward the beauty and wonder surrounding him also suggest transcendence from a brutal world. Unlike the other Beats, all of whom were Ivy League educated,

Corso had acquired his hipster lingo from genuine street credentials.

Corso joined his fellow Beats in poking fun at conformity and societal expectations, perhaps best illustrated in the often anthologized poem "Marriage." The protagonist asks if he should get married and be good, knowing that he is the type to take a date not to the movies, but to cemeteries to tell "about werewolf bathtubs and forked clarinets." He imagines trembling before the priest, and not knowing "what to say say Pie Glue!" (The lengthy poem so charmed actor Ethan Hawke that when he was a teenager, he memorized it to recite on dates.)

After the fame of the Beat movement faded, Corso struggled to support himself, his difficulties compounded by drug and alcohol addiction. Despite his personal battles, he always remained steadfast in his vision of the poet as societal seer. In the late 1990s, documentary filmmaker Gustave Reininger was working on a film about the poet and the Beat

Gregory Corso seeking the Muse in Greece. Corso's poetry combined the dark and the sublime.

movement. Knowing that Corso's life had been defined by his early abandonment, Reininger hired a detective to try to track down his mother. Sam Corso had told Gregory that Michelina went back to Italy, so the filmmaker first looked for her there. But he found her instead in Trenton, New Jersey, a middle-class housewife with a family of her own. Reininger reunited mother and son, and Michelina explained that she had been badly beaten and abused by Corso's father, who knocked out her teeth, and the scared and impoverished sixteen-year-old had fled. In 2001, Gregory Corso would succumb to prostate cancer, but the discovery closed the circle that had haunted him. One of the leaders of America's counter-culture movement finally found some personal peace discovering his Italian mamma.

"Blessed be the revolutionaries of the Spirit!" Corso wrote about those who "boot tyrannical values" without spilling blood. He was referring to the role of the poet, but surely he would have approved of the student leading a campus sit-in.

On December 2, 1964, at the University of California at Berkeley, Mario Savio took the microphone to protest the administration's decision to suppress political activity and shut down a free-speech area on campus grounds. The twenty-one-year-old had become a known figure on campus, standing in his socks on top of police cars and addressing a student body increasingly frustrated with the actions of the administration. That day, he spoke with an originality and power to move people into action reminiscent of Arturo Giovannitti, the gifted leftist orator who had roused Lawrence millworkers in 1912 and persuaded a jury of his innocence. Savio famously proclaimed:

> There's a time when the operation of the machine becomes so odious, makes you so sick at heart, that you can't take part; you can't even passively take part. And you've got to put your bodies upon the gears and upon the wheels, upon the levers, upon all the apparatus, and you've got to make it stop. And you've got to indicate to the people who run it, to the people who own it, that unless you're free, the machine will be prevented from working at all.

Those words launched a thousand students to occupy Sproul Hall, Berkeley's main administrative building, in a massive sit-in. Most of the students, including Savio, remained there until they were dragged away by police. Their actions represented the largest act of civil disobedience ever to take place at an American univer-

Gifted orator Mario Savio helped to start the Free Speech Movement on college campuses.

sity. A week later, UC Berkeley president Clark Kerr gave in to the students' demands and allowed political activity on campus.

Savio, receiving much of the credit for the administration turnaround, helped create what became known as the Free Speech Movement on college campuses, which strongly influenced student activism later in the decade against the Vietnam War. His speech dazzled students and professors alike; most amazing was that Savio had spent much of his young life battling a terrible stutter.

Mario Savio came to Berkeley by way of Queens, New York, where he was raised in an immigrant working-class Italian household. Although Savio spoke Italian fluidly with his parents, Joseph and Dora, in English he struggled with a debilitating stutter. Political battles were also not new to him; he had grown up listening to heated and frequent arguments between his grandfather, a Mussolini supporter, and his father, a machine punch operator and FDR Democrat.

Until college, Savio was known as "Bob" after a priest made fun of the name Mario in class. The incident so upset his parents that they decided to call him by his middle name, Robert. Savio later observed that the episode had taught him that "to be an American" meant "to hide your Italian-ness."

The young Savio wanted to go away to college and hoped to apply to Harvard, but his father insisted that he stay nearby. As valedictorian of his high school class, he won a full scholarship to the Roman Catholic Manhattan College in the Riverdale section of the Bronx. Traditionally, the valedictorian addresses the graduating class, but administration officials, concerned about Savio's stutter, said he didn't have to make a speech. Savio refused to give up this role and, after a halting start, eloquently delivered his remarks (an achievement Savio later deemed a "miracle"), criticizing American materialism and urging student involvement to better the world.

At Manhattan College, Savio was unhappy, finding the Catholic atmosphere oppressive, so he transferred to the tuition-free Queens College. Still not content, he considered dropping out of college but transferred once again, this time to Berkeley.

In California, he seemed to thrive. After his first year at Berkeley he volunteered for the Mississippi Freedom Summer campaign, where he helped register disenfranchised African Americans to vote. Savio reclaimed part of his Italian-American identity, using his birth name Mario, and began to conquer his stutter, which was still pronounced in small-group conversations but disappeared when he took the microphone.

A former altar boy, Savio considered entering the priesthood, but he became disillusioned with the faith and found salvation studying Greek history, philosophy, and literature. His embrace of, and later disillusionment with, the church was akin to Arturo Giovannitti's experience, and their similar interest in classical studies may have helped shape the rhetoric of two formidable Italian-American orators. Both believed in equality and compassion toward the poor, fundamental tenets of the faith they abandoned; Giovannitti embraced the egalitarianism of socialism, and Savio became a voice of the New Left. But Savio rejected political labels. His biographer, Robert Cohen, calls him a reformer and a revolutionary who "wanted immediate egalitarian change, disdained compromise, loathed bureaucracy, and worked for a total transformation of race relations and university life."

Yet Savio's student activism came with great personal cost. UC Berkeley suspended Savio, and the hero of the Free Speech Movement was sentenced to four months in prison after a judge decided that student sit-ins were acts of trespassing and the civil disobedience posture of going limp amounted to resisting arrest. Savio eventually dropped out of the movement, believing that the glare of his media fame hurt its nonhierarchical structure. He also battled depression and panic attacks, and in the seventies he struggled to support his wife and children. The following decade, Savio earned bachelor's and master's degrees from San Francisco State University, and he taught math and philosophy at Sonoma State University. On the twentieth anniversary of the Free Speech Movement, Savio returned to Berkeley as the keynote speaker and passionately decried the politics of Ronald Reagan and the administration's intervention in Central America.

Mario Savio was fifty-three years old when he died from heart problems. He was fighting at the time on behalf of his working-class students against a fee hike at Sonoma State. Shortly after his death, the University of California renamed the spot at Sproul Hall where he had made his unforgettable extemporaneous speech the "Mario Savio Steps."

D O C U M E N T   I

FROM DIANE DI PRIMA'S *RECOLLECTIONS OF MY LIFE AS A WOMAN*

Diane Di Prima was born in Brooklyn, New York, in 1934. A talented student, she gained admission to the selective Hunter High School—an occasion that provoked her father to remind her to never "expect too much, always remember you are Italian." She attended Swarthmore College for two years but dropped out to move back to New York City and establish herself as a woman poet in the emerging all-male Beat movement. She coedited a literary magazine called The Floating Bear *with Amiri Baraka (then known as LeRoi Jones) and was cofounder of the Poet's Press and New York Poets Theatre. Di Prima is the author of over forty books and was named San Francisco's poet laureate in 2009.*

In the following excerpt from her memoir Recollections of My Life as a Woman, *Di Prima describes how the anarchist spirit of her grandfather, Domenico, influenced her days working in the Phoenix bookstore in Greenwich Village and supporting herself as a poet. It was a time of literary repression: Allen Ginsberg's poem "Howl" was on trial, and the works of writers such as Henry Miller and Jean Genet had been banned. Di Prima worked on a scheme with her boss, Larry Wallrich, to bring banned books to the United States.*

(continued on next page)

Larry was a quiet, gentle man as I have said—and an anarchist and utter radical. With everything that word meant at the cusp of the 1960s. Political exasperation, all the frustration of the '50s, looking for an outlet. And as far as I was concerned: while I held onto my healthy suspicion of all "organizations" as such, I would eagerly do whatever came to hand to help to bring down the established order. Nothing that had happened—from the times when I went with my grandfather to rallies in Bronx River Park, all the way to working here in this bookstore, with my baby beside me—had changed my point of view . . .

The Phoenix had its own underground railroad for books, its own method of importing desired but forbidden literature. Most of it was printed in France by Olympia Press, and booklike packages coming from France to the U.S. would have been suspect—likely to be examined by customs. In the system that Larry Wallrich had worked out, the books went from

France to Turkey, where a friend of his lived. In Turkey, they were wrapped in small packages (about three books to a package) and *stamped with the return address of an Episcopalian funeral home in Ankara.* They were then duly labeled as somebody's ashes, and sent to an address (ostensibly a relative of the deceased) in New York City. Each two- or three-book package was sent to a different address of course (Larry had plenty of friends in New York to receive them), and the mailing was spread out over a period of weeks. It seemed that no one at customs felt a strong urge to open packages of Episcopalian bones and ashes—the books got through.

CHAPTER SEVENTEEN

Crime and Prejudice

The star power of Frank Sinatra, Dean Martin, Perry Como, and Tony Bennett helped associate Italian Americans with mellifluous voices, laid-back ease, and urban cool; and figures such as Gregory Corso, Diane Di Prima, and Mario Savio laid the groundwork for a growing counterculture movement. But the majority of the ethnic group was still struggling to lift itself out of its blue-collar status and battle a lingering prejudice. Making these circumstances worse, public attention focused on a nefarious connection that would plague Italian Americans for the rest of the twentieth century.

The fruits of Prohibition, that "noble experiment," had fully ripened: former thugs plucked from the streets had turned into sophisticated criminals. These gangsters moved up in the world, not only dealing in gambling, smuggling, narcotics, and prostitution, but infiltrating legitimate businesses like the garment industry, construction, nightclubs, hotels, and liquor companies. Irish and Jewish gangsters, especially men like Benjamin ("Bugsy") Siegel and Meyer Lansky, were part of this criminal network and invested in and later controlled multimillion-dollar casino enterprises.

The two largest crime syndicates, however, were Italian-American, based in Chicago and New York, heirs to Al Capone's early bootlegging business and a criminal network led by East Harlem's Frank Costello, who had emerged as one of the most powerful mob figures in the country. Costello even made the cover of *Time* maga-

New York mob boss Frank Costello wanted to convince the public that he was a legitimate businessman.

In the 1940s and '50s, many ordinary, law-abiding Italian Americans moved to the suburbs to distance themselves from urban crime and live the American dream. Preserving traditions like the Sunday afternoon family meal helped fortify them against ongoing prejudice.

zine in 1949; behind an illustration of his thick-featured face poured shimmering silver slot machine coins.

In 1950, the year after Costello's *Time* cover, Americans received a public civics lesson on how organized crime was carving up the nation's coffers, siphoning an estimated $20 billion alone through illegal gambling. A freshman senator from Tennessee named Estes Kefauver, who had introduced bills to ban slot machine shipments, became the head of the Special Committee to Investigate Organized Crime in Interstate Commerce. Known as the Kefauver Committee, it began a fifteen-month investigation to uncover whether a national, possibly international, syndicate or "commission" controlled organized crime. Some experts disparaged Kefauver's theory from the start, arguing that the Mafia consisted of ruthless competing groups trying to dominate these lucrative industries.

While the word *mafia* had arisen first during the New Orleans trial and lynchings in 1891 for the murder of police chief David Hennessy, and by the 1930s it frequently appeared in disparaging remarks about Italian Americans, this was the first time an American senator posed the question "What is the Mafia?" before a congressional committee.

The senator couldn't have appeared more opposite from the high school dropouts he collected, questioned, and, at six feet three inches tall, towered over. Estes Kefauver was the grandson of a Baptist preacher who had grown up in the foothills of the Great Smoky Mountains and graduated from Yale Law School in 1927. The Esteses, his mother's family, had settled in Tennessee during colonial times and traced their roots to Renaissance Italy. The senator's namesake was a derivation of the noble Este lineage, which held its family seat, the Villa d'Este, in Tivoli outside of Rome.

Kefauver's mother wrote moral counsel to her son each day— "Do good while life shall last," her words harkened—and Estes Kefauver became a progressive southerner who supported New Deal legislation and school desegregation before the civil rights era. Kefauver had little experience in Washington when he sought the chairmanship of the investigative committee, but he had national aspirations, and the high-profile spot provided enough recognition for him to twice pursue the presidency. Although Kefauver failed to win the Democratic nomination, he was chosen to be the vice-presidential running mate for nominee Adlai Stevenson in 1956.

The Kefauver Committee traveled around the country, grilling gangsters, hoodlums, and gun molls in fourteen cities, including Philadelphia, Miami, and Los Angeles. The public learned about the close connection between bad cops and gangsters and the illegal gambling kickbacks lining the pockets of sheriffs and police. Initially, the hearings received only local coverage, but by the time

The freshman senator from Tennessee, Estes Kefauver, led a fifteen-month investigation into organized crime.

the committee had concluded its investigation in New York, the bright lights of the television media illuminated the room.

With cameras ready, Kefauver brought out his biggest names: longshoreman head Anthony ("Tough Tony") Anastasio, gambling kingpin Joe Adonis, and mob boss Frank Costello. The key moment that captivated American attention and sparked a decades-long fascination with the mob took place during Costello's testimony. Most gangsters called before the committee used the Fifth Amendment to remain silent, but Costello decided to talk.

The televised Senate-organized crime hearings became so popular that they were shown in movie theaters.

Perhaps it was hubris, the belief he could convince Congress and the public that he was a legitimate businessman. Costello held a lifelong grudge against corrupt politicians and judges who earned the public's respect while he was denounced for a life of crime, even after he invested in legitimate businesses. Costello did purchase real estate, nightclubs, and other legal pursuits, but his dark history stained the money backing these interests.

Americans had been exposed to mob characters in movies like *Scarface* and *Little Caesar*, but now an estimated twenty to thirty million viewers were watching real-life gangsters on television at home. Before the cameras rolled, Costello complained to the senators that the bright lights bothered him. As a compromise, the committee told the media that they could only film Costello's hands. Although the director of NBC television news protested the restriction on behalf of all the broadcasters, the committee's decision proved riveting. Costello's hands were the sole image on the black-and-white screen, offering a cinematic angle as artfully composed as one by Martin Scorsese.

"Costello turned his automatic pencil a thousand times," the *Chicago Tribune* reported. "He crumpled papers, he fiddled with book matches, he shuffled income tax returns, he clasped his hands tightly, he unclasped them, he crushed papers, he twisted fingers, he held one hand up to his head, he hung an arm over a chair, he tried a dozen positions, each one reflecting his tension more vividly than the masked face of a gambler could have done."

"Women by the thousands deserted their household duties, afternoon bridge, and canasta for the second day to eavesdrop on the big show," the story continued. "There'll be more watching today. The women may not even get their dishes done."

Costello became so frustrated during

After the gangster Frank Costello complained that the camera lights bothered him, the Kefauver Committee agreed to film only his hands. The committee's decision proved cinematically riveting.

his testimony that he stormed out on the third day, and though he finally returned, this act of contempt, along with tax evasion, would send him to prison later in the decade. The New York hearings provided the prime-time climax to the committee's fifteen months on the road, during which over six hundred witnesses had been interviewed and America had become acquainted with men called "Greasy Thumb" and "Trigger Mike."

Despite all of its efforts and over ten thousand pages of testimony, the Kefauver Committee never found substantial evidence that a national syndicate existed. But it exposed millions of Americans to some big-time criminals. The committee's investigation also led to deportations and the creation of a rackets squad in the IRS that convicted nearly nine hundred gangsters. Illuminating Tammany Hall's close connection with Costello and other underworld figures, the hearings ultimately weakened the political machine that had regained power after the end of La Guardia's tenure in New York.

Estes Kefauver died of a heart attack in August 1963, one month shy of the opportunity to see the fruition of his efforts to expose the inner workings of organized crime, which by then was taking in about $40 billion a year. A new Senate investigation began that September, backed by the power and influence of Bobby Kennedy as the nation's attorney general. This time the committee had an inside informer, the first willing to break the honored code of Mafia silence known as *omertà*.

His name was Joseph Valachi, a five-foot-three convicted murderer, narcotics dealer, and low-level mobster who decided to talk while serving a life sentence. Fearing that a $100,000 price tag had been put on his head, he badly needed government protection. While in prison, Valachi murdered with a metal pipe a fellow inmate who he believed was out to kill him, but he got the wrong guy. He arrived before Congress chain-smoking and disguised from his pursuers with brightly dyed red hair. Valachi was the first man to offer another name for the Mafia: *La Cosa Nostra* ("Our Thing").

Today, mob experts believe that Valachi was too low in the organization's food chain to know as much as he claimed and that he was being used by the feds to present information they had already obtained from prior informants. But his stories riveted a public that, for thirteen years since Costello's flailing hands, had not seen this kind of a show.

Valachi described a secret initiation ritual that began by repeating in Sicilian dialect an oath to live and die "by the gun and knife." The initiate is told to toss a burning paper from hand to hand and say, "This is the way I burn if I expose this organization." Next came the prick of the finger drawing blood as a sign of brotherhood and absolute loyalty. Each inductee was designated a "godfather" to initiate the oath with the finger prick.

Most important, Valachi revealed how five "families" ruled this murderous organization. A "boss" headed the family, followed by an underboss, counselor (*consigliere*), captain, and finally soldiers. The Mafia had cleverly used the cohesiveness of the Italian family—the culture's bedrock value—to create the loyalty and tight structure necessary to dominate organized crime in America. Valachi also named heads of the five leading families at the time: Vito Genovese, Carlo Gambino, Giuseppe Magliocco (Joseph Colombo later took his place), Joseph Bonanno, and Gaetano Lucchese.

The Senate committee illustrated how five "families" ruled this murderous organization.

The grudge-holding Valachi proved an even better show than the Kefauver witnesses, offering salacious details and turning illiterate bit players like himself into major criminals on a national stage. His tantalizing testimony riveted the American public: the Judas-like kiss on the cheek signaling one's impending death; the godfather to whom one owed unquestioning loyalty; the violin case hiding a machine gun; the memorable line, "Once you're in you can't get out." As a reporter covering the hearings presciently noted, "A writer of crime fiction would have gathered plenty of material in listening to Valachi."

Our Ancestors

Florence Scala

While the country's eyes were glued to Valachi's talk of blood oaths and Sicilian bonds, a daughter of Italian immigrants was challenging both the thugs controlling her neighborhood and an all-powerful Mayor Richard J. Daley's plans to demolish Chicago's Little Italy. This story of quiet heroism, however, fell outside the spotlight of a national media obsessed with Italian-American mobsters.

Florence Scala (née Giovangelo) grew up at 1030 West Taylor Street in the Near West Side, where her family lived above their father's first-floor tailor and dry-cleaning shop. Hull House, the famed settlement founded by reformer Jane Addams, stood nearby, and a teacher suggested that Florence's mother take her there—a decision that helped change Scala's life. She told the oral historian Studs Terkel, "The neighborhood was dominated by gangsters and hoodlums. They were men from the old country, who lorded it over the people in the area . . . Hull House gave you a little insight into another world. There was something else to life besides sewing and pressing."

Jane Addams's nephew introduced Scala to the idea of city planning. She enrolled in continuing-education classes at the University of Chicago and began working with the Near West Side Planning Board. The neighborhood remained a pocket of urban blight, but Scala was hopeful that newly targeted urban renewal money from the federal government could transform the area.

These aspirations came to an abrupt halt in 1961 when Daley announced his decision to tear down large parts of the neighborhood to house a campus of the University of Illinois. Daley doomed a beloved Catholic church and Hull House to the wrecking ball, along with eight hundred houses and two hundred businesses. Scala led

Scala led the opposition to the mayor's heavy-handed plan, organizing, picketing, and occupying City Hall with fellow Italian-American women.

the opposition to the mayor's heavy-handed plan, organizing, picketing, and occupying City Hall with fellow Italian-American women during a two-hundred-person sit-in composed mostly of mothers trying to protect their family homes and shouting furiously that the rich always take away from the poor. After someone mysteriously bombed Scala's home with dynamite, she and her husband Charles moved into an apartment at Hull House.

Scala took the case against Mayor Daley to the Supreme Court but lost—a decision that condemned one of Chicago's oldest ethnic enclaves. Her sole success was preserving the original Hull House building. The family home at 1030 West Taylor Street had never been slotted for demolition—her advocacy had always been on behalf of the neighborhood—and she and Charles moved back, remaining there for the rest of their lives.

In 1964, still fresh from the wounds of the destruction, Scala ran for First Ward alderman, declaring that she was determined to "mark the beginning of the end for the hoodlums who have dominated the ward since the beginning of this century." Despite support from young people and independents, she was badly defeated. Florence Scala, who died in 2007, has been described as a "Rosa Parks of the Italian-American neighborhood." Studs Terkel called her "my heroine," who "tried with intelligence and courage to save the soul of our city. She represented to me all that Chicago could have been."

Florence Scala (left), picketing to save her Italian-American neighborhood from Chicago mayor Richard J. Daley's wrecking ball.

CHAPTER EIGHTEEN

Mythmakers

A crime fiction writer was gathering material, poring over thousands of pages of the Kefauver report and absorbing the ready-made pulp fiction of Joe Valachi's words. Mario Puzo understood that a nation avidly tuned in to the testimony of street thugs and turncoats would devour a sweeping gangster story. His two earlier works of fiction had received some minor critical acclaim—no doubt a major achievement for a man born in 1920 to illiterate southern Italian peasants—but pride wasn't putting food on the family table for this husband with five children. *The Dark Arena* and *The Fortunate Pilgrim* had produced only $6,500 in royalties. His next novel would earn him over $6 million.

"I was forty-five years old and tired of being an artist. Besides, I owed $20,000 to relatives, finance companies, banks and assorted bookmakers and shylocks," Puzo explained about his decision to write *The Godfather.* He had never met "an honest-to-god" gangster; even his lifelong love of gambling connected him merely with local bookies. Instead, he drew on memories of tough guys from the streets of his Hell's Kitchen neighborhood and wove tales from government testimony. "You can write and get transcripts of all their investigative committees," Puzo explained. "For ten bucks, I got one hundred volumes."

Puzo's easy lifting and embellishment of real-life anecdotes gave his fiction a verisimilitude that the public accepted as fact. The writer also recognized that the necessary alchemy to transform

Marlon Brando's romanticized Mafia don in *The Godfather* was not a ruthless thug but a judicious leader of a criminal enterprise.

Mario Puzo quipped that he wrote *The Godfather* because he was "tired of being an artist" and in debt.

nonfiction into a successful novel depended not just on the unassailable lure of crime, sex, and violence, but on the reader's sympathy with the story's protagonist. In Puzo's hands, a Mafia don was not a ruthless thug, but a tough yet judicious leader of a criminal enterprise that existed in parallel with a similarly corrupt and hypocritical civic government.

The public first turned the pages of *The Godfather* in 1969 as a deeply divided country debated the Vietnam War and the limits of authority. For many Americans, government had become the villain. Puzo found the perfect moment to publish a novel whose protagonist, Don Corleone, offered a family-centered (albeit murderous) model of governance ready to exact justice.

Though *The Godfather* sold millions of copies, its everlasting place in American popular culture didn't gain its footing until after the 1972 release of the movie directed by Francis Ford Coppola and written by Coppola and Puzo. Coppola's lavishly re-created scenes of first- and second-generation Italian life in America brought these images to the screen, accompanied by a lush musical score from the Italian composer Nino Rota. Coppola followed this cinematic achievement two years later with *The Godfather: Part II*; after a hiatus, Coppola released his long-awaited third and final installment in 1990.

The movies tapped into nostalgia for the immigrant past, using period details to reenact the spectacle of an Italian-American wedding or the terror and loneliness of the Ellis Island journey. Italian Americans either embraced the *Godfather* movies as great filmmaking or rejected them as perpetuating damaging stereotypes.

Ironically, Puzo's novel was published a year before the federal government implemented the Racketeer Influenced and Corrupt Organizations Act (RICO), a statute that, by the 1980s, would significantly crush the power of organized crime. RICO enabled the government to bring groups, rather than single individuals, to trial

Director Francis Ford Coppola on the set of *The Godfather*. The popularity of the trilogy cemented the myth of the Mafia in the minds of Americans.

by presenting a pattern of racketeering. If *The Godfather* cynically implied that organized crime was an inescapable part of a corrupt society, the RICO statute showed how law enforcement, while never obliterating these groups, could make serious inroads in stanching the activity of Italian-American organized crime and the subsequent infiltration of Chinese and Russian mobsters.

Despite this significant decline in the power and reach of the mob, the *Godfather* trilogy perpetuated the myth of a tightly controlled, impenetrable network of criminal masterminds. Few other gangster films, with perhaps the exception of Martin Scorsese's *Goodfellas*, contained *The Godfather*'s cinematic breadth and skill. Scorsese's film, based on the nonfiction book by Nicholas Pileggi, is decidedly unromantic, however, depicting the psychotic life of an Italian- and Irish-American mob turncoat named Henry Hill in all its ugliness.

The *Godfather* trilogy made the genre ripe for parody as well, inspiring a string of comedies that included *Married to the Mob*, *Bullets over Broadway*, *The Freshman*, *Mickey Blue Eyes*, *Analyze This*, *Analyze That*, and even a husky-voiced mob shark played by Robert De Niro in the children's film *Shark Tale*. This steady stream of fictional portrayals eventually influenced real-life criminals, who began to imitate their screen personae. Gambino family crime head John Gotti played *The Godfather*'s musical score at his notorious hangout, the Ravenite Social Club on Mulberry Street in Manhattan's Little Italy; and federal prosecutors listening to electronic surveillance began noticing that mobsters were appropriating dialogue created by Coppola and Puzo.

Yet by the dawn of the twenty-first century, most of the romance was gone from being a gangster. Unlike the aristocratic Corleones, mobsters like John Gotti dealt in drugs, invested in topless bars, and murdered indiscriminately. Breaking the code of Mafia silence (the *omertà*) became almost commonplace, allowing federal prosecutors to put street thugs and the five families' heads alike in prison. Even John Gotti, nicknamed "Teflon Don" because of his ability to elude criminal convictions, spent his last days in prison, dying of cancer in 2002. His underboss Salvatore ("Sammy the Bull") Gravano had turned state's evidence against him.

By this time, Puzo's descriptions of honor-bound families and criminal geniuses seemed close to comical. Vincent ("The Chin") Gigante, a Gambino boss, roamed the streets of his neighborhood in a bathrobe and slippers, hoping the feds would believe he was insane (they didn't). When federal agents went through John Gotti Jr.'s basement and found a typed list of the top-secret organization's "made

Fiction becomes fact: Gambino family crime head John Gotti played *The Godfather*'s musical score at his notorious social club.

men," the *Daily News* published the story under the headline "Dumbfella."

From this new landscape of dark humor, cold-blooded killings, and hapless thugs, David Chase created the landmark cable television series *The Sopranos*, transferring the idea of "men of honor" to a far grittier contemporary reality. In Tony Soprano, American audiences met a New Jersey mob boss with money worries, a nightmare of a mother, and ever-demanding family. He turned to an analyst and a prescription for Prozac.

The show's dark humor, continual references to the *Godfather* films, and willingness to journey through emotional and cultural terrain rarely before seen on television made *The Sopranos*, which ran from 1999 to 2007, a postmodern drama adored by critics. But it also outraged some Italian Americans who resent the roles cast for them long ago by popular culture's easy identification of organized crime with Italian ethnicity.

The Sopranos transferred the idea of "men of honor" to a far grittier contemporary reality.

John Travolta in *Saturday Night Fever*. The film created a disco dance craze, but also fostered the stereotype of the dim-witted Italian American.

One fact is certain in the depiction of Italian Americans by Hollywood mythmakers: blockbuster ticket sales and high Nielsen ratings mean repeating a formula ad infinitum. After the success of *The Godfather*, Italian-American characters in movies and television have been portrayed by one of two predominant stereotypes: the don or the dimwit. Films like *Saturday Night Fever*, *My Cousin Vinny*, and *Moonstruck*, along with a cast of television characters, from Arthur Fonzarelli ("Fonzie") on *Happy Days* to Joey Tribbiani on *Friends*, created the portrait of the dumb but sympathetic Italian American.

With the decline of scripted television shows for the bargain production costs of reality TV, Italian Americans have been caricatured more than ever, defined by big hair or biceps, gaudy jewelry, and foul mouths on shows like *Jersey Shore*, *Mob Wives*, and *The Real Housewives of New Jersey*. Because it has become increasingly difficult to portray the nuanced ways in which ancestral roots shape the character of third-, fourth-, and fifth-generation hyphenated Americans, subtlety has bowed to the sledgehammer.

Younger generations, far removed from the immigrant experience and more confident of their social status, may not be as bothered by these stereotypes as their parents or grandparents are. They can laugh at and ultimately sympathize with the "guido" character, and imitate lines from a film that came out decades before they were born. But for Italian Americans growing up after World War II and establishing themselves professionally when *The Godfather* first captured the imagination of the country, the stigma of the Mafia was very real, shadowing their accomplishments.

Jersey Shore and *Mob Wives*. Because it has become increasingly difficult to portray the nuances of third-, fourth-, and fifth-generation ancestry, subtlety has bowed to the sledgehammer.

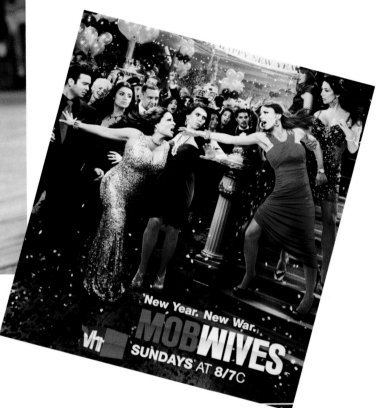

David Chase

David Chase is a writer, director, television producer, and creator of the acclaimed series The Sopranos. *A multiple Emmy Award winner, Chase has among his other television credits* The Rockford Files *and* Northern Exposure. *Chase also wrote and directed the film* Not Fade Away, *an autobiographical coming-of-age story about aspiring teenage rock singers. Chase's paternal grandparents came from the towns of Roccamonfina and Caserta in the province of Caserta, and his maternal grandparents, from Ariano Irpino in the province of Avellino, which served as the origin of his fictional Sopranos family.*

Q: You've described your family as not the happiest group of people.

Chase: My immediate family—my mother, my father—while we had many happy moments and a lot of good times, there was a certain pall over the house. My mother was almost medieval in her thinking. She would say, "Don't let the cat get near the baby, it will suck the breath away." We had a relative who died at a very young age of a brain aneurysm. She was going to graduate school, and my mother said, "You see, David, she was too smart." It was that kind of thinking.

Q: Growing up, how aware were you of being Italian-American?

Chase: I was very aware of it. My mother's father and mother spoke only Italian, period. My grandfather always wore a black suit and tie, and we used to go there for Saturday night dinners. He was the only one who spoke. There would be fifteen people at the table, and only he would talk . . . One time we were having Thanksgiving dinner, and my grandfather took this peach and started crying because it reminded him of the peaches back in the Old Country.

Q: Tony Soprano, the character you created, is very nostalgic. Is that part of you?

Chase: Yeah, very much. I'm a nostalgic person. I try not to be, but I am.

Q: Did you like growing up Italian?

Chase: I've always felt lucky to be Italian. I think it is a nice thing to be. Probably as time goes on it is going to . . . kind of vanish.

Q: Why did your family change its name?

Chase: My grandmother came here at twelve and worked in the mills in Providence. She was illiterate. She married an older guy named DeCesare. She had three or four kids with him. Then, when she was in her early twenties, a boarder, a young man from Roccamonfina, moved into the house and they hooked up. She had two kids with that guy, but she told DeCesare they were his. One of those two kids was my father, so my father's name was DeCesare. The new guy's name was Joe Fusco. Anyway, things fell apart. She and Joe Fusco took all the kids, the DeCesare kids and the two Fusco kids, and ran away from Providence to Newark, New Jersey. They chose the name Chase because it sounded a little like DeCesare, but they wouldn't be able to be tracked down in any of the Italian neighborhoods.

Q: Do you ever think about changing it back?

Chase: I've thought about it a couple of times, and when *The Sopranos* was coming on the air I thought I should go back to my Italian name. I talked it over with the people at HBO, and they said, "Don't do that," and I listened to them. They said, "You're known as David Chase. Don't do it now." I knew it was going to create some problems with Italian-American antidefamation groups because I

> My mother was almost medieval in her thinking. She would say, "Don't let the cat get near the baby, it will suck the breath away."

didn't have an Italian name, but I didn't change it back, and it wouldn't have made any difference anyway.

Q: How aware were you of the Mafia when you were growing up? Were there "made" guys around?

Chase: I didn't know there was such a thing as a made guy until I was maybe a teenager, and I'm not even sure I knew that it was called a "made guy" then. I knew there were people in the neighborhood who were gangsters, as my parents called them.

Q: Why do people love seeing gangster films?

Chase: The director John Boorman, who made the Irish crime film *The General*, suggested that in a time of atomization of the family, the community, and the dissolution of old ideals, it is the last tribal thing we've got. It is really tribal—it is not your family, it is your tribe. That is a nurturing feeling for people.

Q: Were you conscious of wanting to portray a real, not romanticized, family when you created *The Sopranos*?

Chase: I wasn't consciously trying to do anything. I wasn't trying to do any kind of exposé. I wrote what I knew. I had a pretty good idea that a lot of it or some of it was funny. I was very particular that the humor was in the details. A lot of the dialogue in the first season of *The Sopranos* that comes out of the mother [Livia Soprano] is really just my mother talking.

John Turturro

The actor John Turturro has appeared in numerous films, including Do the Right Thing, Barton Fink, Quiz Show, *and* O Brother, Where Art Thou? *Turturro is also a writer and director, whose first film,* Mac, *about three brothers working together in construction, won a Golden Camera award for best first feature at the 1992 Cannes Film Festival. Turturro has written and directed several other films, including* Passione, *a documentary released in 2010 about the rich musical tradition of the city of Naples.*

Q: Where did you grow up?

Turturro: I was born in Brooklyn and grew up in Hollis Queens—the home of rap—and it was a very mixed neighborhood. We lived in a garden apartment. We all slept in the same room—my mother, my father, my brother, and me. I grew up in a black neighborhood until I was five or six, when we moved to Rosedale, which was more of an Italian, Irish, and somewhat Jewish neighborhood. It was very segregated at that time. I was considered very dark, and people kept calling me a Puerto Rican, and they called me a little black kid. I didn't like that neighborhood as much as Hollis, I have to say.

Q: In your work as a director and writer, you often focus on family. What is it about family that draws you in as an artist?

Turturro: Well, when you don't have opportunities to travel and go places, a lot of your life is defined within this one place—around the table with everybody pitching in. My father worked with his father, and he worked with his brothers. My mother also was part of his [masonry] business and she worked in the dressmaking business with her cousin. We shared holidays together and there was always a lot of family around.

Q: What are some of your childhood memories?

Turturro: I worked with my father every summer of my life since I was ten years old. We never had money to send me to camp. It was always to clean his houses, but I loved being with him. It is how I got to know my father. I got up in the morning and would leave at six-thirty with Dad. He was very nice in the car; then when we got on the job, he was like, "Get the hell out of the way." But I learned. I used to feed lumber; I used to clean. My father was very suspicious. He always said, "Never trust an Italian." I said, "Well, who do you trust?" "I don't trust anybody." He was a very interesting guy.

Q: Do you think Italian families have a generalized distrust of people outside the family?

Turturro: I still have it. I don't trust people immediately. I feel first of all, trust is earned. I don't distrust them, but at the same time I don't give away my trust easily. The more charming someone is, the more I'm suspicious, because you think, what do they want? What are they trying to get from me?

Q: As an actor you are not known for taking roles in Mafia films. Is this a conscious choice?

I'm not averse to Mafia films . . . As a genre, I sometimes feel it is limited. I mean, playing a bad guy is always interesting, but there is more to life than that.

Turturro: I'm not averse to Mafia films. I loved the *Godfather* films. It is a genre like cowboys and Indians. I've played gangsters. I did *Men of Respect*. I did *Miller's Crossing*. I was a Jewish gangster. What made *The Godfather* a film that people wanted to revisit was that it was more about a family than about the Mafia, and Coppola infused that into it. As a genre, I sometimes feel it is limited. I mean, playing a bad guy is always interesting, but there is more to life than that. When I see these guys and they play versions upon versions of versions of it, it is reductive.

Q: So why are we stuck in this genre?

Turturro: When I did *Mac*, it was very, very hard to get the money for that. Then Stanley Tucci did his movie *Big Night*. Those things are really the exceptions to the rule. You can't just tell Italian-American stories.

Q: Does it bother you when people equate television shows like *Jersey Shore* with being Italian-American?

Turturro: Oh, I've hated it for years. I don't want to come out and condemn stuff, because I would rather just try to do something and say, "Well, here's what I like." I wish *Passione*, the documentary I made, would get out to more people. Not because I made it, but because it is a part of a group of us, the Neapolitans, who gave a lot to the rest of the world. I guess we've been so disorganized, we've allowed people to do that [*Jersey Shore*]. We've never really said, "No more, we don't want this anymore."

CHAPTER NINETEEN

Breaking Through

A cover story for the *New York Times Magazine* declared in 1983 that Italian Americans finally were "coming into their own." Spotlighting success stories in politics, business, the arts, and academia, the article signaled a long-eluded mainstream acceptance. It certainly was a far cry from the newspaper of record's 1891 description of Italian immigrants in New Orleans as those "sneaking and cowardly Sicilians, the descendants of bandits and assassins, who have transported to this country the lawless passions, the cut throat practices and the oathbound societies." What a difference a century makes in America.

The list of achievers included Mario Cuomo, then governor of New York; Eleanor Cutri Smeal, former president of the National Organization for Women; Lee A. Iacocca, then chairman of Chrysler; New York congresswoman Geraldine Ferraro; architect Robert Venturi; US senators Pete V. Domenici of New Mexico and Alfonse D'Amato of New York; and A. Bartlett Giamatti, president of Yale.

Focusing mainly on East Coast Italian Americans, the story didn't mention another rising star in Democratic politics, San Francisco's Nancy Pelosi, daughter of Thomas J. D'Alesandro, a New Deal congressman and the first Italian American to be elected mayor of Baltimore. At the time, Pelosi had not yet run for office but served as chair of the California Democratic Party and the host committee for the 1984 Democratic National Convention. Held in San Francisco, the convention catapulted two Italian Americans

Mario Cuomo inverted the century-long knock on the insularity of the Italian family, describing it instead as a means of support and strength.

appearing on the *New York Times Magazine*'s cover the year before further into national spotlight.

Presidential candidate Walter Mondale selected three-term congresswoman Geraldine Ferraro from the borough of Queens to be his running mate—the first time in US history that a major party named a woman to the ticket. Another Queens resident, Governor Mario Cuomo, delivered the keynote address at the nominating convention. Both Ferraro and Cuomo made historic speeches—the first for its progress toward female equality, the second for a dazzling rhetoric that captured the nation's attention.

Using the image of his father, Andrea, the New York governor called for a Democratic vision of government that combined compassion and capability: "I watched a small man with thick calluses on both his hands work fifteen and sixteen hours a day. I saw him once literally bleed from the bottoms of his feet, a man who came here uneducated, alone, unable to speak the language, who taught me all I needed to know about faith and hard work by the simple eloquence of his example. I learned about our kind of democracy from my father and I learned about our obligation to each other from him and my mother."

Cuomo inverted the century-long knock on the Italian family—that its insularity rendered the ethnic group incapable of civic participation and achievement—describing family instead as a means of support and strength. As governor, Cuomo consistently used the image of his mother's southern Italian village, where the peasants lived in shacks with no heat and dirt floors and found consolation in "the sharing of benefits and burdens." This communal lesson became the basis for Cuomo's "family of New York" metaphor, an alternative to the nation's individualistic, go-it-alone credo.

The message of the "family of New York"— that mutually supportive communities matter not only to the health of the individual but to the state and the nation—could in some ways

Presidential candidate Walter Mondale's selection of Geraldine Ferraro as his running mate marked the first time in US history that a major party named a woman to the ticket.

be seen as a public policy version of what doctors two decades earlier had dubbed the "Roseto Effect." So popular was the governor's convention speech that speculation began that he might run for president—a consolation perhaps for the resounding defeat of Mondale and Ferraro to incumbent Ronald Reagan and his running mate George Bush.

Throughout this breakthrough decade, the ethnic group's achievements continued to soar. In 1986, President Reagan nominated the first Italian American to the Supreme Court: Antonin Scalia, a man whose conservative legal philosophy matched the president's own. The Senate unanimously confirmed Scalia. Today, looking back on his appointment, the associate justice wondered whether part of the Senate's overwhelming support came from understanding the meaningful symbolism of naming an Italian American to the court.

"Many of the Senators who might otherwise have voted against

The bedrock values of the Italian family helped shape Mario Cuomo's political message.

me, who came from states with a large Italian-American population, I'm sure they were aware of it," said Scalia. "I think, for Italian Americans, given what they most abhor, which is their identification with crime and the Mafia, I wouldn't be surprised if they would be more proud to have an Italian-American justice than to have an Italian-American president."

Yet if one man continued to fuel the idea of an Italian-American president, it was Mario Cuomo. Memories of his convention speech lingered in the minds of Democrats looking for a strong candidate. Italian Americans took particular delight in this speculation because the governor was defined, and in many ways

Nominated by President Ronald Reagan in 1986, Justice Antonin Scalia became the first Italian American to serve on the US Supreme Court.

defined himself, by his "Italianness"—the rolling vowels in his name, the broad southern Italian face. Cuomo had established himself as a principled governor, an intellectual Italian-American politician, and an astute observer of the effects of ethnic prejudice on one's identity. He spoke of graduating tied for first place in his law school class, only to be urged by the dean to change his last name in order to find a job on Wall Street.

The notion that the Mafia stereotype continued to taint the careers of successful Italian Americans of his generation also infuriated Cuomo. He recounted how, when John Lindsay tried to persuade him to join his administration, he invited Cuomo and his wife, Matilda, to the mayor's mansion to see *The Godfather*. "How can you invite me to see *The Godfather*?" Cuomo responded. "This is the guy who kills people, murders them, plucks their eyes out, drugs them, and he's treated as a great guy, the whole community loves him. What are you saying with this movie?" He recalled that Lindsay replied, "Oh, it's only a movie, you're too sensitive." (Cuomo finally saw *The Godfather* for the first time in 2013 and, according to the *New York Times*, "somewhat grudgingly" offered "maybe this thing was a masterpiece.")

In the 1980s, Cuomo watched how Geraldine Ferraro's candidacy was severely damaged by the business practices of her husband, John Zaccaro, along with the rumors of his association with organized crime figures. During the 1992 presidential campaign, Cuomo endured then-candidate Bill Clinton's remark that the New York governor acted like a "Mafioso." Cuomo supporters wondered whether the albatross of the Mafia had added to his indecision about seeking the presidency, a persistent wavering that earned him the sobriquet "Hamlet on the Hudson."

Cuomo decided not to run—a choice that dismayed admirers across the country. He never revealed his reasons, other than an unconvincing declaration that he needed to fulfill his obligations in the state capital. Did he fear the ugliness of the Mafia stereotype in a national campaign? Or was his decision made, in part, by an apprehension and cautiousness common to the southern Italian temperament? Cuomo once admitted, "The idea that I could come from behind my mother and father's grocery store in South Jamaica, that we could come, in one generation, to this: the highest seat in the state of New York. That's enough for a lifetime."

If, in the 1990s, a Mafia stereotype could still dissuade talented public servants from seeking national office, by the new millennium its mythic power, like the real-life mob, was fading. When former US attorney and mayor of New York City Rudolph Giuliani ran for president in 2007, his name recognition created an early buzz among fellow Republicans, even if his candidacy ultimately never sparked. But the specter of the Mafia in the presidential campaign didn't make Giuliani flinch—a rather amazing achievement, considering that seven years earlier an investigative journalist had reported that Giuliani's father, who grew up in East Harlem, had been arrested as a young man and sentenced to prison for robbing someone at gunpoint. His father had also worked in a bar as the designated loan collector for a family member tied to the mob. Despite the sins of the father, the public accepted the son for his achievements as mayor and remembered his earlier work as a tough prosecutor who put mobsters behind bars.

In the same year that Giuliani ran for president, an Italian-American woman and mother of five children ascended to the third highest elected office in the nation. San Francisco congress-woman Nancy Pelosi, who served as House minority whip and leader, became Speaker of the House. After the Democrats lost control of the House of Representatives in 2011, Pelosi stepped down as Speaker but resumed her former post as minority leader, the only woman to hold either position in US history.

Ultimately, Mario Cuomo, the fifty-second governor of New York, placed his faith for a Cuomo political future in his eldest son, Andrew, who on January 1, 2011, was sworn in as the state's fifty-sixth governor. Hoping to build on his father's progressive legacy, the son passed marriage equality legislation during his first year in office and tougher gun control the following year. Today, two Italian Americans lead the state: Andrew Cuomo as governor, and Bill de Blasio as mayor of New York City.

More than a century since Italy's mass migration, as the immigrant experience becomes more and more diluted, many Italian Americans wonder about the future of Italian-American identity. Will the culture's memorable characteristics—the fragrant scents and tastes, family stories, and lessons imparted from ancestors—soon be at risk of disappearing through assimilation? De Blasio's story offers some clues about the new forms Italian-American identity might take.

Born Warren Wilhelm Jr. to a German-American father and Italian-American mother, and called Bill from an early age, de Blasio is an example of an American who made his ethnic identification a conscious choice rather than a passive inheritance. Warren Wilhelm Sr.'s struggles with alcoholism caused his wife, Maria, to divorce him and raise their three sons by herself. The father's decline ultimately led to

Congresswoman Nancy Pelosi and her father, Thomas J. D'Alesandro, former mayor of Baltimore, at the swearing-in ceremony when she was first elected, in 1987.

New York governor Andrew Cuomo with daughters (left to right) Cara, Mariah, and Michaela.

suicide, and an adolescent Bill found solace in his mother's family and their Old World values. He officially changed his last name from Wilhelm to de Blasio, his maternal surname, and has described the "strength, warmth, and coherence" of his mother's family as an "antidote" to the difficulties he faced in his teenage years. He cherished the family's ties to Italy and encouraged his mother to write *The Other Italy*, about the partisan resistance to Mussolini's Fascist regime.

De Blasio continues to express his passion for the culture by speaking conversational Italian, returning to his grandfather's ancestral village of Sant'Agata de' Goti near Naples, and naming his children Chiara and Dante. During his election night victory, de Blasio mentioned the Neapolitan town and offered a "Grazie a tutti!" to its residents, who stayed up all night to watch the televised speech.

De Blasio's identity as an Italian American took on broader political significance as he campaigned with his biracial family. De Blasio is married to Chirlane McCray, a Caribbean American and

A poster in the ancestral southern Italian town of Bill de Blasio's mother declares its support for New York's mayor.

former coworker in the administration of David Dinkins, the city's first African-American mayor. Dinkins's election in 1989 affirmed the desire of New Yorkers to ease racial tensions that had been fulminating during the eighties, which included several highly publicized murders of African-American men by Italian-American youths angry about the presence of "outsiders" in their dwindling ethnic enclaves.

The breakthrough decade of the 1980s signaled the long-awaited emergence of Italian Americans from the shadow of the past to achieve positions of prominence in every major profession—a success that has grown stronger with each passing year. That so many prominent Italian Americans would continue to point to the strength of the family to offer lessons, comfort, and a sense of identity also seemed a minor miracle in an increasingly atomized society. But who could have imagined that this once-maligned ethnic group would be able to maintain a cultural cohesion that many Americans turn to today for influence and inspiration.

Nancy Pelosi

Nancy Pelosi was born in Baltimore, Maryland, and grew up in the city's Little Italy section. She is the daughter of former Baltimore mayor Thomas D'Alesandro and Annunciata Lombardi. Her father's family came from Genoa and the region of Abruzzo, and her mother's side was from the region of Molise and Sicily. Pelosi, the mother of five children, made US political history in 2007 when she became both the first woman and the first Italian American to hold the office of Speaker of the House of Representatives.

Q: Your father was a very prominent politician. How did he get into politics?

Pelosi: My father had in his DNA a feel for people, an obligation to help one another, and a sense of public service. The way I've heard the story is that when he was a little boy, his mother took him to the convention that was held in Baltimore and nominated Woodrow Wilson for president of the United States. She carried him on her shoulders, and he felt the spark and then it just continued. When he was twenty-one, when he voted the first time, he voted for himself for House of Delegates. My father had it in his blood that that was what he would do, and my brother [Thomas D'Alesandro III] followed in his footsteps. He, too, was mayor of Baltimore.

Q: Your father became mayor in 1947. Did he have the opportunity to know Fiorello La Guardia?

Pelosi: He did know La Guardia. La Guardia served in Congress, and my father served in Congress later. I remember him telling me that La Guardia said: if you want to go statewide stay in the Congress, don't run for mayor. When you're mayor you are identified with the city. Which he did—he ran for mayor of Baltimore. When he ran statewide he didn't win, but as he said, "I won every election that was important." He loved being mayor of Baltimore.

Q: Growing up in a household full of men, what was your model for Italian-American female life? Can you talk about your mother? Did she feel tethered to the home?

Pelosi: If my mother were in this generation, she would be president of the United States. She was very, very talented, and she was mom. My mother and father were a team. I don't think he would ever have been as successful as he was without her strong support. She had seven children, six boys and one girl. I was the youngest. She didn't spend a whole lot of time cooking. We all managed to eat very well, but it wasn't as if she was stirring a pot of stew. She cooked, but she was more a person of the community. My brother Tommy used to tell the story that during the Depression people would knock on our door all the time needing a job or a place to live. Sometimes they were just hungry. And he said that with mamma you never knew who was going to be sitting at the dinner table because if you were hungry she took you in.

Q: In 1984, you were the head of the host committee at a Democratic convention that was very important to Italian Americans. What was that moment like?

Pelosi: I was very proud that Mario Cuomo was going to be the keynote speaker and that Geraldine Ferraro was going to be the chair of

the platform committee. So I was host committee, Geraldine was platform, Mario was the keynote speaker, and then, of course, lo and behold, just a few days before the convention it was announced that Geraldine would be the candidate for vice president . . . Nothing could describe what happened on the floor of that house when she was nominated and accepted the nomination for that convention. Really in my life, there are very few things that would match when Geraldine Ferraro was nominated, and when she accepted the nomination. The response was thunderous.

Q: The two of you were both trailblazers for women.

Pelosi: I understood in some ways why it took so long to have a woman Speaker of the House, because this is a male-dominated institution. It always has been. But I never could really understand why it took so long to have an Italian-American Speaker of the House, because we had many great leaders in Congress from our community. And so to be both at once was quite remarkable . . . I've always thought I have more energy than anyone because I'm an Italian-American woman. I don't know that I would have the drive, and the energy, and the enthusiasm, and the spirit if I were not Italian American. I really believe that.

I understood in some ways why it took so long to have a woman Speaker of the House, because this is a male-dominated institution . . . But I never could really understand why it took so long to have an Italian-American Speaker of the House.

CHAPTER TWENTY

We're All Italian!

Over 150 years after the first immigrant journey, Italian-American culture is deeply infused into the landscape: in government, business, education, film, food, theater, television, literature, art, and sports, the contributions are countless. The immigrants' values and traditions not only have given Americans things that we love, but remind us of what we lack.

To look back on the Italian-American experience is to see how nineteenth-century traditions continue to influence the way we live today. The peasant instinct to preserve the tastes of Italy, for example, has been refined from the early pushcarts to fruit and produce shops to specialty stores to contemporary temples of gastronomy like Eataly, which occupies fifty-eight thousand square feet in New York City and sixty-two thousand square feet in Chicago.

Though social workers once lectured immigrants about proper nutrition and Americans patronizingly smiled at southern Italians eating "weeds" such as dandelions, escarole, chicory, and broccoli rabe, today these bitter greens not only are served in the best restaurants but are known to contain properties that may offer protection against certain cancers. Olive oil and basement wine have turned out to be good for the heart, and the Mediterranean diet has moved from shameful food to superfood.

In what we eat and drink, Italians have always seemed to be ahead of the curve. Missing the flavor of dark-roasted coffee, Anto-

The peasant instinct to preserve the tastes of Italy that began with pushcarts, and then grocery stores, continues today in fifty-eight thousand square feet of space in New York's Eataly food store.

nio Ferrara began serving espresso and Italian pastries in a New York Little Italy café in 1892 that still bears his name. Caffe Reggio, which opened in Greenwich Village in 1927, claims to be the first in North America to have served cappuccino. It would take more than half a century for America to replace its typical watery brew with frothy cappuccinos and venti-sized lattes.

An espresso machine from the 1940s. Italian Americans sought dark-roasted coffee since first arriving in the nineteenth century.

In Greenwich Village, the café Sant Ambroeus— local dialect in Milan for the city's patron saint, Sant' Ambrogio— attracts today's coffee connoisseurs with its stand-up espresso bar.

Confectioner Domenico Ghirardelli introduced fine chocolates to San Francisco in 1852. The immigrant tradition of making fresh pasta and ravioli is practiced today by Mario Batali, Lidia Bastianich, Alfred Portale, Tom Colicchio, Michael Romano, Mario Carbone, and Rich Torrisi, who are among the many talented chefs creating innovative cuisines that combine Italian and Italian-American culinary traditions and rival the dishes of the best restaurants in Italy.

Yet the current American love for all things Italian, and the desire among many to be Italian, extends deeper than this appreciation of food or wine or cozy cafés. Some of the culture's most distinctive values—the security of family and community, the pleasure of craftsmanship, the yearning for *dolce far niente* (literally, the "sweetness of doing nothing")—speak to the void left by a mechanized, productivity-obsessed way of life.

Celebrity chefs like Mario Batali have created innovative cuisines that rival the dishes of the best restaurants in Italy.

Take the delicate fig tree, a symbol of Italian tradition forming its roots in America. Botanists say that there would be no fig trees in New York if southern Italian peasants had not brought and planted branches here, which they had carried with them in the ships' steerage. Once the fig trees began to grow, the immigrants would tenderly wrap and blanket the roots during the long harsh winter, replanting them each year in the softened spring soil. Thus they produced one of the New World's most delightful fruits, whose sweet, juicy bursts on the tongue reveal the small pleasures cultivated through time, patience, and effort.

Yet the immigrants detected early on that America didn't share these values—if it meant losing profit. Diary entries of the first wave of immigrants reveal these sentiments and fears. "The Dollar is King in America and truly represents the life in this country," one man wrote. Although the Italians came here to earn badly needed dollars, they were surprised at the supremacy placed on work above all else and at the lack of interest in crafts-manship. An artisan complained that while Italians sought perfection in their handiwork, the typical American response was, "Never mind your art; we want efficiency." At the start of the twen-tieth century, the immigrants already anticipated the country's long-standing affinity for fast production over the painstaking pro-cess of creation.

Michael La Sorte, who compiled numerous diary entries into a book on the immigrant experience, noted that the early arrivers "considered American cultural priorities to be perverted. Italian culture emphasized simplicity, beauty, temperance, love of family, a spirit of economy—values that transcended the individual, and time and place. Americans were concerned with the here and now."

These values—of community over individual, beauty over mass production, time over profit—continue to be part of the magnetic pull that leads Americans to Italy today, in search of an attitude toward life lost between the Old World and the New. The appeal of Frances Mayes's best-selling memoir *Under the Tuscan Sun*, along with its numerous sequels, and Elizabeth Gilbert's *Eat, Pray, Love* were all based on the premise that time spent in Italy offers renewal for a depleted spirit.

Mayes, who lived in San Francisco, left a region in large part shaped by Italians from Tuscany for a more authentic Tuscan expe-rience. Recovering from divorce, she suggested that happiness and a back-to-basics approach to life were deeply intertwined: restoring an old farmhouse with one's hands, planting in cycle with the sea-sons, mingling with locals, cooking with garden-grown ingredi-ents. After the success of Mayes's books, American real estate companies began scooping up thousands of acres in Tuscany to build and renovate homes that offer the benefits of this slower, sim-pler life. Today, purchasing a time-share in a farmhouse restored by one of these American companies can cost a million dollars for a three-week annual stay.

To walk through villages in southern Italy today, meeting local artisans and hearing their stories, is to listen to echoes of the early

The timeless values of Italian culture that the early immigrants found lacking here—community over individual, beauty over mass production, time over profit—still attract Americans to Italy today.

immigrants' diary musings. When an American businessman, for example, tried to persuade an artist to mass-produce his beautiful hand-painted ceramics to sell in Target, he briefly considered the highly profitable offer but ultimately refused. Craftsmanship had shaped his pride and sense of purpose in life and he wasn't going to risk the reputation of his product to the flaws of assembly line production. "We live in a nice house. We have a nice life. How much money do we need?" he concluded.

A greengrocer from the same town expressed confusion at an American's annoyance that his shop didn't stock seedless grapes. "But there is no such thing as a seedless grape!" he emphatically declared. He had been in the grocery business for thirty-five years, yet was unaware that fruit is often genetically modified to fit consumers' needs.

Handcrafted work over mass production, seasonal harvests over genetic modification. Italians characteristically prefer the relationship of hand to object, seed to soil. They do not like to tamper with the essential nature of things—the modern-day quest to manipulate life's rhythm to fit our ever-changing and unquenchable desires.

But the immigrants came to a land defined by such tampering—this restless search for the new on a vast untried canvas. Each generation fearless enough to pull up roots to heed this call to adventure has absorbed the competing ideals of harboring tradition and embracing change. The alliance has not always been easy, but at its best it created dreamers who combined Italy's eternal values with America's boundless imagination—people with the equanimity to build a supportive neighborhood and business community that gained national attention for staving off heart disease; the innovation to restore San Francisco after its colossal earthquake, teach a population of poor people how to save money, and create the largest bank in the world; the courage to tell workers that they're not machines, but humans with dignity who deserve roses as well as daily bread; the humbleness of faith to bow to life's mystery; the passion to reimagine a beleaguered New York City as a gleaming metropolis; the artfulness to redefine music and film; the talent and dedication to become public servants at the highest levels of the land—all of these men and women re-creating the past and imagining the future, contributing to the palimpsest of ideas, dreams, and visions written onto the American landscape.

Today it's hard to imagine that the twentieth century began with austere and venerated Americans pronouncing southern Italians as nothing but trouble. Or, considering the wide-ranging artistic achievement of Italian Americans, to look back to those darker days when a sociologist prophesied with italicized emphasis that the south of Italy was, and would always be, *utterly sterile as creators of beauty.* Creators of beauty define the way America sees the many Italian Americans of southern descent who became its most beloved actors, filmmakers, singers, composers, writers, architects, chefs, and designers.

In fashion, southern Italians created a style that reflected elements of their ancestral roots, and these choices, at first considered brash and in bad taste, eventually redefined contemporary haute couture. Designer Gianni Versace, who lived in Italy and America, flamboyantly putting his stamp on fashion here, adopted the sunburst colors of the Mediterranean for his palette. Versace's wildly ornate designs often appropriated Greek and Roman influences from his homeland of Reggio di Calabria. His choices defiantly contrasted the subdued earth tones of his chief rival, Giorgio Armani, who was born outside of Milan. While Armani clothes reflected the casual elegance of the north of Italy, a Versace wardrobe, worn by cultural icons as varied as Madonna and Princess Diana, heralded the exuberance of the south.

In the visual arts, Massimiliano Gioni became, in 2013, the youngest artistic director in the 118-year history of the Venice Biennale, the most prestigious art exhibition in the world. Gioni grew up outside of Milan and lives in New York with his Milanese wife, who is also a curator; they represent the latest wave of first-generation Italians, well-educated men and women who seek America's vibrant multiculturalism. For the Biennale, Gioni, then thirty-nine, chose to showcase the *Encyclopedic Palace of the World*, the work of an Italian-American auto mechanic and self-taught Pennsylvania artist named Marino Auriti. By making Auriti's work the theme of the exhibition, Gioni embraced the idea of this outsider artist in order to charge the imagination of the world's leading artists.

In the 1950s, Auriti built in his backyard the *Encyclopedic Palace of the World*, an eleven-foot-tall architectural model made of wood, brass, plastic, and celluloid to showcase his dream: a 136-story skyscraper museum that would contain all the world's knowledge "from the wheel to the satellite." Auriti imagined that the building and its surrounding piazza would encompass sixteen blocks in Washington, DC.

His eccentric vision, long before the Internet, of amassing and

The self-taught Italian-American painter Ralph Fasanella depicted the ethnic group's struggles. In *Iceman Crucified #3* (1956), Fasanella's father, who was an iceman, is crucified on a block of ice.

showcasing the world's knowledge would have remained in storage if his family hadn't taken up its cause. His granddaughter B. G. Firmani explored the American Folk Art Museum but initially thought that its objects of pure Americana—weather vanes, quilts, and Shaker wood—portended an unlikely fit for her grandfather's baroque vision. But hanging on a wall was *Iceman Crucified #3*, by

Ralph Fasanella, the self-taught Italian-American painter whose bright colors and thick brush strokes depicted the ethnic group's struggles and icons. The painting portrayed Fasanella's father, who was an iceman, crucified on a giant block of ice. "I felt such a mixture of grief and hope," wrote Firmani, "that I burst into tears. And then I thought: this is the place!"

The American Folk Art Museum first displayed Auriti's *Encyclopedic Palace of the World* in 2004; in 2012 it became the centerpiece of a new exhibition and soon after led the Biennale. In Venice, the *Encyclopedic Palace*, standing in the opening gallery of the cavern-

The theme for the 2013 Venice Biennale, the international art world's most prestigious exhibition, was the *Encyclopedic Palace of the World*, the work of an Italian-American auto mechanic and self-taught artist, Marino Auriti.

ous exhibition space, welcomed nearly half a million people who visited the six-month-long art event. The model, with four entrance points, greeted its visitors in English, Italian, French, and Spanish; Auriti printed above its Doric columns aphorisms for how to live ethically:

WATCH THAT YOU DON'T BECOME GREEDY WITH YOUR PROFITS.

THE LESS YOU DESIRE, THE GREATER YOUR HAPPINESS.

SURROUND YOURSELF WITH HONEST FRIENDS AND LIVE LONG AND HAPPILY.

LIVE BY YOUR WORK.

Above the columns of his *Encyclopedic Palace,* Marino Auriti printed aphorisms about how to live ethically.

These sentiments, deeply Italian in spirit, mirror the egalitarian credo that guided the settlers of Roseto, Pennsylvania, in the late nineteenth century and the many others who followed. Auriti,

born in 1891, a decade after the first eight men from Roseto Valfortore made the New World their home, set forth on an immigrant journey that echoed the struggles of millions of Italian Americans caught in the tumult of history. After Auriti published satirical anti-Fascist poems in a local paper in the 1920s, Fascist goons force-fed him castor oil and took over his home. His wife was born in America, but her family, among the early "birds of passage" who had returned to Italy, could not reenter the country, because of the restrictive 1924 Johnson-Reed Act, nor could Auriti secure a legal emigration. By going first to Brazil, Auriti and his wife eventually found their way to America.

At the time Auriti designed his *Encyclopedic Palace*, he had retired as an auto mechanic, yet he still possessed a dream particular to the immigrant experience: he was audacious and bold enough to imagine synthesizing and sharing the world's knowledge. The amateur craftsman would never live to see streams of international artists paying homage to his vision, but years after his death, Auriti's daughter had a dream in which her father stood one more time in his backyard, the place where he loved to tinker with oversized ideas. He was holding "a tiny, living tree with its root ball intact" and offering the words that every child who has lost a beloved parent wants to hear: *Io vivo* ("I live").

The roots planted by immigrants in a once inhospitable New World soil are not only intact but thriving. Each subsequent generation, preserving and passing along pieces of Italian-American culture that fed and sustained them, continues to strengthen the stem and nourish the branches. *Noi viviamo.* We live.

A NOTE ON SOURCES

The Italian Americans: A History draws on the scholarly and popular works, along with thousands of pages of transcript interviews, of the people who participated in the PBS documentary series. This book is the product of the rich histories composed by academics, journalists, biographers, and cultural historians and told by generations of Italian Americans, including distinguished jurists and government officials; San Francisco fishermen; residents of Roseto, New Orleans, and Little Italies across the country; World War II veterans; and descendants of the documentary's subjects. We urge readers to explore the extensive bibliography to delve deeper into the history and complex identity of the ethnic group.

In addition, I would like to credit the books that guided my thinking during the course of writing *The Italian Americans: A History.*

Introduction

In the Introduction, the discussion of the hero's journey is from Joseph Campbell's *The Hero with a Thousand Faces.* The material on Roseto, Pennsylvania, in "*Cent' Anni!*" is drawn from the work of John Bruhn and Stewart Wolf, who conducted the community health study and wrote *The Roseto Story* and *The Power of Clan.* In addition, Italian anthropologist Carla Bianco's *The Two Rosetos* compared life in Roseto, Pennsylvania, to the original Italian ancestral village Roseto Valfortore.

Part One: 1860–1910

Source material for Chapter 1 ("La Famiglia") included Jasper Ridley's *Garibaldi*; Giuseppe Garibaldi's *My Life*; Donna Gabaccia's *Italy's Many Diasporas*; *A Concise History of Italy* by Christopher Duggan; *Between Salt Water and Holy Water* by Tommaso Astarita; and *In the Shadow of Vesuvius* by Jordan Lancaster. I relied on both Astarita's and Lancaster's works for subsequent discussions about popular art, religious celebration, and customs in Naples and southern Italy. For "Our Ancestors," the account of Garibaldi's life in Staten Island was drawn from Jasper Ridley's *Garibaldi*, as was the discussion in Chapter 2 of Garibaldi's interest in the American Civil War.

For Chapter 2 ("Who Killa da Chief?"), *Bread and Respect*, written by Anthony Margavio and Jerome Salomone, provided details about the early settlement of Italians in New Orleans, along with Vincenza Scarpaci's "Walking the Color Line: Italian Immigrants in Rural Louisiana, 1880–1910," in *Are Italians White?*, edited by Jennifer Guglielmo and Salvatore Salerno. The Booker T. Washington quote is taken from his book *The Man Farthest Down*. Tom Smith's *The Crescent City Lynchings* provided details about the trial and lynching. Other source material about the Hennessy murder included Thomas Reppetto's *American Mafia*, Humbert S. Nelli's *The Business of Crime*, and Richard Gambino's *Vendetta*.

Chapter 3 ("Birds of Passage") drew upon Michael La Sorte's compilation of early immigrant diary accounts in *La Merica* and B. Amore's *An Italian American Odyssey*. Other source material included Humbert Nelli's *Italians in Chicago 1880–1930* and *La Storia* by Jerre Mangione and Ben Morreale.

For Chapter 4 ("A Secret History"), John Mariani's *How Italian Food Conquered the World* helped inform the discussion of food and immigrant life. I drew upon Humbert Nelli's and Thomas Reppetto's work on the history of Italian Americans and crime for the discussion of the Black Hand, along with Robert Lombardo's *The Black Hand*. Laurie Fabiano provided details about her grandmother's kidnapping previously described in her historical novel *Elizabeth Street*. For the "Our Ancestors" account of Giuseppe Petrosino's life, in addition to reporting in the *New York Times*, I relied on the book *Joe Petrosino*, by Arrigo Petacco.

The history of early Italian settlement in California discussed in Chapter 5 ("Up from the Ashes") was informed by Deanna Gumina's *The Italians of San Francisco*, along with Dino Cinel's *From Italy to San Francisco*. For the life of A. P. Giannini, I drew primarily upon Gerald Nash's biography, *A. P. Giannini and the Bank of America*, along with Todd Buchholz's *New Ideas from Dead CEOs*.

Part Two: 1910–1930

Leonard Covello's magisterial *The Social Background of the Italo-American School Child* and his memoir, *The Heart Is the Teacher*, informed Chapter 6 ("Becoming American"). Emily Leider's biography of Rudolph Valentino (*Dark Lover*), as well as Robert Oberfirst's and Irving Shulman's biographies, provided details of the actor's life in "Our Ancestors."

In Chapter 7 ("Fruits of Thy Labor"), I drew upon the work of Bruce Watson's *Bread and Roses*, along with Ardis Cameron's *Radicals of the Worst Sort*, Mary Heaton Vorse's *A Footnote to Folly*, Peter Carlson's *Roughneck*, and Margaret Sanger's "The Fighting Women of Lawrence," originally published in the February 18, 1912, issue of the *New York Call*. Arturo Giovannitti's courtroom speech is taken from *Rebel Voices: An IWW Anthology*, edited by Joyce L. Kornbluh.

In Chapter 8 ("Taking the Streets"), the discussion of Italian-American devotion and the East Harlem *festa* was drawn primarily from Robert Orsi's *The Madonna of 115th Street*; and of religious devotion in southern Italy, from Tommaso Astarita's *Between Salt Water and Holy Water*.

Bruce Watson's *Sacco and Vanzetti* informed Chapter 9 ("Guilt by Association"), along with *The Letters of Sacco and Vanzetti*, edited by Marion Denman Frankfurter and Gardner Jackson. For the discussion of anarchist Luigi Galleani and his followers, I referred to Paul Avrich's *Sacco and Vanzetti*, along with Marcella Bencivenni's *Italian Immigrant Radical Culture*. The "Our Ancestors" portrait of Angela Bambace was drawn from interviews with her grandchildren Mindy and Tim Camponeschi, as well as Jennifer Guglielmo's *Living the Revolution*.

The discussion of Prohibition in Chapter 10 ("A Shortcut") was informed by Stephen Fox's *Blood and Power*, along with Humbert Nelli's The *Business of Crime* and Thomas Reppetto's *American Mafia*.

Part Three: 1930–1945

In Chapter 11 ("The Little Flower"), I drew upon Thomas Kessner's *Fiorello H. La Guardia and the Making of a Modern New York*, Arthur Mann's *La Guardia* and *La Guardia Comes to Power*, and Howard Zinn's *LaGuardia in Congress*. Jennifer Guglielmo's *Living the Revolution* provided details about Italian-American women in the garment industry; and Nick Taylor's *American-Made*, about the WPA program.

The discussion of Fascism in America in Chapter 12 ("Faith in the Fatherland") was informed primarily by John Diggins's *Mussolini and Fascism* and original newspaper accounts. Dorothy Gallagher's *All the Right Enemies* provided details about Carlo Tresca's anti-Fascist activities. Stefano Luconi of the University of Padua helped sort out the fractious history of Columbus Day. The quote about Mussolini enabling four million Italian Americans to hold up their heads comes from Caroline Ware's *The Cultural Approach to History*. The story of La Guardia's efforts to curtail Generoso Pope is from Thomas Kessner's *Fiorello H. La Guardia and the Making of a Modern New York*. Paul David Pope's *The Deeds of My Fathers* added to the account of Generoso Pope. Harvey Sachs's biographies of Arturo Toscanini (*Arturo Toscanini from 1915 to 1946* and *Toscanini*) informed the "Our Ancestors" portrait of the conductor.

For Chapter 13 ("Why We Fight"), I drew upon Salvatore LaGumina's *The Humble and the Heroic*; William M. Tuttle Jr.'s *Daddy's Gone to War*; Nancy Carnevale's *A New Language, A New World*; and William Murray's *Janet, My Mother, and Me*. The story of Hector Boiardi in "Why We Fight" and "Our Ancestors" was informed by interviews with Joseph and Anna Boiardi, as well as by Anna Boiardi and Stephanie Lyness's *Delicious Memories*.

In Chapter 14 ("Enemy Aliens"), I included stories from the anthology *Una Storia Segreta*, edited by Lawrence DiStasi, as well as Stephen Fox's *The Unknown Internment*. I also drew upon Jerre Mangione's *An Ethnic at Large* and cited material from the *Report to the Congress of the United States: A Review of the Restrictions on Persons of Italian Ancestry during World War II* (Washington, DC: US Department of Justice, 2001).

Part Four: 1945–Present

The discussion of Italian-American crooners in Chapter 15 ("American Dreams") was informed by Mark Rotella's *Amore* and Tony Bennett's *The Good Life*. For the life of Frank Sinatra, I drew upon *Frank: The Voice* by James Kaplan, *Why Sinatra Matters* by Pete Hamill, and *Sinatra in Hollywood* by Tom Santopietro.

For the portrait of Gregory Corso in Chapter 16 ("Cultural Outlaws"), I drew upon Corso's collected letters in *An Accidental Autobiography*; *American Writers*, edited by Jay Parini; and *Exiled Angel*, by Gregory Stephenson. Gustave Reininger's 2009 documentary film *Corso: The Last Beat*, as well as an interview with Peter Sourian, additionally informed my account. The portrait of Mario Savio is drawn primarily from Robert Cohen's *Freedom's Orator*, along with Gil Fagiani's "Mario Savio: Resurrecting an Italian American Radical," in *The Lost World of Italian-American Radicalism*, edited by Philip V. Cannistraro and Gerald Meyer.

In Chapter 17 ("Crime and Prejudice"), I relied on newspaper accounts from the *New York Times*, *Washington Post*, and *Chicago Tribune* for the discussion of the Kefauver and Valachi hearings, along with Stephen Fox's *Blood and Power*,

Thomas Reppetto's *American Mafia*, and Humbert S. Nelli's *The Business of Crime*. For "Our Ancestors," details of Florence Scala's activism came from Adam Cohen and Elizabeth Taylor's *American Pharaoh*, along with Studs Terkel's *Division Street* and *Chicago Tribune* articles.

For Chapter 18 ("Mythmakers"), I drew upon George De Stefano's *An Offer We Can't Refuse*, and Mario Puzo's *The Godfather* and *The Godfather Papers and Other Confessions*.

Chapter 19 ("Breaking Through") was informed by documentary interviews, newspaper accounts, and Wayne Barrett's biography of Rudy Giuliani (*Rudy!*). The portrait of Mario Cuomo was drawn from my book *Were You Always an Italian?*

Source material for Chapter 20 ("We're All Italian!") included Simone Cinotto's *The Italian American Table*; *The Big Book of Italian American Culture*, edited by Lawrence DiStasi; and Michael La Sorte's *La Merica*. The story of Marino Auriti and his *Encyclopedic Palace* comes from his granddaughter B. G. Firmani's blog, *Forte e Gentile*, along with articles from the *New York Times*.

BIBLIOGRAPHY

Alba, Richard. *Italian Americans: Into the Twilight of Ethnicity.* Englewood Cliffs, NJ: Prentice-Hall, 1985.

Amore, B. *An Italian American Odyssey: Life Line—Filo Della Vita: Through Ellis Island and Beyond.* New York: Center for Migration Studies, 2006.

Astarita, Tommaso. *Between Salt Water and Holy Water: A History of Southern Italy.* New York: W. W. Norton, 2005.

Avrich, Paul. *Sacco and Vanzetti: The Anarchist Background.* Princeton, NJ: Princeton University Press, 1991.

Barrett, Wayne. *Rudy!: An Investigative Biography of Rudolph Giuliani.* New York: Basic Books, 2000.

Barzini, Luigi. *The Italians.* New York: Simon & Schuster, 1996.

Bencivenni, Marcella. *Italian Immigrant Radical Culture: The Idealism of the Sovversivi in the United States, 1890–1940.* New York: New York University Press, 2011.

Bennett, Tony. *The Good Life.* With Will Friedwald. New York: Pocket Books, 1998.

Bianco, Carla. *The Two Rosetos.* Bloomington: Indiana University Press, 1974.

Boiardi, Anna, and Stephanie Lyness. *Delicious Memories: Recipes and Stories from the Chef Boyardee Family.* New York: Stewart, Tabori & Chang, 2011.

Bonadio, Felice A. *A. P. Giannini: Banker of America.* Berkeley: University of California Press, 1994.

Bondanella, Peter. *Hollywood Italians: Dagos, Palookas, Romeos, Wise Guys, and Sopranos.* New York: Continuum, 2004.

Bruhn, John G., and Stewart Wolf. *The Power of Clan: The Influence of Human Relations on Heart Disease.* Transaction, 1993.

Bruhn, John G., and Stewart Wolf. *The Roseto Story: An Anatomy of Health.* Norman: University of Oklahoma Press, 1979.

Buchholz, Todd G. *New Ideas from Dead CEOs.* New York: Harper Collins, 2007.

Cameron, Ardis. *Radicals of the Worst Sort: Laboring Women in Lawrence, Massachusetts, 1860–1912.* Urbana: University of Illinois Press, 1993.

Campbell, Joseph. *The Hero with a Thousand Faces.* Novato, CA: New World Library, 2008.

Cannistraro, Philip V. *Blackshirts in Little Italy: Italian Americans and Fascism 1921–1929.* West Lafayette, IN: Bordighera, 1999.

Cannistraro, Philip V., and Gerald Meyer, eds. *The Lost World of Italian-American Radicalism.* Westport, CT: Praeger, 2003.

Capeci, Jerry, and Tom Robbins. *Mob Boss: The Life of Little Al D'Arco, The Man Who Brought Down the Mafia.* New York: St. Martin's Press, 2013.

Carlson, Peter. *Roughneck: The Life and Times of Big Bill Haywood.* New York: W. W. Norton, 1983.

Carnevale, Nancy C. *A New Language, A New World.* Champaign: University of Illinois Press, 2009.

Cinel, Dino. *From Italy to San Francisco: The Immigrant Experience.* Stanford, CA: Stanford University Press, 1982.

Cinotto, Simone. *The Italian American Table: Food, Family, and Community in New York City.* Urbana: University of Illinois Press, 2013.

Clapps Herman, Joanna, ed. *Our Roots Are Deep with Passion.* New York: Other Press, 2006.

Cohen, Adam, and Elizabeth Taylor. *American Pharaoh: Mayor Richard J. Daley: His Battle for Chicago and the Nation.* Boston: Little, Brown, 2000.

Cohen, Robert. *Freedom's Orator: Mario Savio and the Radical Legacy of the 1960s.* Oxford: Oxford University Press, 2009.

Collins, Richard. *John Fante: A Literary Portrait.* Toronto: Guernica Editions, 2000.

Corso, Gregory. *An Accidental Autobiography: The Selected Letters of Gregory Corso.* Edited by Bill Morgan. New York: New Directions, 2003.

Covello, Leonard. *The Heart Is the Teacher.* New York: McGraw-Hill, 1958.

Covello, Leonard. *The Social Background of the Italo-American School Child.* Leiden, Netherlands: E. J. Brill, 1967.

Cramer, Richard Ben. *Joe DiMaggio: The Hero's Life.* New York: Simon & Schuster, 2000.

D'Epiro, Peter, and Mary Desmond Pinkowish. *Sprezzatura: 50 Ways Italian Genius Shaped the World.* New York: Anchor, 2001.

DeSalvo, Louise, and Edvige Giunta, eds. *The Milk of Almonds: Italian American Women Writers on Food and Culture.* New York: Feminist Press, 2002.

De Stefano, George. *An Offer We Can't Refuse: The Mafia in the Mind of America.* New York: Faber and Faber, 2006.

Di Donato, Pietro. *Christ in Concrete.* New York: Penguin, 2004.

Diggins, John P. *Mussolini and Fascism: The View from America.* Princeton, NJ: Princeton University Press, 1972.

Di Prima, Diane. *Recollections of My Life as a Woman.* New York: Viking, 2001.

DiStasi, Lawrence, ed. *The Big Book of Italian American Culture.* New York: Harper Perennial, 1990.

DiStasi, Lawrence, ed. *Una Storia Segreta: The Secret History of Italian American Evacuation and Internment during World War II.* Berkeley, CA: Heyday, 2001.

Dubofsky, Melvyn. *We Shall Be All: A History of the Industrial Workers of the World.* Chicago: Quadrangle, 1969.

Duggan, Christopher. *A Concise History of Italy.* Cambridge: Cambridge University Press, 1994.

Eco, Umberto. *Five Moral Pieces.* Translated from the Italian by Alastair McEwen. San Diego, CA: Harcourt, 2002.

Fabiano, Laurie. *Elizabeth Street.* New York: First Mariner, 2011.

Fante, John. *The Wine of Youth: Selected Stories of John Fante.* New York: HarperCollins, 2002.

Ferraro, Thomas. *Feeling Italian.* New York: New York University Press, 2005.

Fox, Stephen. *Blood and Power: Organized Crime in Twentieth-Century America.* New York: William Morrow, 1989.

Fox, Stephen. *The Unknown Internment: An Oral History of the Relocation of Italian Americans during World War II.* Boston: Twayne, 1990.

Frankfurter, Marion Denman, and Gardner Jackson, eds. *The Letters of Sacco and Vanzetti.* New York: Penguin, 1997.

Gabaccia, Donna R. *From Sicily to Elizabeth Street: Housing and Social Change among Italian Immigrants, 1880–1930.* Albany: State University of New York, 1984.

Gabaccia, Donna R. *Italy's Many Diasporas.* London: Routledge, 2003.

Gabaccia, Donna R. *Militants and Migrants: Rural Sicilians Become American Workers.* New Brunswick, NJ: Rutgers University Press, 1988.

Gallagher, Dorothy. *All the Right Enemies: The Life and Murder of Carlo Tresca.* New Brunswick, NJ: Rutgers University Press, 1988.

Gambino, Richard. *Blood of My Blood: The Dilemma of the Italian American.* Garden City, NY: Anchor/Doubleday, 1974.

Gambino, Richard. *Vendetta.* New York: Doubleday, 1977.

Gardaphé, Fred. *From Wise Guys to Wise Men.* New York: Routledge, 2006.

Garibaldi, Giuseppe. *My Life.* Translated by Stephen Parkin. London: Hesperus, 2004.

Giovannitti, Arturo. *Arrows in the Gale*. Riverdale, CT: Hillacre, 1914.

Guglielmo, Jennifer. *Living the Revolution: Italian Women's Resistance and Radicalism in New York City, 1880–1945*. Chapel Hill: University of North Carolina Press, 2010.

Guglielmo, Jennifer, and Salvatore Salerno, eds. *Are Italians White?: How Race Is Made in America*. New York: Routledge, 2003.

Gumina, Deanna Paoli. *The Italians of San Francisco: 1850–1930*. New York: Center for Migration Studies, 1978.

Hamill, Pete. *Why Sinatra Matters*. Boston: Little, Brown, 1998.

Horowitz, Joseph. *Understanding Toscanini: How He Became an American Culture-God and Helped Create a New Audience for Old Music*. New York: Knopf, 1987.

Johanek, Michael C., and John L. Puckett. *Leonard Covello and the Making of Benjamin Franklin High School*. Philadelphia: Temple University Press, 2007.

Kaplan, James. *Frank: The Voice*. New York: Anchor, 2010.

Katz, Ephraim. *The Film Encyclopedia*. New York: Putnam, 1979.

Kessner, Thomas. *Fiorello H. La Guardia and the Making of a Modern New York*. New York: McGraw-Hill, 1989.

Kornbluh, Joyce L., ed. *Rebel Voices: An IWW Anthology*. Ann Arbor: University of Michigan Press, 1964.

LaGumina, Salvatore J. *The Humble and the Heroic: Wartime Italian Americans*. Youngstown, NY: Cambria, 2006.

Lancaster, Jordan. *In the Shadow of Vesuvius: A Cultural History of Naples*. London: I. B. Tauris, 2005.

La Sorte, Michael. *La Merica: Images of Italian Greenhorn Experience*. Philadelphia: Temple Unversity Press, 1985.

Laurino, Maria. *Old World Daughter, New World Mother: An Education in Love and Freedom*. New York: W. W. Norton, 2009.

Laurino, Maria. *Were You Always an Italian?: Ancestors and Other Icons of Italian America*. New York: W. W. Norton, 2001.

Leider, Emily W. *Dark Lover: The Life and Death of Rudolph Valentino*. New York: Macmillan, 2004.

Levi, Carlo. *Christ Stopped at Eboli*. Translated from the Italian by Frances Frenaye. New York: Farrar, Straus and Giroux, 1987.

Lombardo, Robert M. *The Black Hand: Terror by Letter in Chicago*. Urbana: University of Illinois Press, 2010.

Mangione, Jerre. *An Ethnic at Large: A Memoir of America in the Thirties and Forties*. New York: Putnam, 1978.

Mangione, Jerre, and Ben Morreale. *La Storia: Five Centuries of the Italian American Experience*. New York: HarperCollins, 1992.

Mann, Arthur. *La Guardia: A Fighter against His Times 1882–1933*. Philadelphia: Lippincott, 1959.

Mann, Arthur. *La Guardia Comes to Power: 1933*. Chicago: University of Chicago Press, 1965.

Margavio, A. V., and Jerome J. Salomone. *Bread and Respect: The Italians of Louisiana*. Gretna, LA: Pelican, 2002.

Mariani, John F. *How Italian Food Conquered the World*. New York: Palgrave Macmillan, 2011.

Meyer, Gerald. *Vito Marcantonio: Radical Politician 1902–1954*. Albany: State University of New York Press, 1989.

Mormino, Gary. *The Impact of World War II on Italian Americans*. New York: Bordighera, 2008.

Murray, William. *Janet, My Mother, and Me: A Memoir of Growing Up with Janet Flanner and Natalia Danesi Murray*. New York: Simon & Schuster, 2000.

Nash, Gerald D. *A. P. Giannini and the Bank of America*. Norman: University of Oklahoma Press, 1992.

Nelli, Humbert S. *The Business of Crime: Italians and Syndicate Crime in the United States*. Chicago: University of Chicago Press, 1976.

Nelli, Humbert S. *Italians in Chicago 1880–1930: A Study in Ethnic Mobility*. New York: Oxford University Press, 1970.

Oberfirst, Robert. *Rudolph Valentino: The Man behind the Myth*. New York: Citadel Press, 1962.

Orsi, Robert. *The Madonna of 115th Street: Faith and Community in Italian Harlem, 1880–1950*. New Haven, CT: Yale University Press, 2010.

Parini, Jay, ed. *American Writers: A Collection of Literary Biographies*, suppl. 12. New York: Scribner, 2002.

Pernicone, Nunzio. *Carlo Tresca: Portrait of a Rebel*. New York: Palgrave Macmillan, 2005.

Pernicone, Nunzio. *Italian Anarchism, 1864–1892*. Oakland, CA: AK Press, 2009.

Petacco, Arrigo. *Joe Petrosino*. Translated by Charles Lam Markmann. New York: Macmillan, 1974.

Pope, Paul David. *The Deeds of My Fathers: How My Grandfather and Father Built New York and Created the Tabloid World of Today*. Lanham, MD: A Philip Turner Book with Rowman & Littlefield, 2010.

Porter, Katherine Anne. *The Never-Ending Wrong*. Boston: Little, Brown, 1977.

Pozzetta, George E., ed. *Pane e Lavoro: The Italian American Working Class*. Toronto: Multicultural History Society of Ontario, 1980.

Puzo, Mario. *The Godfather*. New York: New American Library, Penguin Group, 1969.

Puzo, Mario. *The Godfather Papers and Other Confessions.* New York: Putnam, 1972.

Reppetto, Thomas. *American Mafia: A History of Its Rise to Power.* New York: Henry Holt, 2004.

Ridley, Jasper. *Garibaldi.* New York: Viking, 1976.

Riis, Jacob August. *How the Other Half Lives: Studies among the Tenements of New York.* New York: Penguin, 1997.

Ross, Edward Alsworth. *The Old World in the New: The Significance of Past and Present Immigration to the American People.* New York: Century, 1914.

Rotella, Mark. *Amore: The Story of Italian American Song.* New York: Farrar, Straus and Giroux, 2010.

Sachs, Harvey. *Arturo Toscanini from 1915 to 1946: Art in the Shadow of Politics.* Turin, Italy: Edizioni di Torino, 1987.

Sachs, Harvey. *Toscanini.* London: Robson, 1993.

Sante, Luc. *Low Life.* New York: Farrar, Straus and Giroux, 1991.

Santopietro, Tom. *The Godfather Effect: Changing Hollywood, America, and Me.* New York: St. Martin's Press, 2012.

Santopietro, Tom. *Sinatra in Hollywood.* New York: St. Martin's Press, 2008.

Scirocco, Alfonso. *Garibaldi.* Translated by Allan Cameron. Princeton, NJ: Princeton University Press, 2007.

Sforza, Carlo. *The Real Italians: A Study in European Psychology.* New York: Columbia University Press, 1942.

Shulman, Irving. *Valentino.* New York: Simon & Schuster, 1967.

Silone, Ignazio. *Fontamara.* Translated from the Italian by Harvey Fergusson II. New York: Atheneum, 1960.

Smith, Tom. *The Crescent City Lynchings: The Murder of Chief Hennessy, the New Orleans "Mafia" Trials, and the Parish Prison Mob.* Guilford, CT: Lyons, 2007.

Stein, Leon. *The Triangle Fire.* Ithaca, NY: Cornell University Press, 2001.

Stephenson, Gregory. *Exiled Angel: A Study of the Work of Gregory Corso.* London: Hearing Eye, 1989.

Talese, Gay. *Honor Thy Father.* New York: Ballantine, 1971.

Talese, Gay. *Unto the Sons.* New York: Knopf, 1993.

Taylor, Nick. *American-Made: The Enduring Legacy of the WPA: When FDR Put the Nation to Work.* New York: Bantam, 2008.

Terkel, Studs. *Division Street: America.* New York: Pantheon, 1967.

Tuttle, William M., Jr. *Daddy's Gone to War: The Second World War in the Lives of America's Children.* Oxford: Oxford University Press, 1993.

Vorse, Mary Heaton. *A Footnote to Folly.* New York: Arno, 1980.

Ware, Caroline F., ed. *The Cultural Approach to History.* New York: Columbia University Press, 1940.

Washington, Booker Taliaferro. *The Man Farthest Down: A Record of Observation and Study in Europe.* Garden City, NY: Doubleday, 1912.

Watson, Bruce. *Bread and Roses: Mills, Migrants, and the Struggle for the American Dream.* New York: Penguin, 2005.

Watson, Bruce. *Sacco and Vanzetti.* New York: Penguin, 2007.

Wilhelm, Maria de Blasio. *The Other Italy: Italian Resistance in World War II.* New York: W. W. Norton, 1988.

Zinn, Howard. *LaGuardia in Congress.* New York: W. W. Norton, 1969.

ACKNOWLEDGMENTS

Writing the companion book to the PBS documentary series *The Italian Americans* allowed me the opportunity to take part in a project that for years I had admired from afar, having shared cappuccino and conversation with a few of the people involved in its creation and development. As I dug into the project, the team at Ark Media, a group of smart, talented, and generous filmmakers, were always available and eager to share their voluminous material with me.

Special thanks to Maia Harris, who reached out during the project's earliest stages; Jeff Bieber at WETA Television, who offered ideas and encouragement; and WETA's intrepid interns Robert Gabriel and Lyndsi Bosco. My talented research assistant, Shayna Garkofsky, delved deep into the subject matter, gamely tackling historical and contemporary research. At Ark Media, Julia Marchesi and Muriel Soenens were the source of many engaging discussions, along with Josh Gleason, whose commanding memory aided my own. The illustrations in this book are possible only because of the tenacity and skill of Ark Media's wonderful Hannah Olson, who always seemed to have photos and facts at her fingertips, along with Michael Shorris, who applied his walker-in-the-city photographic eye to my research requests and, in an unforgettable feat, tracked down from a photograph the city bus on which I had left a canvas bag with all of my notebooks for this project. And most of all, my thanks to Ark Media's John Maggio, who not only created a superb documentary film, but generously offered his advice and friendship, always accompanied by lots of laughter, making this companion book a joy to write.

Friends and colleagues provided excellent ideas, observations, facts and figures, and objects that made their way onto these pages. My thanks to Stefano Albertini, B. Amore, Wayne Barrett, Paul Berman, Mary Brown, Alan Christian,

Rose Marie Cleese, Adam Cohen, Lawrence DiStasi, Geoffrey Dunn, Laurie Fabiano, Donna Gabaccia, David Giovannitti, Edvige Giunta, Joanna Clapps Herman, Aldo Mansi, Tom Robbins, Stephanie Romeo, Joseph J. Salvo, Matthew Santirocco, Joseph Scelsa, Joseph Sciorra, Anthony Tamburri, and Andrew Zambelli. A special thanks to Wallis Wilde-Menozzi for cherished lunches discussing Italian and Italian-American culture.

My thanks to friends and family for hand-holding during the course of an intense year: Jennifer Brown (who held stepladders, too, in pursuit of this project), LynNell Hancock, Gary Lang, Ruth Pastine, and Vincent Santoro. Thanks to my mother-in-law, Sylvia Shorris, who provided additional Mediterranean wisdom; James and Cindy Shorris; my brother Bob, for his love, good humor, and continued encouragement of my work; and my late mother, Connie, who enthusiastically supported this project.

I couldn't find a better advocate—and friend—in my agent, Susan Ramer, whose constant support and reassuring presence guided me along the way. Anna Mageras at W. W. Norton always graciously offered her assistance and answers to my many, many questions. Designer Chris Welch and copy editor Stephanie Hiebert each provided an elegant and attentive eye to every page. Alane Salierno Mason was, quite simply, the perfect editor for this book. I'm always grateful for Alane's intelligence, insights, and graceful editorial suggestions, but this illustrated project gave us the opportunity to search for objects from Italian-American childhoods long ago, finding a shared madeleine in homely nutcrackers and pastel-colored wedding almonds.

There is no greater gift than imagining the meaning and lessons of the past with the people who guide you through the present, and whose presence adds meaning to each day. My son Michael, my joy, my husband Tony, my love, thank you for teaching and inspiring me.

CREDITS

TEXT:

"The Odyssey of a Wop" (excerpt of about 500 words from pp. 138–39) from *The Wine of Youth: Selected Stories* by John Fante. Copyright © 1940 by John Fante. Copyright © 1985 by Joyce Fante. Reprinted by permission of HarperCollins Publishers.

IMAGES:

Ship manifest: Laurie Fabiano personal collection

Group at table: Laurie Fabiano personal collection

Italian couple: Alan Christian personal collection

Italian-American family in kitchen: Maria Laurino personal collection

Cassata Siciliana: Photograph by Paul Cary Goldberg

Eataly counter: Photograph by Virginia Rollison

Roseto banner: Courtesy of *The Italian Americans* documentary

Men in box being lowered: Photograph by Steve Schapiro

Women working at sewing machines: Photograph by Steve Schapiro

Baker holding two bread loaves: Photograph by Steve Schapiro

Gold horn (*cornetto*): Photograph by Chris Leary

Woman in crown and white dress: Photograph by Steve Schapiro

Girl in white dress: Courtesy of *The Italian Americans* documentary

Prosecco glass: Shutterstock stock photograph

Adriana Trigiani: Photograph by Tim Stephenson

Espresso pot: Photograph by Chris Leary

Two women on donkey: Library of Congress, Prints & Photographs Division [LC-USZ62-73453]

Peasants and donkey in courtyard: Library of Congress, Prints & Photographs Division [LC-USZ62-73730]

Family of peasants: Library of Congress, Prints & Photographs Division, National Child Labor Committee Collection [LC-USZ62-93129]

Peasants picking lemons in Sicily: Library of Congress, Prints & Photographs Division [LC-USZ62-73485]

Italian peasant girl: Library of Congress, Prints & Photographs Division [LC-DIG-ppmsca-08349]

Waiting to board ship: Paolo Cresci Foundation

Garibaldi on horse: Library of Congress, Prints & Photographs Division [LC-DIG-pga-02437]

Peasants on street: Library of Congress, Prints & Photographs Division [LC-USZ62-73454]

Two men hanging: Special and Digital Collections, Tampa Library, University of South Florida

Banana vendors: Library of Congress, Prints & Photographs Division [LC-USZ62-131516]

David Hennessy: Courtesy of The Historic New Orleans Collection, Acc. No. 2006.024.11

"To Hunt the Assassins" newspaper clip: Courtesy of *The Italian Americans* documentary

"Assassinated" newspaper clip: Courtesy of *The Italian Americans* documentary

Mafia cartoon: © Bettmann/Corbis

"None Guilty" newspaper clip: Courtesy of *The Italian Americans* documentary

Parish prison: Courtesy of The Historic New Orleans Collection, Acc. No. 1974.25.3.259

Inmates in courtyard: Courtesy of The Historic New Orleans Collection, Acc. No. 1974.25.25.228

Mulberry Street: Library of Congress, Prints & Photographs Division [LC-USZC4-1584]

Immigrants waiting on dock: Library of Congress, Prints & Photographs Division [LC-USZ62-11203]

Inspection of arriving immigrants: Library of Congress, Prints & Photographs Division [LC-USZC4-4656]

Laborer shoveling: Center for Migration Studies

Derogatory sheet music: "I Break-a da Stones" sheet music, Balch Institute Sheet Music Collection [3141], Historical Society of Pennsylvania

Women working in silk mill: Center for Migration Studies

Workers at macaroni factory: Center for Migration Studies

Collage of immigration photographs and documents: Courtesy of B. Amore

Ancestor panel (great-grandmother): Courtesy of B. Amore

Nineteenth-century artifacts: Courtesy of B. Amore

Ancestor panel (great-grandfather): Courtesy of B. Amore

Clam vendor: Library of Congress, Prints & Photographs Division [LC-D401-13642]

Bread sellers: Library of Congress, Prints & Photographs Division [LC-USZ62-63005]

Black Hand members: Courtesy of *The Italian Americans* documentary

Lt. Joseph Petrosino escorting a Black Hand criminal with other police officers: Library of Congress, Prints & Photographs Division [LC-USZ62-137644]

"Bomb shakes" newspaper clip: Laurie Fabiano personal collection

Angelina Siena: Laurie Fabiano personal collection

Giuseppe Petrosino: Library of Congress, Prints & Photographs Division [LC-DIG-ggbain-03609]

Black Hand letters: Courtesy of The Italian American Museum

Main Street, San Francisco: J. B. Monaco Photograph Collection, San Francisco History Center, San Francisco Public Library

Crab fisherman: © Bettmann/Corbis

Man with fish on line: Geoffrey Dunn personal collection

Grocery store: Courtesy of the California Historical Society, CHS2014.160

San Francisco earthquake: Library of Congress, Prints & Photographs Division [LC-USZ62-47147]

A. P. Giannini: J. B. Monaco Photograph Collection, San Francisco History Center, San Francisco Public Library

Souvenir scavengers: U.S. National Archives

Bank of Italy: J. B. Monaco Photograph Collection, San Francisco History Center, San Francisco Public Library

Spoons: Photograph by Chris Leary

Mother with three children: Library of Congress, Prints & Photographs Division, National Child Labor Committee Collection [LC-DIG-nclc-04116]

Rolling pin and ravioli cutter: Photograph by Chris Leary

Social worker visiting family: © Underwood & Underwood/Corbis

Family in crowded home, Providence, Rhode Island: Library of Congress, Prints & Photographs Division, National Child Labor Committee Collection [LC-DIG-nclc-02721]

Leonard Covello: Portrait of Leonard Covello, Leonard Covello Papers [MSS 040], Historical Society of Pennsylvania

Passport: Alane Salierno Mason personal collection

Schoolboy: Library of Congress, Prints & Photograph Division [LC-DIG-ggbain-14196]

Schoolgirls: Library of Congress, Prints & Photograph Division [LC-DIG-ggbain-14198]

Embroidered heart: Courtesy of B. Amore

Family in front of store: Courtesy of The Italian American Museum

Rudolph Valentino: Library of Congress, Prints & Photograph Division [LC-USZ62-90327]

"A Wop" cartoon: Stock Montage/Archive Photos/Getty Images

Lawrence strike meeting: Library of Congress, Prints & Photographs Division [LC-DIG-ggbain-10185]

Striking millworkers: Walter P. Reuther Library, Archives of Labor and Urban Affairs, Wayne State University

Giovannitti and Ettor postcard: David Giovannitti personal collection

Children of Lawrence strikers: Library of Congress, Prints & Photographs Division [LC-USZ62-98168]

Children's exodus: Library of Congress, Prints & Photographs Division [LC-DIG-ggbain-10241]

Child working in mill: Library of Congress, Prints & Photographs Division, National Child Labor Committee Collection [LC-DIG-nclc-01668]

Group of child millworkers: Library of Congress, Prints & Photographs Division, National Child Labor Committee Collection [LC-DIG-nclc-02370]

IWW "Bread or Revolution" hat card: Library of Congress, Prints & Photographs Division [LC-USZ62-22190]

Giovannitti writing collage: David Giovannitti personal collection

San Gennaro festival: Photograph by Michael Shorris

Communion girls: Alan Christian personal collection

Communion boys: Alane Salierno Mason personal collection

Our Lady of Sorrows: Photograph by Michael Shorris

Our Lady of Mount Carmel procession: Alane Salierno Mason personal collection

Communion collage: Photograph by Chris Leary

Crucifix: Photograph by Chris Leary

Our Lady of Mount Carmel float: Courtesy of *The Italian Americans* documentary

Madonna and bread loaves: Photograph by Paul Cary Goldberg

Ransacked room: Joseph A. Labadie Collection, University of Michigan

La Cronaca Sovversiva pamphlet: Center for Migration Studies

Anarchists marching: Library of Congress, Prints & Photographs Division [LC-USZ62-33538]

Gruppo Autonomo pamphlet: Center for Migration Studies

Palmer house after explosion: Library of Congress, Prints & Photographs Division [LC-DIG-npcc-33288]

Sacco and Vanzetti: © Bettmann/Corbis

Sacco and Vanzetti poster: Daily Worker/Daily World Photographs Collection, Tamiment Library, New York University

Angela Bambace and mother: Mindy Camponeschi personal collection

Angela Bambace and sons: Mindy Camponeschi personal collection

Dumping whiskey during Prohibition: Library of Congress, Prints & Photographs Division [LC-USZ62-12142]

Women at a speakeasy: Keystone-France/Gamma-Keystone/Getty Images

Italian-American social club: Alane Salierno Mason personal collection

Genna family: Popperfoto/Popperfoto/Getty Images

St. Valentine's Day massacre: © Bettmann/Corbis

Nut cracker and picks: Photograph by Chris Leary

La Guardia and Rossi: Rose Marie Cleese personal collection

Tammany Tiger: Library of Congress, Prints & Photographs Division [LC-USZC4-10303]

La Guardia with wife and child: The La Guardia and Wagner Archives, La Guardia Community College/The City University of New York

Organ grinder: © Bettmann/Corbis

Sewing machine and dresses: Courtesy of B. Amore

La Guardia pouring alcoholic beverage: © Bettmann/Corbis

La Guardia and Vito Marcantonio: Gerald Meyer collection

WPA and union card: Alane Salierno Mason personal collection

Daniel Celentano painting: Smithsonian American Art Museum, Washington, DC/Art Resource, NY

La Guardia smashing slot machines: Hulton Archive/Archive Photos/Getty Images

Union art: Alane Salierno Mason personal collection

Fascist gathering in New Jersey: Center for Migration Studies

Giovannitti poem: David Giovannitti personal collection

Mussolini: Library of Congress, Prints & Photographs Division [LC-USW 33-000890-ZC]

President Franklin Roosevelt and Generoso Pope: Paul D. Pope and the Pope Media Center LLC collection

Arturo Toscanini poster: Library of Congress, Prints & Photographs Division [LC-DIG-ggbain-32153]

Albert Onesti with soldiers: Ron Onesti personal collection

"Keep 'em Flying" poster: Library of Congress, Prints & Photographs Division, FSA/OWI collection [LC-USW3-015095-D]

"Stamp 'Em Out!" poster: Library of Congress, Prints & Photographs Division [LC-USZC2-1142]

Rosina Bonavita and fellow worker: Joseph T. Hickey personal collection

World War II flag raising ceremony: Library of Congress, Prints & Photographs Division, FSA/OWI collection [LC-USW 3-006904-E]

Tony Bennett and mother: Tony Bennett family personal collection

Women celebrating child's birthday: Alan Christian personal collection

Locals celebrating Italy's surrender: Daily Worker/Daily World Photographs Collection, Tamiment Library, New York University

Chef Boy-Ar-Dee ad: Apic/Hulton Archive/Getty Images

Gay Talese: Courtesy *The Italian Americans* documentary

Missoula, Montana internment camp: Courtesy of the National Japanese American Historical Society. Donated by Goro and Nobi Asaki

Celestina Stagnaro Loero: Geoffrey Dunn personal collection

Men in internment camp: Courtesy of the National Japanese American Historical Society. Donated by Goro and Nobi Asaki

Men on wharf: Library of Congress, Prints & Photographs Division [LC-USF34-081790-E]

Joe DiMaggio with parents: Underwood Archives/Archive Photos/Getty Images

Angelo J. Rossi with siblings: Rose Marie Cleese personal collection

Knock 'Em on Their Axis: National Archives photo no. 179-WP-772

ID cards (beginning upper left): Geoffrey Dunn personal collection, Anthony Tamburri personal collection, Geoffrey Dunn personal collection, Stephanie Romeo personal collection

Notice to Enemy Aliens poster: Courtesy of the Japanese American National Library

Alessi espresso pot: "La cupola, Espresso coffee maker," designed in 1988 by Aldo Rossi. Courtesy of Alessi

Theater marquee: Photofest Digital

Dean Martin: Photofest Digital

Tony Bennett: Photofest Digital

Frank Sinatra: Photofest Digital

Davis, Martin, and Sinatra: Photofest Digital

Madonna on cross: Dave Hogan/Getty Images Entertainment/Getty Images

Lady Gaga: Photofest Digital

Dion DiMucci: Courtesy of *The Italian Americans* documentary

Gasoline book cover: Copyright © 1958 by City Lights Books. Reprinted by permission of City Lights Books. Photograph by Michael Shorris

Gregory Corso: Loomis Dean/The LIFE Picture Collection/Getty Images

Mario Savio: Steven Marcus Photograph, The Bancroft Library, University of California, Berkeley

Diana Di Prima: Photograph by William F. Wilson

Frank Costello: Library of Congress, Prints & Photographs Division [LC-USZ62-120716]

Family on patio: Alane Salierno Mason personal collection

Estes Kefauver: © Bettmann/Corbis

Kefauver billboard: Michael Rougier/The LIFE Picture Collection/Getty Images

Frank Costello's hands: Alfred Eisenstaedt/The LIFE Picture Collection/Getty Images

Carlo Gambino "family" chart: © Bettmann/Corbis

Florence Scala: Casa Italia, Chicago

Marlon Brando: Photofest Digital

Mario Puzo: Bernard Gotfryd/Premium Archives/Getty Images

Francis Ford Coppola directing *The Godfather*: Photograph by Steve Schapiro

John Gotti: Photofest Digital

The Sopranos: Photofest Digital

John Travolta: Photofest Digital

Jersey Shore's Pauly D.: Photofest Digital

Mob Wives: Newscom

David Chase: Courtesy of *The Italian Americans* documentary

John Turturro: Courtesy of *The Italian Americans* documentary

Mario Cuomo: Photograph by Janie Eisenberg

Geraldine Ferraro and Walter Mondale: © Bettmann/Corbis

Italian grandmothers: Stephanie Romeo personal collection

Justice Antonin Scalia: The Collection of the Supreme Court of the United States

Political buttons: Photograph by Chris Leary

Nancy Pelosi swearing-in: Pelosi family personal collection

Andrew Cuomo and daughters: Courtesy of the Governor's Office

De Blasio "One of Us" poster: Photograph by Luigi Maria Mongillo

Nancy Pelosi: Courtesy of *The Italian Americans* documentary

Eataly counter: Photograph by Virginia Rollison

Sant Ambroeus espresso bar: Photograph by Michael Shorris

1940s espresso machine: Library of Congress, Prints & Photographs Division, FSA/OWI collection [LC-USW 3-006923-E]

Mario Batali: Photograph by Melanie Dunea

Tuscan countryside: Photograph by Michael Shorris

Painting: *Iceman Crucified #3*, Ralph Fasanella (1914–1997). New York, 1956. Oil on canvas. 48¾ x 37¾ in. Collection American Folk Art Museum, New York. Gift of Patricia L. and Maurice C. Thompson Jr., 1991.11.1. Photograph by Gavin Ashworth, New York

Encyclopedic Palace: Photograph by Michael Shorris

Encyclopedic Palace detail: Photograph by Michael Shorris

Fig tree: Shutterstock stock photograph

INDEX

Page numbers in *italics* refer to illustrations.

Ferlinghetti, Lawrence, *211*, 212
Ferrara, Antonio, 259–60
Ferraro, Geraldine, 247, 248, *248*,
    249, 251, 256–57
Ferrone, Margaret, 176
fifth column, 186, 187
fig trees, 261
Fiorito, Jennie, 177
Firmani, B. G., 266–67
First Communion, *108*
Fischer, Marie, 151
Fisherman's Wharf, 4, 63, *64*, 188, 190
fishing industry, 31, 61, 63–64, *64*,
    189–90, *189*
Five Points, 50
Floating Bear, The, 219
Florida, 146
Flynn, Bina, 212
Flynn, Elizabeth Gurley, 212
Foggia, 146
Fontana, M. J., 65–66
Fontane, Johnny (char.), 203
Fonzarelli, Arthur "Fonzie" (char.), 238
Fortunate Pilgrim, The (Puzo), 233
Fortune, 166
Forty Thieves, 50
Four Horsemen of the Apocalypse, The,
    88
France, 19, 20, 24, 117, 168, 220–21
Francis, Connie, 198
Frankfurter, Felix, 128
Free Speech Movement, 215–17, *216,*
    218
free speech, 163–64
Freshman, The, 236
Friends, 238
From Here to Eternity, 202
Fuller, Alvan T., 128
Fusco, Joe, 241

gabellotti, 33, 34
Gaga, Lady, 206–7, *206*
Galleani, Luigi, 118, *118,* 120, 121, 123,
    123
Galleanisti, 121, 122, 141

Gambino, Carlo, 229
Gambino family, 236, *236*
gambling, 136, 139, 141, 156, *156,* 224,
    225, 233
gangsters:
    arrests of, 155–56
    Hollywood films about, 73, 228,
        233, 234–36, 242, 245
    Kefauver Committee hearings and,
        225–29
    Prohibition and, 136–37, *138,* 223
    violence and, 139–40
Gardner, Ava, 202–3
Garibaldi, Anita, 25
Garibaldi, Giuseppe, 19–21, *21,* 22, 23,
    24–25, *24,* 29, 169
Garibaldi-Meucci Museum, 24, 25
garment industry, 14, 131, 133, 150–51,
    150, 175
Gasoline (Corso), 211, 212
Gatsby, Jay (char.), 88
Gazzetta del Massachusetts, 163
General, The, 242
Genet, Jean, 219
Genna brothers, 138, *138*
Gennaro, Saint, *107,* 109
Genoa, 19, 62, 63, 65, 66
Genovese, Vito, 229
Gentile, Don, 178
Georgia, 14, 122
German Americans, 5, 7, 56, 107, 175,
    185, 186, 187, 188
Germany, 117
Ghirardelli, Domenico, 65, 261
Giacosa, Giuseppe, 44
Giamatti, A. Bartlett, 247
Giannini, Amadeo Peter (A. P.), 4, 66,
    67–74, *68, 70,* 164
Giannini, Luigi, 66–67
Giannini, Virginia, 66–67
GI Bill, 180
Gigante, Vincent "the Chin," 236
Gilbert, Elizabeth, 262
Gilded Age, 93
Gimbel Brother bombs, 121–22

League of Nations, 167
Le Donne's, 6
Lehman, Herbert, 159
Leonardo da Vinci, 61
Letters of Sacco and Vanzetti, 129
Levi, Carlo, 17–19, 26–27, *27*
"Like a Virgin," 206
Lincoln, Abraham, 29, *157*
Lindsay, John, 250
literacy, 82, 83, 84, 185–86, 188–89
Little Caesar, 227
Little Italies, 49, 56, 86, 107
loans, 68–69, 70, *70,* 71
Loero, Celestina Stagnaro, *186*
Lombardi, Annunciata, 255
LoPizzo, Anna, 97, 100
Los Angeles, Calif., 73, 138
Louisiana, 4, 30–32, *31*
Lucania, 18, 26, 39
Lucchese, Gaetano, 229
Luce, Henry, 166
Luciano, Charlie "Lucky," 140–41,
      202, 212–13
Lucy, Saint, 109
Lupo, Ignazio, 51
Luzzatto-Coen, Irene, 146
lynching, *29,* 36–37, *36, 37,* 225

Mac, 243, 245
macaroni factory, 45
Madeiros, Celestino, 126, 128
Madonna (singer), *204,* 205–7, 265
Madonna (Virgin Mary), 9, 11, 108, 109,
      110, 111–13, *112, 113,* 114–115, *114,* 207
Mafia, 32–34, 36, 61–62, 141, 242
   Black Hand tied to, 51, 80
   five "families" of, *229, 229,* 236
   Hollywood's portrayal of, *233, 234,*
      235, 236, 238, 244–45
   Italians stereotyped as, 35, 37, 56,
      80, 202, 250, 251
   Kefauver Committee hearings and,
      224–25, 228–29
   silence code (*omertà*) of, 228, 236
   use of term, 33, *34,* 225
   see also organized crime

Maggio, Angelo (char.), 202, 204
Magliocco, Giuseppe, 229
Maida, 182
malocchio (evil eye), 8, *8*
Mangione, Jerre, 173–74
Manhattan College, 217
Marcantonio, Vito, 78, 152–53, *152,* 160
"March on Rome," 161, 169
"Marriage," 214
Married to the Mob, 236
Martello, Il, 163
Martin, Dean, 198, *199, 203,* 205, 223
Martin, Peter, 211–12, *211*
Martini, Allen V., 178
Maryland, 133, 255
Massachusetts, 4, 94, 120, 124, 125–
      26, 128–29
Massachusetts state militia, 95
Massachusetts Supreme Court, 128
Matera, 26
materialism, 8, 11, 211, 217
Mathis, June, 88
Matranga (Italian stevedore), 34–35
Mayes, Frances, 262
Mayor La Guardia Calling Rome, 178
Mazzini, Giuseppe, 19, 96, 168
McCormick, Anne O'Hare, 161
McCray, Chirlane, 253–54
McGill University, 96
McKinley, William, 124
Medicare, 190
Mencken, H. L., 90, 163–64
Men of Respect, 245
Messina, 33
Metropolitan Opera, 170
Metternich, Prince Klemens von, 21
Meucci, Antonio, 25
Michelangelo, 61
Mickey Blue Eyes, 236
Milan, 82, 91, *260,* 265
military, U.S., 173, 176
Millay, Edna St. Vincent, 129
Miller, Henry, 219
Miller's Crossing, 245
Milton, Pa., 181
Mission District, San Francisco, 63